Art by Chance: Fortuitous Impressions

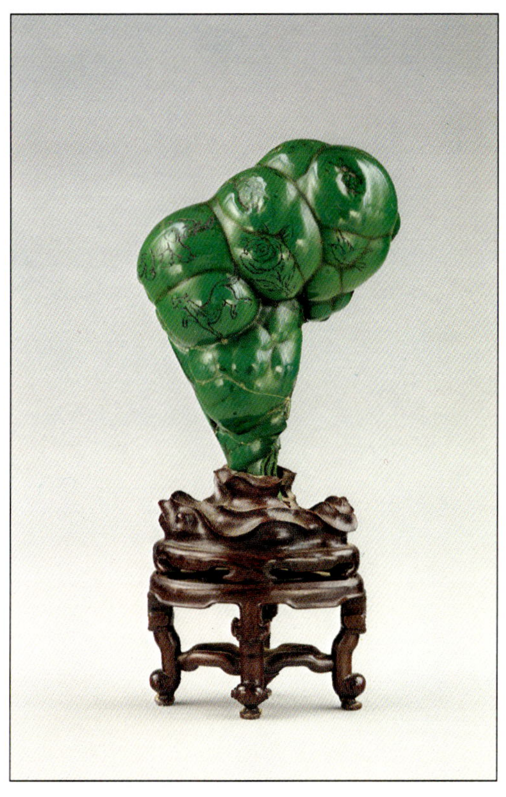

No. 7

By George L. McKenna

July 22-September 3, 1989

The Nelson-Atkins Museum of Art

Kansas City, Missouri

Financial assistance for the exhibition has been provided by
Fred. S. James & Co. of Missouri, Inc.
The Missouri Arts Council
The National Endowment for the Arts
The Nelson Gallery Foundation
The Print Society

This catalogue has been supported by the Andrew W. Mellon Foundation, the
Grace M. Frick Bequest, and the Emily B. and Louis S. Rothschild Bequest.

Cover: No. 93, Sandra K. Nicht, *Another Green World/Sunrise,*
cliché-verre C-print, 1984

Title page: No. 7, Chinese malachite stone, 1745

Library of Congress Cataloging-in-Publication Data

McKenna, George L.
Art by chance: fortuitous impressions/by George L. McKenna.
p.   cm.
Exhibition held July 22-Sept. 3, 1989.
Bibliography: p.
ISBN 0-942614-13-5: $14.95
1. Art, European—Exhibitions.   2. Art, American—Exhibitions.
I. Nelson-Atkins Museum of Art.   II. Title.
N6750.M34   1989   89-30073
707'.4'0178411—dc19   CIP

Printed in the United States of America by The Lowell Press, Inc.
Kansas City, Missouri

Table of Contents

Lenders to the Exhibition iv

Donors of Works of Art in the Museum Collection Shown
   in the Exhibition. v

Preface vi

Acknowledgments vii

Introduction x

Introduction Notes xix

Catalogue

    I.   Unpremeditated and Invented Tracks: Random Loci 1

   II.   Dreams, Miracles, Disasters, and Coincidences 21

  III.   Captured Transiences and Appearances of Spontaneity. 33

  IV.   Expectations Confounded and Realizations Deferred. 49

   V.   Harbingers and Manipulators of Fate 55

  VI.   Forces of Circumstance: Involuntarily Altered States
        and Unforeseen Versions 61

Sources of Quotations 66

Catalogue Notes 67

Bibliography 69

Lenders to the Exhibition

Albright-Knox Art Gallery, Buffalo
Museum of Fine Arts, Boston
Art Institute of Chicago
Crown Point Press
Davison Art Center, Wesleyan University,
    Middletown, Connecticut
Des Moines Art Center
Fogg Art Museum, Harvard University
John Gibson Editions, New York
Solomon R. Guggenheim Museum, New York
Hallmark Collections, Hallmark Cards, Inc.
The High Museum of Art, Atlanta
Heyeck Press, Woodside, California
The Museum of Fine Arts, Houston
Mr. Douglass Morse Howell
Dr. James N. Hueser
Mr. Gunnar A. Kaldewey, Poestenkill, New York
Indiana University Art Museum
Editions Ilene Kurtz, New York
Mr. Victor Landweber
The Lilly Library, Indiana University
Marion Koogler McNay Art Museum, San Antonio
Milwaukee Art Museum
The Minneapolis Institute of Arts
Museum of Art and Archaeology, University of
    Missouri
The Museum of Modern Art, New York
Mr. Kenji Nakahashi

National Gallery of Art
University Art Museum, University of New Mexico
New Orleans Museum of Art
The New Pyramid Press, London, England
North Carolina Museum of Art, Raleigh
The Art Museum, Princeton University
Private collections
Harry Ransom Humanities Research Center,
    University of Texas at Austin
Mr. Robert Rauschenberg
The Red Gull Press, Hitchin, England
Arthur M. Sackler Museum, Harvard University
Sheldon Memorial Art Gallery, University of
    Nebraska - Lincoln
Spencer Museum of Art, University of Kansas
Mr. Robert Stanley
The Toledo Museum of Art
Twinrocker Handmade Paper, Brookston, Indiana
Edwin A. Ulrich Museum, Wichita State University
Vermillion Editions, Minneapolis
Walker Art Center, Minneapolis
Whitney Museum of American Art, New York
Yale Center for British Art
Yale University Art Gallery
The Jane Voorhees Zimmerli Art Museum, Rutgers -
    The State University of New Jersey, New
    Brunswick

Donors of Works of Art in the Museum Collection
Shown in the Exhibition

Thomas Agnew and Sons
Anonymous Donors
*Anonymous Fund
Mr. and Mrs. Adam Aronson
Mr. John H. Bender
Mr. and Mrs. Robert L. Bloch
Mrs. George H. Bunting, Jr.
Frank P. and Harriet C. Burnap
Mr. Robert W. Carlson
Mrs. William H. Chapman
Dr. and Mrs. George Colom
Mr. John Donnelly
Paula N. Dorman
David Douglas Duncan
Mr. Daniel Farber
Mr. John F. Fennelly
Mr. Joseph C. Fennelly
Mr. Robert B. Fizzell
Friends of Art
*Friends of Art Memorial Fund
Mr. Paul Gardner
The Greenberg Family
Mr. and Mrs. Irving Groupp
Guild of the Friends of Art
Miss Peggy Guggenheim
Bequest of Joseph H. Heil
Dr. and Mrs. Joseph F. Jacobs

Anne Foster Kriehn
Mr. David Kluger
Mrs. David M. Lighton
Mrs. Jean S. Lighton
Mrs. Jacob L. Loose
Mr. and Mrs. Sidney B. Lurie
Mrs. James C. Lysle
Diane Philipoff Maurer
Mr. Paul Maurer
Mr. Milton McGreevy
Mr. and Mrs. Milton McGreevy
    through the Mission Fund
Mr. and Mrs. George L. McKenna
Dr. Carl W. Melcher
*NBC Fund
*Nelson Fund
*Nelson Gallery Foundation Funds
*Roy S. Odell Memorial Fund
The Print Collectors
The Print Society
*Richard Shields Fund
Mr. Laurence Sickman
Mrs. Louis Sosland
Connie Sullivan
Mr. and Mrs. Stephen Tabb
Jane Wade

* Donors of funds for purchasing

Preface

Art by Chance: Fortuitous Impressions is an outgrowth of a previous exhibition *Repeated Exposure: Photographic Imagery in the Print Media*, 1982, organized by the curator, which considered the impact of photography on ink-printed graphics. In the course of assembling it, he became more aware of the accidental, experimental aspects of the discovery of photographic processes (with their application to printing methods) and of Senefelder's no less fortuitous prior invention of lithography. The chance naming of such movements as Dada and Impressionism, among others, also came to mind. Aside from these piquant phenomena, the more numerous other associations of chance with art of many kinds—in technique and theme, theory and practice—began to seem a rewarding field for exploration.

Others have produced exhibitions on the subject: *Against Order: Chance and Art,* Institute of Contemporary Art, University of Pennsylvania, 1970; *Toeval* (Chance), Rijksuniversiteit, Utrecht, 1972; and *Chance and Change; a century of the avant-garde,* Auckland, New Zealand City Art Gallery, 1985. Among the works represented to some extent within the three were sculpture, records of happenings, documentation of earthworks, and three-dimensional motor-driven and electronic kinetic art. These, this organizer, with the bias of a graphics curator, has largely eschewed. It is felt that the range of the present exhibition, encompassing an extensive variety of two-dimensional art, from Paleolithic times to the present, and including surface embellishment of decorative art, affords viewers an appropriately focused experience.

Like all special exhibitions of loans obtained from many collections, carefully selected for relevance to the theme, the final reality represents as close an approximation as possible to the ideal showing initially envisioned. What is sought may not always be available, for reasons of fragility, reluctance of owners to lend, or prior commitments. The Trustees of one Eastern art museum, debating the merits of the request for loans to *Art by Chance,* took exception to the possible ambiguity of the title, on the ground that the artists whose works were desired as examples of random effects had worked hard and purposefully to obtain just such results. It was no matter, moreover, that the artists themselves had often published accounts of their enthusiastic, dedicated exploitation of accident in forming their pictures. Fortunately, in the end, we were granted the loans.

Curators assembling exhibitions are familiar with the unanticipated vagaries of fate that beset the lengthy process. In this instance, there were such interventions of chance as the disappearance between London and Kansas City of a set of stereographs of the earthquake in Messina and as the coincidental arrival in the mail of a long-awaited pertinent book at just the very moment one was writing on the subject of Stieglitz's *Equivalents.* When the compilation of the catalogue had progressed beyond the halfway point, it was suddenly noticed that the arrangement of the exhibition, devised years ago into six parts, some devoted to the passive absorption of chance into art and others to the active initiative of artists in utilizing the accidental, reflected the symbol of the fifty-fifth hexagram, the symbolic representation of *Fêng*, or Abundance, in the Chinese classic oracular book, the *I Ching*. This is not only a fair characterization of the following contents, but, we hope, an auspicious omen for organizer and observer alike.

The succeeding general introduction is truly an overview, touching upon the variabilities of the use of chance in art, with examples adduced but not shown in the exhibition. The six sectional introductions are more particularized, with specific attention to the objects on view and described in detail in the catalogue entries.

Acknowledgments

Assembling an exhibition of the scope of "Art by Chance" has been enabled by the interest and willingness of my colleagues at the Museum, of many persons at other cooperating institutions, and of artists, gallery personnel, and publishers. I am beholden to all of them for the gracious assistance which has made this showing possible.

First, one must record the encouragement always offered by our late Director, Laurence Sickman, with whom I had the privilege of being associated for thirty-six years. What prized knowledge I have of Oriental art is derived from the collections he founded here and from the explanations of them he was ever ready, as a profound connoisseur, to extend to persons like myself who, until enlightened by his instruction, had admired the works without otherwise fully understanding them. When the theme of this exhibition was first mentioned to him, he responded sympathetically to it and forthwith proposed the welcome loan from his collection of the Chinese malachite stone illustrated on the title page of this catalogue.

Our present Director, Marc F. Wilson, also an accomplished Orientalist, possesses as did his mentor Mr. Sickman, an abiding sensitivity to the distinctive qualities of Occidental art. Mr. Wilson fosters in the Museum an atmosphere conducive to organizing exhibitions, permanent and temporary, with related publications, that explore in a scholarly manner diverse subjects related to the Museum collections. His informed receptiveness is truly heartening.

An equal receptivity has been demonstrated by the generous lenders to the exhibition who have entrusted to the Museum works of art from their collections. These individuals and institutions have been named with appreciation in the list at the beginning of this catalogue: their important contributions are highly valued. It is a pleasure to cite thankfully here the persons, many of them museum colleagues, who have facilitated my efforts by providing vital assistance and information:

Mr. Douglas G. Schultz, Ms. Laura Catalano, Albright-Knox Art Gallery, Buffalo; Mr. Alan Shestack, Dr. Barbara Shapiro, Ms. Barbara Butts, Ms. Linda Thomas, Ms. Karen L. Otis, Museum of Fine Arts, Boston; Ms. Edwina B. Evers, Califia Books, San Francisco; Mr. James N. Wood, Ms. Suzanne Folds McCullagh, Ms. Gloria Teplitz, Ms. Mary Solt, Ms. Mary Mulhern, Art Institute of Chicago; Ms. Kathan Brown, Ms. Valerie Wade, Ms. Janice Capecci, Crown Point Press, San Francisco; Mrs. Ellen D'Oench, Mr. Richard H. Wood, Davison Art Center, Wesleyan University, Middletown, Connecticut; Ms. Julia Brown Turrell, Ms. Margaret A. Willard, Des Moines Art Center; Mr. Edgar Peters Bowron, Ms. Ada Bortoluzzi, Ms. Elizabeth Gombosi, Fogg Art Museum, Arthur M. Sackler Museum, Harvard University, Cambridge.

Mr. John Gibson, Ms. Valerie Del-Sol, John Gibson Editions, New York; Mr. Thomas M. Messer, Ms. Diane Waldman, Ms. Lisa Dennison, Ms. Nina Schroeder, Solomon R. Guggenheim Museum, New York; Ms. Amy Hauft, Printed Matter, Inc., New York; Mr. Keith F. Davis, Ms. Pat Fundom, Hallmark Collections, Hallmark Cards, Inc., Kansas City; Miss Kathy Hamilton, Lakewood, Colorado; Mr. Gudmund Vigtel, Ms. Marge Harvey, Ms. Frances R. Francis, Ms. Carolyn B. Padwa, High Museum of Art, Atlanta; Ms. Robin Heyeck, Heyeck Press, Woodside, California; Mr. Peter C. Marzio, Ms. Anne W. Tucker, Mr. Charles Carroll, Ms. Diane Arnold, Museum of Fine Arts, Houston; Mr. Douglass Morse Howell, Hackettstown, New Jersey; Dr. James N.

Hueser, Columbia, Missouri; Adelheid M. Gealt, Ms. Diane Drisch, Terry Harley-Wilson, Indiana University Art Museum, Bloomington; Mr. Gunnar A. Kaldewey, Poestenkill, New York; Ms. Ilene Kurtz, Ms. Yvonne Muranushi, Editions Ilene Kurtz, New York.

Mr. Victor Landweber, Berkeley, California; Dr. William R. Cagle, Miss Marcia Morrison, Lilly Library, Indiana University, Bloomington; Mr. Larry Frye, Lilly Library, Wabash College, Crawfordsville, Indiana; Mr. Paul and Ms. Diane Maurer, Centre Hall, Pennsylvania; Mr. John Palmer Leeper, Mr. Norris J. Fergeson, Torri Wilson, Bann Williams, Marion Koogler McNay Art Museum, San Antonio, Texas; Mr. Russell Bowman, Mr. James Mundy, Miss Cisley Celmer, Milwaukee Art Museum; Mr. Timothy Fiske, Mr. John Ittmann, Mr. Richard Campbell, Ms. Karen Duncan, Ms. Melissa M. Moore, Minneapolis Institute of Arts; Mr. Forrest McGill, Ms. Patricia Condon, Mr. Jeffrey B. Wilcox, Museum of Art and Archaeology, University of Missouri - Columbia; Mrs. Cynthia Rogers, Linda Hall Library, Kansas City, Missouri; Mr. Richard E. Oldenburg, Ms. Riva Castleman, Ms. Audrey Isselbacher, Ms. Beatrice Kernan, Mr. Thomas D. Grischkowsky, Museum of Modern Art, New York; Mr. Kenji Nakahashi, New York; Mr. J. Carter Brown, Mr. Andrew Robison, Ms. Mary Suzor, Mr. Ira Bartfield, National Gallery of Art, Washington, D. C.

Mr. Peter Walch, Mr. Kevin Donovan, Ms. Jackie Chavez-Cunningham, University Art Museum, University of New Mexico, Albuquerque; Mr. E. John Bullard, Mr. Daniel Piersol, Mr. Paul Tarvar, New Orleans Museum of Art; Mr. Robert Hadrill, The New Pyramid Press, London, England; Mr. Richard S. Schneiderman, Mrs. Peggy Jo D. Kirby, North Carolina Museum of Art, Raleigh; Mr. Allen Rosenbaum, Mr. Robert H. Lafond, The Art Museum, Princeton University; Mr. Roy Flukinger, Ms. Devon Susholtz, Ms. Carey Thornton, Leslie S. Kronz, Harry Ransom Humanities Research Center, University of Texas at Austin; Mr. Robert Rauschenberg, Mr. David White, Curator for Mr. Robert Rauschenberg, New York; Mr. Michael Gullick, The Red Gull Press, Hitchin, Herts, England; Mr. George W. Neubert, Sheldon Memorial Art Gallery, University of Nebraska - Lincoln.

Mr. Douglas Tilghman, Mr. Stephen H. Goddard, Miss Janet Dreiling, Spencer Museum of Art, University of Kansas, Lawrence; Mr. Robert Stanley, New York; Mr. Roger Mandle, Miss Patricia J. Whitesides, Toledo Museum of Art; Ms. Kathryn Clark, Twinrocker Handmade Paper, Brookston,

Indiana; Mr. Martin H. Bush, Ms. Maria Ciski, Edwin A. Ulrich Museum, Wichita State University, Wichita, Kansas; Mr. Steven Andersen, Vermillion Editions, Ltd., Minneapolis, Minnesota; Mr. Martin Friedman, Ms. Elizabeth N. Armstrong, Ms. Carolyn Clark DeCato, Walker Art Center, Minneapolis; Mr. Thomas N. Armstrong, III, Ms. Nancy McGary, Ms. Roberta LeMay, Ms. Anita Duquette, Whitney Museum of American Art, New York; Mr. Duncan Robinson, Mr. Timothy A. Goodhue, Ms. Marilyn Hunt, Yale Center for British Art; Ms. Mary Gardner Neill, Mr. Richard S. Field, Mr. Anthony Hirschel, Ms. Susan Frankenbach, Ms. Diane Hart, Mr. William Cuffe, Yale University Art Gallery, New Haven, Connecticut; Mr. Phillip Dennis Cate, Ms. Barbara S. Trelstad, Jane Voorhees Zimmerli Art Museum, Rutgers - The State University of New Jersey, New Brunswick.

Through the years, devoted patrons of the Museum have donated works of art that assuredly are germane to this exhibition, and it is with gratitude that we list their names on the page after that specifying the lenders.

Leaving nothing to chance, my confreres here in all departments have marshaled their redoubtable talents to aid in the realization of this showing of the fortuitous. The logistics involved in arranging the timely arrival of the loans at the Museum have been adroitly handled by our Registrar, Ann Erbacher, and her associate Cindy Cart. Their colleague Linda Dost nimbly scheduled the considerable photographing required, which our staff cameraman Melville McLean performed with dispatch and distinction. Painstaking care was bestowed on the packing, handling, and installation of the art objects by Bobby Hornaday and his staff, Craig Bruns, David Dieleman, and Brent Powell.

Michael Hagler brought to his handsome design of the exhibition his customary flair for the telling harmonization of a wealth of disparate works of art from many eras, in a way that permits the particular qualities of each object to be fully manifest. Our conservator of paper, Christine Young, with the help of her assistant Steve Bonham, refurbished to peak condition many of the Museum prints and drawings included in the exhibition, as well as some of the privately owned loans, and improved the means of their mounting and presentation.

To two of my fellow curators—Deborah Emont Scott in the 20th century department and Wai-kam Ho in the Oriental—I am indebted for their cheerfully granted permission to deploy under the rubric of "Art by Chance" relevant objects in their care. I am further thankful to Mr. Ho for his kindness in preparing a translation of a Chinese inscription.

Obtaining innumerable publications and providing expert guidance in threading through a collection in cataloguing transition, our Museum librarian Stanley Hess and his staff, especially Karen Meizner, have contributed significantly to the accurate and easeful writing of this publication. The range of the bibliography attests to their efforts.

Michael Churchman and his aide Mary Ellen Young were unfailingly helpful throughout the arduous process of applying for grants which furnished the wherewithal to underwrite the costs of the exhibition. In the area of education, Ann Brubaker and her ally Carol Inge have enthusiastically rallied to devise ancillary programs pertinent to the theme of the showing.

My dear wife Jan, always my mainstay in sustaining morale and offering wise counsel, has, as Museum slide librarian, secured many needed color prints and slides. My assistant Lisbeth Lurey has attended faithfully to the exacting chore of proofreading.

To all those, near and far, cited or inadvertently unnamed, who have collaborated in achieving the actuality of this unusual exhibition, I am immensely grateful.

George L. McKenna

Pied Beauty

Glory be to God for dappled things—
For skies of couple-colour as a brinded cow;
For rose-moles all in stipple upon trout that swim;
Fresh-firecoal chestnut-falls; finches' wings;
Landscape plotted and pieced—fold, fallow, and plough;
And áll Trádes, their gear and tackle and trim.
All things counter, original, spare, strange;
Whatever is fickle, freckled (who knows how?)
With swift, slow; sweet, sour; adazzle, dim;
He fathers-forth whose beauty is past change:
Praise him.

Gerard Manley Hopkins, 1844-1889

Introduction

The reproductions accompanying this introduction are shown only for purposes
of illustration, and the works of art in them are not included in the exhibition.

Accident! Take a chance! It happens!

These somewhat stirring utterances, expressive of alarm, exhortation, and acceptance, are familiar responses in the presence of the unexpected, whether encountered in mundane daily existence or in the process of fashioning pictures. In art, as in other manifestations of life, change is an ineluctable constant, and often its impetus is chance. From earliest times, chance has served the artist in both method and content. Art, which some of its practitioners have frequently aspired to equate with the seeming certainties of science, can now be perceived, in the recently developed scientific theory of chaos, to be suitably in accord with the predictability of the unpredictable in the objective world. In his 1836 talks on landscape painting at the Royal Institution, London, the artist John Constable stated:

> I hope to show that ours is a regularly taught profession; that it is *scientific* as well as *poetic;* that imagination alone never did, and never can, produce works that are to stand by a comparison with *realities.* [1st lecture]

> Painting is a science, and should be pursued as an inquiry into the laws of nature. Why, then, may not landscape be considered as a branch of natural philosophy, of which pictures are but the experiments? [5th lecture][1]

Chance Beginnings

Realities were early faced and, as far as is known, first transmuted into art by prehistoric beings about thirty thousand years ago, in the Aurignacian era of the Upper (Later) Paleolithic period. Found objects, such as agreeably shaped and colored stones, or teeth, bits of bone and ivory acquired in hunting reindeer and mammoths were worn as ornamentation on the (sometimes painted) body. Lines incised in the objects may have been intended originally to indicate ownership or, in the case of spear points, awls, and other instruments and weaponry, to aid one's hands in gripping them or to improve the holding ability of the devices themselves when fastened to shafts. The continued repetition and elaboration of such engraved designs, beyond their utilitarian function, would seem to denote an in-born concern for beauty of appearance. As Luquet concluded, "I consider as established at the very beginning of prehistoric art, independent of any other preoccupation, the existence and desire for pleasure produced by certain sensorial impressions, here visual, which is the very essence of aesthetic and artistic sentiment."[2]

From such non-objective incisions on tools and from contemporaneous linear drawings or paintings (sometimes designated as 'macaroni') on cave walls, it was but a short step to their resolution, as in a child's random scrawlings, into recognizable partial figural forms—human, animal, or avian. It is believed that such shapes first may have been copied after imprints in soft earth of human or beastly tracks of hand or foot. The earliest intentional art marks are the stenciled likenesses on cave walls of hands defined by blowing pigments around them while the fingers were held against the surface (reproduced in a panel in the exhibition). When whole figures of such creatures as men, women, bison, or horses were represented in polychrome paintings, the artists often made use of existing natural rock projections, cracks, or depressions whose contours in part suggested those of the subjects. Luquet doubts that the painter deliberately searched for these accidental indications of known physical resemblance, but converted them to

x

completed plausible images after chancing to find them.[3]

Endlessly observant in his quest for pragmatic and artistic knowledge of the world, Leonardo da Vinci (1452-1519), living centuries before the discovery of prehistoric cave painting, wrote of the similar potential for form discernible in the lineaments of aged manmade walls:

A Way To Stimulate and Arouse the Mind to Various Inventions

I will not refrain from setting among these precepts [Precepts of the Painter] a new device for consideration which, although it may appear trivial and almost ludicrous, is nevertheless of great utility in arousing the mind to various inventions.

And this is that if you look at any walls spotted with various stains or with a mixture of different kinds of stones, if you are about to invent some scene you will be able to see in it a resemblance to various different landscapes adorned with mountains, rivers, rocks, trees, plains, wide valleys and various groups of hills. You will also be able to see divers combats and figures in quick movement, and strange expressions of faces, and outlandish costumes, and an infinite number of things which you can then reduce into separate and well-conceived forms. With such walls and blends of different stones it comes about as it does with the sound of bells, in whose clanging you may discover every name and word that you can imagine.[4]

In his chronicle of artists, Vasari recorded a similar attention to stained walls by Leonardo's contemporary Piero di Cosimo (1462-1521).[5] Leonardo reproached another contemporary, Sandro Botticelli (1447?-1510), for asserting that a sponge of various colors thrown against a wall would leave a stain "wherein was seen a fine landscape," but that for lack of finish and detail in the scenery he derived from that stain "such a painter makes wretched landscapes."[6]

Sketches Induced by Chance

The last of his several publications presenting, for the guidance of artists, the procedures he had developed for training his pupils, Alexander Cozens (1717-1786) named *A New Method of assisting the Invention in Drawing Original Compositions of Landscape,* alluding to Leonardo's title; it contains engravings after Cozens's original blots and after completed brush drawings he made from them. Noting in the introduction to his treatise the paucity

of inspirational stains on walls when one most needed them, Cozens spoke of his improved method of obtaining them at will by producing equally provocative ink blots on paper. These he regarded as wholly "accidental" formations (though directed with some mental idea of the desired subject) intended to serve as the foundation for more finished sketches to be traced over them[7]—not seemingly a Botticellian ideal.

In his first, earlier publication, 1771, sometimes issued with copies of the *New Method* in 1786, Cozens presented schematic renderings of thirty-two trees, silhouetted masses of each species with some indication of foliage, but no elaborate detail. There is sufficient indication of structural character—trunk and branches, general over-all appearance, and outer contour (but without the linear outlining usually practiced) for each tree to be recognizable. To this diagram it was expected that additions would be made by the artist to establish singularity of the particular tree being represented. As Ching Hao, an early 10th century Chinese artist, wrote in his "Notes on Brush-Work": "As you like to paint clouds, forests, and landscapes, it is necessary for you to understand the origin of every phenomenon. Every tree grows according to its natural disposition."[8]

Or, as Kenneth Feigenbaum, a contemporary physicist who has explored the point at which orderly systems tend to become turbulent or chaotic—as we see them in everyday life—speaking of Dutch ink drawings of about 1600, recently observed: "If you look closely, the trees have sort of leafy boundaries, but it doesn't work if that's all it is—there are also, sticking in it, little pieces of twiglike stuff. There's a definite interplay between the softer textures and the things with more definite lines."[9] Nor are Cozens's paradigms, specific as to type, as spare as Leonardo's diagram of the growth of trees, universalizing a generic, all-purpose form of trunk and branches, an approach to embodying one of Plato's essential perfect archetypes.[10] By means of almost endlessly repeated simple mathematical formulae, involving the near approximation of the form of the tiniest element within such an irregularly contoured natural object as a tree to the shape of its largest components—self-similarity in short—it is possible now to produce in computer simulation its exact likeness. In the 1970s, the scientist Benoit Mandelbrot developed the process, which essentially is a recognition of the hidden order underlying seemingly random phenomena.[11] That order, whose origin is unknowable, is maintained through what Rupert Sheldrake hypothesizes as "morphic resonance" of past states of being and is subject to change only through chance, catastrophic or by way of spontaneous mutations through the creative evolution of natural selection.[12]

Apposite are some earlier references in Chinese art history. In commenting on the stories on art by the Chinese author Chuang Tzu (4th-3rd century B.C.), Sakanishi writes, "What then, we ask, is the relation between the subject of the painting and the painting itself? Unlike in literature, where nature appears only as the reflection of personal moods and thoughts, in painting the expression of nature becomes the primary aim. Hence we have the theory of art as imitation [of nature] and of paintings as substitutes or doubles for those depicted."[13] The essay on landscape painting by Wang Wei (415-443 A.D.) refers to the futility of slavish copying: "In painting the form of an object must first fuse with the spirit, after which the mind transforms it in various ways. The spirit, to be sure, has no form; yet that which moves and transforms the form of an object is the spirit. If the spirit is not manifested in the painting, the forms will not move us at all."[14] The Chinese historian, Chang Yen-yuan (about 850 A.D.), discussing the Six Principles of Painting, lamented: "Paintings of the present time may possess an outward likeness, but the operations of the spirit are lacking in them. If only they strive to obtain the spirit resonance, the outward likeness will naturally be in the work."[15] And, finally, in discussing late Ming painting and associated writings, with regard to the importance of calligraphic skill artists should then have wielded, the present-day historian Chu-tsing Li states, "[The] emphasis on brush and ink instead of likeness is the most important development in late Ming literati theory, with Dong Qichang [Tung Ch'i-ch'ang, 1555-1636] its outstanding exponent."[16]

The proliferation of Oriental and Occidental drawing and painting manuals, the well-known reverence of Chinese artists for the styles of predecessors, and the dependence of European and American masters on the ideas of others disseminated by prints—despite all these, the chance occasion of unaltered reproduction in newly constituted works is rare (except for Warhol?), and individual spontaneity—spirit, to use Chinese phraseology—tends irrepressibly to emerge in art of the greatest originality.

The studies of clouds which conclude Cozens's *New Method* and that John Constable copied about 1800 for instructing himself are as schematic as his trees and as carefully titled, though not in the then new technical terms introduced by the first meteorologists. Perhaps Constable was impelled by the rudimentary nature of Cozens's sketches toward his own later more searching, almost documentary picturing of transient skies, which, appropriately, however, endeavors to indicate the evanescence of such rapidly changing forms.

Observable throughout the exhibition are versions of another of nature's most variable elements, water—in the form of waves, falls, and fountains —sometimes in the most summary styles imaginable and sometimes of a character which closely approaches the illusionism of fractal geometry. Fractals, or fractional dimensions, named and defined by Benoit Mandelbrot, are non-Euclidean (in that they exclude regular manmade geometrical forms—the cylinder, sphere, and cone into which Cézanne divided nature) and trace in natural objects their discontinuous, irregular contours which tend to be endlessly repeatable in any scale within them, from miniscule to huge. The study of the behavior of fluids has long been a preoccupation of artist and scientist alike, from Leonardo to the philosospher Theodor Schwenk, who, in 1976, descried the trails of water particles in a flowing stream as forming strings twisting spirally around each other within the larger surge of the current or movement of the waves.[17] The contemporary photographer Michael McGuire stated, "I can think of no more explicitly fractal image than Hokusai's *Great Wave of Kanagawa*. The great capital C of the wave on the left as it threatens to engulf the small sampan like boat repeats itself in ever smaller waves and wavelets throughout the picture." (Fig. 1)[18] Equal in natural fractal detail but less turbulent are the painting *North Sea* by the Chinese artist Chou Ch'ên (1368-1644) (Fig. 2), Vija Celmins's lithographs of waves (No. 231, 240) and Weston's and White's photographs of surf (No. 199, 200; 202, 212).

The Spectator's Role

Cozens and Constable did not seem to identify the rôle of Leonardo's stains on walls with that of equally provocative and more frequently observed puffs of clouds in adumbrating discernible, extraneous shapes—people, animals, sails, etc. Their more purist painterly concern was with the effects of atmosphere and lighting in skies in modifying landscape. But the common practice of discerning lifelike forms in the heavens has a longer history. It was early noted by Philostratus (about 170-245 A.D.) in his account of the life of the Phythagorean philosopher Apollonius of Tyana,[19] was seen in paintings by the 15th century artist Mantegna, and

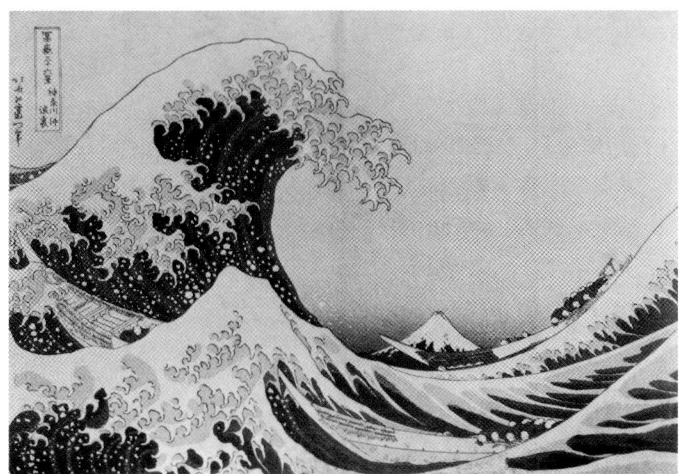

Fig. 1   Katsushika Hokusai (1760-1849)
Great Wave off Kanagawa, from *The Thirty-Six Views of Fuji*
Color woodblock print
Collection: The Nelson-Atkins Museum of Art, Nelson Fund

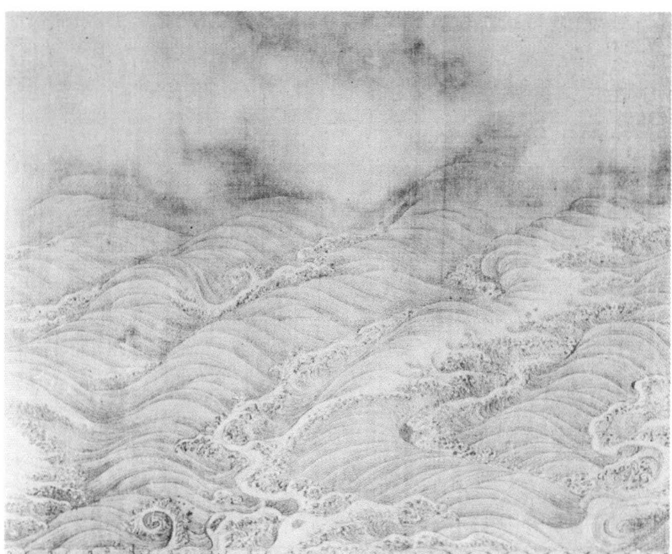

Fig. 2   Chou Ch'ên (about 1455-1536)
The North Sea (detail)
Ink and slight color on silk
Collection: The Nelson-Atkins Museum of Art, Nelson Fund

was expressed later by Shakespeare and other poets. Such chance images are in the eye and mind of the beholder—of skies or pictures. The viewer, collaborating with the artist, as Duchamp stated, "adds his contribution to the creative act."[20]

This contribution is not wholly the harmonizing of the art work with the objective world but involves, also, the spectator's imagination, emotions, and familiarity with other art. Robert Mueller has stated that "you can see things in cloud shapes or in random art, much as if you were looking at a Rorschach inkblot in which you can see faces or animals in the rolling clouds,"[21] but properly specifies that the artist brings to the most seemingly random pictorial creation a sense of order distinctive to himself and perceptible to the observer. Indeed, the spectator's inclination to read recognizable shapes into art created with the aid of chance would appear to be opposed in part to those varieties of painting—abstract expressionist, color field, for instance—that thrive on the objectively indefinable. Harold Rosenberg stated that, in this sort of art, "Form, color, composition, drawing, are auxiliaries, any one of which—or practically all, as has been attempted logically, with unpainted canvases—can be dispensed with ... The innovation of Action Painting was to dispense with the representation of the state [the artist's psychic state or tension] in favor of enacting it in physical movement."[22]

To few of us is given the purported ability of the American artist James Rosenquist (born 1933), who "talks about 'seeing abstraction everywhere, looking at a landscape and seeing abstraction,'"[23] seemingly

the converse of the dark masses and empty, light spaces of Alexander Cozens's elementary ink blots. The capacity for discerning abstraction, akin to viewing out-of-focus or enlarged details of paintings, could serve us well in grasping the essentials of the composition of scenery or art. Or, as Arthur Danto somewhat pejoratively states:

> Think of some great drawing, and then imagine it as seen by you when seized by a kind of pictorial dyslexia, hence as so many splotches and smudges and scratches and puddles. It would be to look at those drawings perhaps as the theory of formalism would enjoin us always to look at everything artistic.[24]

Apropos is the well-known lawsuit by James A. McNeill Whistler (1834-1903) for libel against the writer John Ruskin (1819-1900) who had reviewed, in the publication he edited, *Fors Clavigera,* an exhibition of the artist's work at the Grosvenor Gallery, London, in May, 1877. Alluding to Whistler's canvas, *Nocturne in Black and Gold: The Falling Rocket,* 1874 (a view of fireworks at Cremorne Gardens; now in the collection of the Detroit Institute of Arts), Ruskin opined, "I have seen and heard much of cockney impudence before now, but never expected to hear a coxcomb ask two hundred guineas for flinging a pot of paint in the public's face."[25] In his courtroom testimony, Whistler defined a nocturne as "... an arrangement of line, form and colour first, and I make use of any incident in it which shall bring about a symmetrical result,"[26] "symmetrical" in this context doubtless meaning "compositionally adroit." Without the title

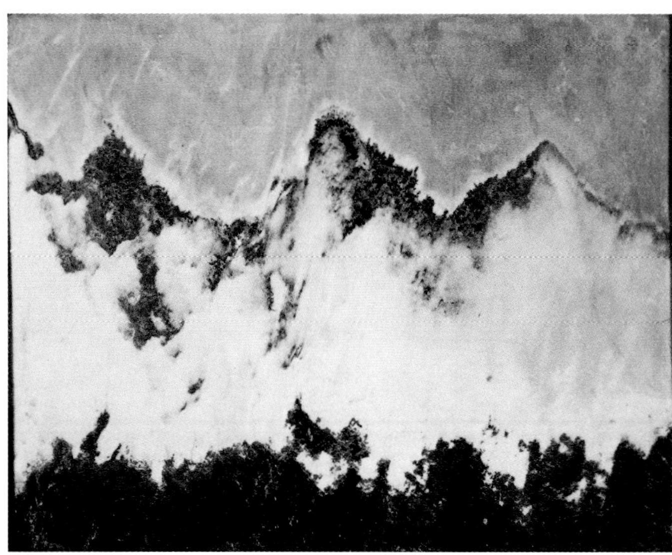

Fig. 3   *Winter Peaks Hoard the Snow,* from a series of *The Four Seasons*
Chinese, 1700-1800
Ta-li marble
Collection: The Nelson-Atkins Museum of Art, Nelson Fund

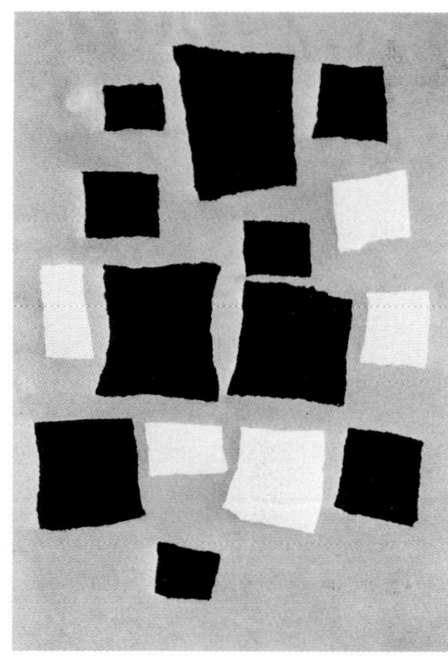

Fig. 4   Jean (Hans) Arp (1887-1966)
Collage Arranged According to the Laws of Chance, 1916-7
Torn and pasted papers
Collection: The Museum of Modern Art, New York, Purchase

appendage of "The Falling Rocket," the picture would not imply a specific model, however transient, and its present-day viewer could be entirely content with Whistler's notion of a non-objective arrangement.

Provocative Conversions

With the advent of the anti-conventional, anti-logical movement of Dada, beginning in Zurich in 1916, and its descendant Surrealism, founded in Paris by the Dadaist André Breton (1896-1966) in 1924, espousing the rôle of the non-rational and marvelous—dreams, the unconscious, "pure psychic automatism"—in forming art, the cultivation of chance became a welcomed procedure. It has continued to be so to the present; in less polemical times it might have been termed "unfettered imagination." Marcel Duchamp (1887-1968) had experimented with chance effects as early as 1913,[27] and Hans Arp (1887-1966) was assembling Dada chance collages from 1916.[28] Duchamp's "ready-mades"—bottle-rack, urinal, bicycle wheel—are essentially found entities selected at random, or as Breton defined them "manufactured objects promoted to the dignity of objects of art through the choice of the artist."[29] The transformation of the commonplace artifact is completed by its new title and by the added signature of the artist.

There is a not too far-fetched older corollary in Chinese marble pictures (known also to a lesser extent in European practice), slabs quarried from natural sources, not artificially created, that embody the semblances of watery, mountainous, or cloudy landscapes (Fig. 3). It has been posited that such rock

scenes may have influenced the "softly furred" styles of the 11th century painters Mi Fu and his son Mi Yu-jen.[30] The translucency of the marble surface, which allows both absorption and reflection of light, is harmonious with the Chinese association of light with clouds, and clouds with mountains: "Just as the moonlight was absorbed into the marble and given forth again, so were clouds described as being sucked into and spewed out of mountains and rocks ... A surface was not an absolute boundary, but a transition from one state of energy to another."[31]

The governing principle here is the chance relocation by the intervening artist of an unaltered object from the realm of the ordinary to that of the esthetic, whether it be a rock form of an aspect pleasing to Oriental taste or a hand- or machine-made Occidental device having a known utilitarian function. Teddy Brunius has summarized the issue:

The point is often made in definitions of art that a work of art is man-made. But we know that the Chinese connoisseurs constructed rules for the use of natural stones just as if they were works of art. These natural stones were taken from the original places, sometimes to be transported far away and put into a garden. They were not changed at all, but nevertheless they were works of art.

Thus the definition of art must be widened. Not all works of art are man-made. It is sophistry to say—as is often said—that man makes a natural work of art when he takes the stone from nature and puts it in a garden. From my point of view, the chief fact is that natural objects are

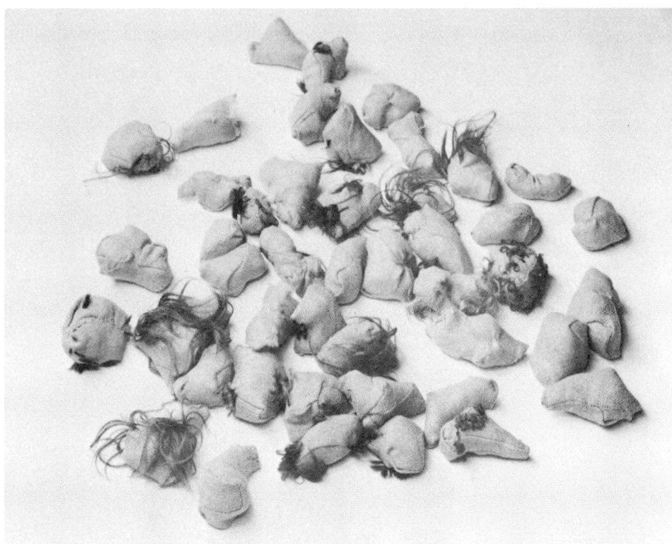

Fig. 5   Kathy Hamilton, American, Contemporary
Untitled (46 Balls)
Burlap and hair
Whereabouts unknown

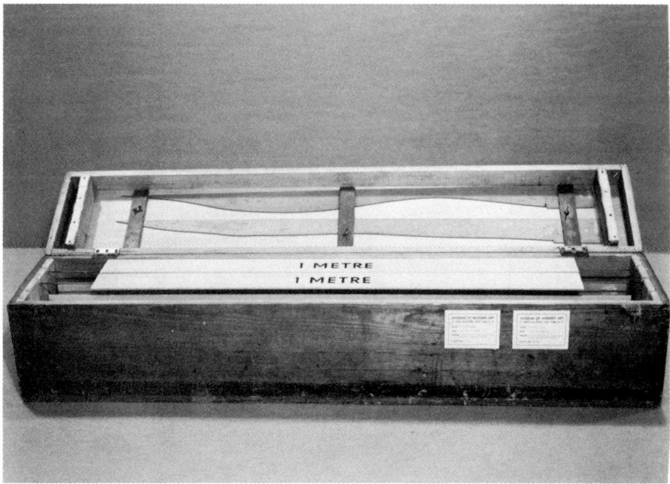

Fig. 6   Marcel Duchamp (1887-1968)
3 Stoppages étalon, 1913-4
Assemblage
Collection: The Museum of Modern Art, New York, Katherine S. Dreier
   Bequest

sometimes used according to the rules of works of art.[32]

In a modern, cleverly simulated Platonic dialogue, the English novelist Iris Murdoch has addressed this very problem:

Acastos *very fast*

... Old statues which don't look like real people are often much better art—and if we just want to imitate real things why have art at all? Real men are more like men than marble men are. Or why not just put a cooking pot on a pedestal and call it art, or a few old bricks or—?

Deximenes

If they were called art at least we'd look at them.[33]

Morse Peckham would seem to have the last word: "A work of art is any perceptual field which an individual uses as an occasion for performing the role of art perceiver."[34]

Proceedings from the Unplotted

Arp's chance collages are the outcome of dropping pieces of paper onto a surface and gluing them there, and thus are not quite of the variety which Braque and Picasso initiated about 1911, composing them from the detritus of urban culture, including whole or partial words from labels or other printed materials, and carefully disposing them within their cubist pictures, usually of still life. *Arrangement According to the Laws of Chance* (Fig. 4), 1916-7 (so titled by the artist many years later), one of Arp's early works in the vein, has an orderliness that seems to belie its supposed haphazard origin.

Although comprised of torn papers (anticipating Arp's looser, fortuitously contoured collages of the 1930s and 1940s) and unlike some of his contemporaneous collages made up of straight-edged fragments sliced with a paper cutter, the picture has an air of conscious deliberation, as Alastair Grieve, William Rubin, and now Jane Hancock have noted.[35] There is considerable intertwining of association at this period between chance visual art and literature—at least words, or random poems, which Pincus-Witten has traced to experiments in the topography of poetry of the last quarter of the 19th century by Stéphane Mallarmé (1842-1898). (Actually such verses in pictorial form were first devised by Greek Rhodian poets about 300 B.C.)[36] They seem to forecast both Cubist collage and Italian Futurist pictographic linguistics.[37] John Cage's lithograph and lithographed plexiglas panels, *Not Wanting to Say Anything about Marcel* (No. 62, 63) use letters as pictorial elements much as they were incorporated in Cubist collages, but they are arranged by chance and are not intended to provide aspects of objective reality as was the practice of Braque and Picasso.

The gracious harmony and the lack of overlapping in Arp's collage, like many of Joan Miró's early automatist prints, fail to suggest the chance formation of a poem assembled by Tristan Tzara's method of drawing random printed lines from a sack. Rather, in its conscious intent, it recalls shaped poetry, or calligrammes, verses in the form of their subject—like Guillaume Apollinaire's sunburst, heart, crown, or rain drops or, even earlier, Lewis

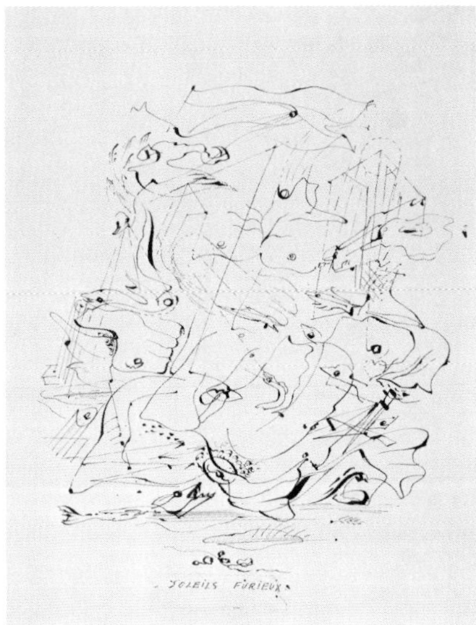

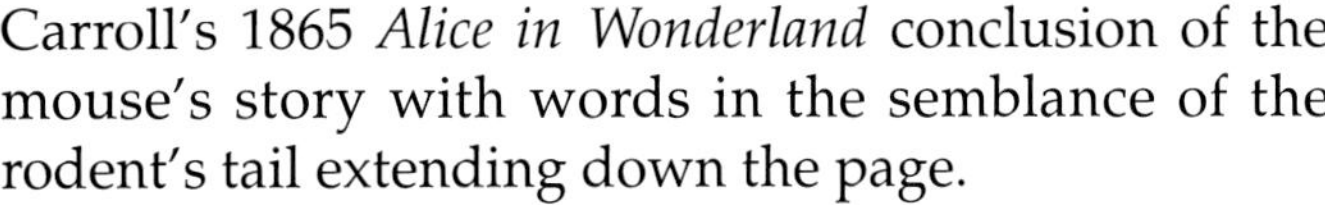

Fig. 7 André Masson (1896–   )
Furious Suns, 1925
Pen and ink
Collection: The Museum of Modern Art, New York, Purchase

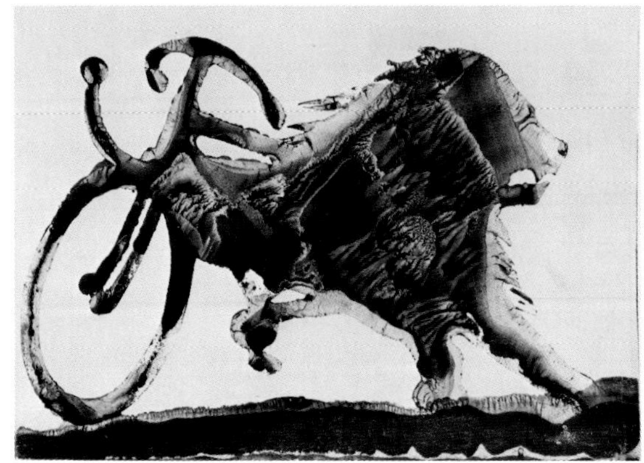

Fig. 8 Oscar Dominguez (1906-1957)
Untitled, 1937
Ink transfer (decalcomania)
Collection: The Museum of Modern Art, New York, Given anonymously

Carroll's 1865 *Alice in Wonderland* conclusion of the mouse's story with words in the semblance of the rodent's tail extending down the page.

Shorn of the control of these and of Arp's collage, and more diffusely evocative is a now vanished work by the contemporary artist Kathy Hamilton shown at our museum, in the Mid-America III exhibition, 1970, an untitled group of forty-six burlap balls, some exuding hair: the fortuitous formation of its final enigmatic appearance was assured by requiring the exhibitor to dump the contents freely from a paper bag (Fig. 5). Sharing in the unpredictability of the result but not eliminating the precipitating act of the author, Marcel Duchamp formed his *3 Standard Stoppages* by dropping threads one meter long from a height of one meter, creating "a new image of length ... the meter dimished,"[38] whose contours converted into wood templates were stored in a box for future use (Fig. 6). Douglass Morse Howell similarly executed *Synchronic Drawings* by adding a dropped string or bits of colored pulp to his paper mash at just the opportune moment for incorporating them as unforeseeable arabesques (No. 59, 60).

Recording on a surface the spoor of the traveling, impulsive hand automatically directed by the unconscious was a technique, derived by the Surrealist theorist André Breton (1896-1966) after 1921 from the idea of free association espoused by Freud, and was at first applied to verbal compositions. No less communicative in its visual incarnation, as in the wandering linearism of André Masson (born 1896) (Fig. 7) or the scattered

placement of imagined objects by Joan Miró (1893-1983) (No. 37), such works "always allude, however elliptically, to a subject ... The Surrealists eschewed perceptual starting points and worked toward an interior image, whether this was conjured improvisationally through automatism or recorded illusionistically from the screen of the mind's eye." [39] The ancient technique of frottage (rubbing over rough surfaces), used by Max Ernst (1891-1976) (No. 36) from 1925 is an automatist method of obtaining images by chance encounters. Like a monotype, decalcomania (taking an impression from a freshly painted original by pressing a sheet of paper over it), practiced from 1936 by Oscar Dominguez (1906-1957) (Fig. 8), produces a transferred image of distinctively fluid, fortuitous texture.

Some of the Surrealist artists—Masson and Miró among them—who had worked with Stanley William Hayter (1901-1988) at his printmaking studio in Paris, Atelier 17, continued to do so when the workshop was relocated to New York during World War II and they exiled themselves from Europe. At the workshop, Jackson Pollock (1912-1956) became familiar with the automatist mode of drawing freely in meandering scribbles and executed his only intaglio prints (No. 42). The practice is regarded as having influenced his later non-objective linear painting with pigments drizzled from above, which in its method of performance is pure automatism. As Pollock describes, "When I am in my painting I am not aware of what I am doing. It is only after a sort of 'get acquainted' period that I see what I have been about. I have no fear about making changes, destroying the image, etc., because the painting has a life of its own. I try to let it come through."[40] While his contextualist approach respects the integrity of the fortuitously forming picture, he nevertheless "'sees' to it that the overall texture is even and balanced and that the elements of shape and color leave each other sufficient freedom."[41]

Plain and Fancy

In science, the simplest adequate explanation for a phenomenon or process is preferred, though not always attained. In art, complicated fullness, subsuming an order however tenuous, seems necessary to correspond with the limitless variety of the objective world and our mental counterpart of it. As Arnhem observes, "The arts, as a reflection of human existence at its highest, have always and spontaneously lived up to this demand of plenitude."[42] The unavoidable requirement for complexity is recognized by such chaos-science theorists as Mitchell Feigenbaum:

> When you look at the early stuff of Van Gogh there are zillions of details that are put into it, there's always an immense amount of information in his paintings. It obviously occurred to him, what is the irreducible amount of this stuff that you have to put in ... With Ruysdael and Turner, if you look at the way they construct complicated water, it is clearly done in an iterative way. There's some level of stuff, and then stuff painted on top of that, and then corrections to that. Turbulent fluids for those painters is always something with a scale idea in it.[43]

In other words, the myriad fractional dimensions that compose the chance contours of waves—unlike the Euclidean averaging approximations of shape—verge on the infinite.

The apparent depreciation of the uncomplicated does not deny spectators the satisfaction of enjoying works of disarming simplicity whose graceful aspect is formed by exceedingly subtle refinements: the Parthenon, Chinese Ch'ing Dynasty porcelains, sculptures by Arp and by Brancusi, for instance. Does not Hogarth's serpentine line of beauty from his 1753 *Analysis of Beauty* suggest such artful simplicity? Perhaps the ultimate reductions are afforded by the white paintings of Rauschenberg (No. 279), which ambient lighting and the transient shadows of viewers are invited to modify; John Cage's silent music, of which the sounds of the audience and the concert hall are the motifs and the performers; and Malevich's endlessly evocative solid black (No. 278) or white squares. In them, simplicity and chance are united, and the potential abundance of complication is limitless. But, according to Arnhem, "A work of art does not ask for meaning; it contains it."[44]

What was called, until the other day, International Style architecture—one of the popular whipping boys for its sterile minimalism—has lately been superseded by buildings with sophisticated vernacular touches. "The vogue for geometrical architecture and painting came and went ... To Mandelbrot and his followers [the theorists of chaos science] the reason is clear. Simple shapes are inhuman. They fail to resonate with the way nature organizes itself or with the way human perception sees the world."[45] While the human demand for naturalistic plenitude is unquestioned, it goes unacknowledged that geometry and chaos theory are both, like art, human concepts seeking to explain the basis of hidden natural order.

But the triangles, circles, and other geometrical shapes, deemed by Galileo and Euclid to be essential to understanding the objective world, are now thought to be inexactly descriptive and to need to be replaced by fractal geometry—the geometry of the irregular—for "clouds are not spheres, mountains are not cones, coastlines are not circles, and bark is not smooth, nor does lightning travel in a straight line."[46]

From nature (and after a glancing blow at the square-on-square pictures of Josef Albers) the fractalists turn to architecture, and, in the latter, from the elegant pristinity of the Seagram building to the elaborate detail of Beaux-Arts design, "with its sculptures and gargoyles, its quoins and jamb stones, its cartouches decorated with scrollwork, its cornices topped with cheneaux and lined with dentils. A Beaux-Arts paragon like the Paris Opera has no scale because it has every scale. An observer seeing the building from any distance finds some detail that draws the eye. The composition changes as one approaches and new elements of the structure come into play."[47] Speaking of Corbusier's city planning, John Cage wrote, "'Art this is called. Its shape is tyranny.'... For situations of too much order, such as programmatic architecture and organizational bureaucracy, he [Cage] champions disorder; for situations of needless disorder, he supports overall ordering ..."[48]

In short, human appreciation for the variability of nature is extended to desire for a like unexpected multifariousness in the built environment. The ornamentation of plain expanses which Louis

Sullivan and Frank Lloyd Wright designed, derived from the forms of growing plants, afforded a rich visual relief from otherwise undifferentiated surfaces. Although stylized in shape, such adornment, viewed at varying angles under changing conditions of light, has a welcome vitality.

Entitled to Arouse

The linguistic labels which artists have chosen to designate their works can have the function of directing viewers to understanding of the themes depicted—or they may not. Such generic appellations as "Landscape" or "Portrait" communicate little information beyond the obvious, but the name of a site or a person furnishes identification, and, for someone familiar with the subject, invites comparison with the known model. Titles like "Improvisation," used by Kandinsky with appended numbers, and "Nocturne" or "Arrangement," favored by Whistler (like his "Arrangement in gray and black," amplified, however, by "Portrait of the painter's mother") indicate the process or declared intention more than the result. Naming a work "Untitled" begs the question, but invites the spectator to an orgy of personal imagination circling around the image and guided only by individual schemata and apperceptions that seem to pertain to what is seen.

The perception of a work of art is a matter of chance interpretation by the viewer, involving memory and expectation: "... we always interpret what we see, even if it is a cloud or an ink-blot."[49] As Danto states, "... in the philosophy of art there is no appreciation without interpretation. Interpretation consists in determining the relationship between a work of art and its material counterpart."[50] The spectator's interpretation may well not be congruent—would that it were!—with the original interpretation of the subject when first confronted (in actuality or in concept) by the artist. The title assigned can be an explanatory clue especially when a Biblical reference, a literary anecdote, or the personification of a mythical creature is portrayed realistically or symbolically. René Magritte's famous image, "This is not a pipe," with the sentence itself inscribed beneath the semblance of the smoker's artifact reminds us that, indeed, the convincing counterfeit is really but a picture of a pipe and fits our classified knowledge of both. When, in 1934, Picasso wedded a bicycle seat and a pair of handlebars and called the bronze cast of them a *Bull's Head* or, in 1951, used a child's toy automobile to serve as the head of the mother in his bronze *Baboon and Young*, the artist directs observers to enjoy the chance veristic resemblances he first detected.

The communicability of a non-objective work of art—abstract, dreamlike, or minimal—can be enhanced by the particularity of the title. As Gombrich concluded, "Let me say in a rough and ready way that language can specify, images cannot. It is an observation which stands in curious contrast to the fact that images are concrete, vivid, and inexhaustibly rich in sensory qualities, while language is abstract and purely conventional."[51] The myriad of colored dots over a pearlescent gray background in Tancredi Parmeggiani's painting is transformed into our recognition of a plausible scene when we know that it is named *Daybreak in Venice* (No. 50). But what can we make of the inscrutable titles of Max Ernst's photogram *Death is something like Cousin Cynthia* (No. 36) or Nancy Graves's color print *Approaches the Limit of II?* (No. 87). These enigmatic captions signify something concretely meaningful to the artist but, veiled in mystery to the beholder, both the pictures and the words are open to inconceivable interpretation. Cryptic encoding of titles is appropriate for visually puzzling intricacies—both stem unpredictably from sources in the unconscious—and the affecting qualities of the pictorial are not diminished by the obscurity of the verbal.

Art arose by chance and has never abandoned the circumstance of its origin.

Introduction Notes

[1]*John Constable's Discourses*, pp. 39, 69.

[2]Luquet, *The Art and Religion of Fossil Man*, p. 116.

[3]*Ibid.*, p. 144.

[4]*The Notebooks of Leonardo da Vinci*, transl. by Edward MacCurdy, Vol. I, p. 250.

[5]Vasari, *Lives of the Most Eminent Painters, Sculptors, and Architects*, transl. by Gaston Du C. de Vere, Vol. II, 811.

[6]Quoted by Yashiro, *Sandro Botticelli and the Florentine Renaissance*, pp. 50-51.

[7]Oppé, *Alexander and John Robert Cozens*, pp. 168-170.

[8]Sakanishi, *The Spirit of the Brush*, p. 90.

[9]Gleick, *Chaos: Making a New Science*, p. 186.

[10]Gombrich, *Art and Illusion*, p. 155.

[11]Gleick, *op. cit.*, pp. 231-232.

[12]Sheldrake, *The Presence of the Past*, pp. 308-313.

[13]Sakanishi, *op. cit.*, pp. 18-19.

[14]*Ibid.*, p. 44.

[15]*Ibid.*, p. 78.

[16]Chu-tsing Li, "Artistic Theories of the Literati," in *The Chinese Scholar's Studio*, p. 18.

[17]Gleick, *op. cit.*, pp. 197-199.

[18]McGuire, "An eye for fractals," in Peitgen and Saupe, *The Science of Fractal Images*, pp. 261-262.

[19]*Ibid.*, pp. 181-182.

[20]Duchamp, "The creative act," p. 29.

[21]Mueller, "The Communication of Art" in *The Science of Art*, p. 105.

[22]Rosenberg, *The Tradition of the New*, p. 26 and n., p. 27.

[23]Tucker, *James Rosenquist*, p. 16, quoting Lippard, "James Rosenquist: Aspects of a Multiple Art," p. 43.

[24]Danto, *The Transfiguration of the Commonplace*, p. 106.

[25]Pennell, *The Life of James McNeill Whistler*, Vol. I, p. 213.

[26]*Ibid.*, p. 234.

[27]Watts, *Chance, A Perspective on Dada*, p. 33.

[28]Hancock, "Arps's Chance Collages" in Foster, ed., *Dada/Dimensions*, 1985, p. 54.

[29]Quoted in Schwarz, *The Complete Works of Marcel Duchamp*, p. 43.

[30]Hay, *Kernels of Energy, Bones of Earth*, p. 86.

[31]*Loc. cit.*

[32]Brunius, "The Uses of Works of Art," p. 127.

[33]Murdoch, *Acastos: Two Platonic Dialogues*, p. 20.

[34]Peckham, *Man's Rage for Chaos; Biology, Behavior and the Arts*, p. 123.

[35]Hancock, *op. cit.*, p. 48 and n. 5.

[36]Boultenhouse, "Poems in the Shapes of Things," p. 65.

[37]Pincus-Witten, "Against Order. Poetical Sources of Chance Art" in Prokopoff, *Against Order: Chance and Art*, n.p.

[38]Duchamp, *Notes and Projects for the Large Glass*, 96.

[39]Rubin, *Dada and Surrealist Art*, p. 150.

[40]Statement in *possibilities* 1, Winter, 1947-8, quoted by Friedman, *Jackson Pollock: Energy Made Visible*, p. 100.

[41]Arnhem, *Entropy and Art: An Essay on Disorder and Order*, p. 23.

[42]*Ibid.*, p. 49.

[43]Quoted in Gleick, *op. cit.*, pp. 186-187.

[44]Arnhem, *op. cit.*, p. 55.

[45]Gleick, *op. cit.*, pp. 116-117.

[46]Mandelbrot quoted in Peitgen and Saupe, *op. cit.*, p. 23.

[47]Gleick, *op. cit.*, p. 117.

[48]Kostelanetz, ed., *John Cage*, p. 206.

[49]Gombrich, "Image and word in twentieth-century art," p. 221.

[50]Danto, *op. cit.*, p. 113.

[51]Gombrich, *op. cit.*, pp. 220-221.

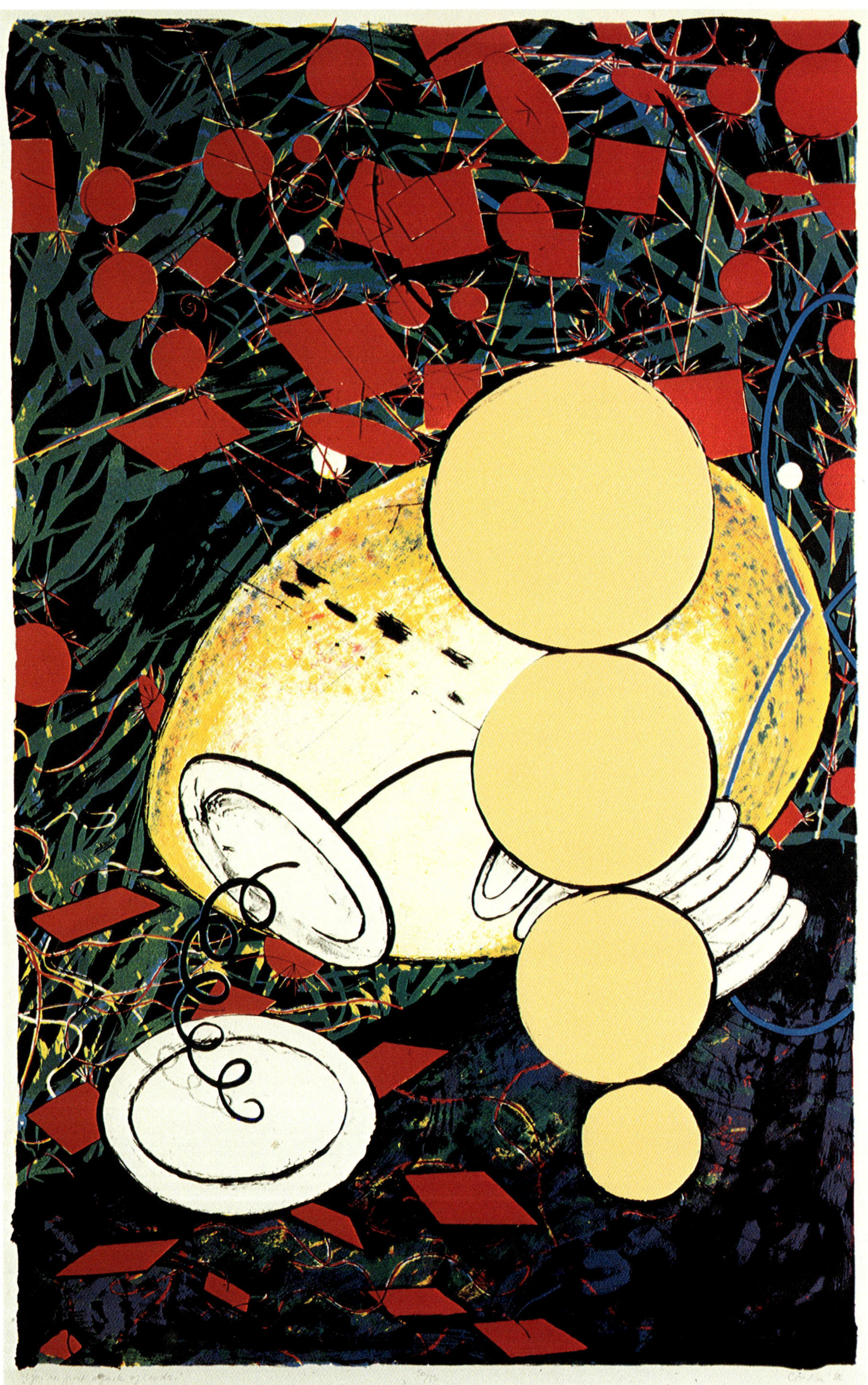

103. Chris Costan
American, contemporary
You're Just a Pack of Cards, 1986, 50/75
Color lithograph
Collection: The Nelson-Atkins Museum of Art, Anonymous Gift

I. Unpremeditated and Invented Tracks: Random Loci

Chosen by human volition, but independent of will in their results, techniques which incorporate chance in making artifacts emulate the indeterminate workings of nature and exalt the unconscious. Human creations, however seemingly subjective in origin, can partake of the chaos with which the objective world is invested. In the works of art in this section of the exhibition, orders of disorder are everywhere discernible. They may be regarded as evidences of the subordination of consciousness to uncontrollable processes dependent on variable conditions: among them, the viscosity of ink or pigment, the strength of air currents, the resistance and texture of materials, the flexibility of a moving limb, the vagaries of dreams.

Some thirty thousand years ago the first known examples of art appeared: paintings of hands in such Upper Paleolithic caves as Altamira and El Castillo in Spain, Gargas and Pech Merle in France.[1] (See illustrated panel in exhibition.) In black, red, or yellow, these likenesses were formed by a prehistoric human blowing from the mouth or through a bone tube the powdered pigments which define on the walls the negative silhouettes of hands. The delicately speckled texture in the surrounding clouds so obtained is entirely random. Most of the impressions are of left hands of women and children. One can only speculate on the pictures' functions.

Many millennia after these enigmatic, blurred images, there is manifest in the decoration of another of man's early arts—pottery—evidences of unpredictability. These include marbled ware, found in ancient Rome and China, as well as in many other civilizations, that is produced by successive layering, cutting, and merging of clay bats of two or more colors, then pressing them into a mold to form an object. The striations are thus wholly the result of chance.[2] By chance, also, the T'ang Dynasty jar (No. 1), resembles 18th century Staffordshire agate wares (No. 10, 13).

In Oriental pottery wares, the effects of mottling, streaking, and crackling, originally accidental, could, through practice, be attained with some degree of prescience.[3] The delicate vertical trails of the tea bowl of *chien* stoneware (No. 2) (known as *Temmoku* in Japan), from northern Fukien, was obtained by dipping the body into the glaze while holding the foot-rim. In the evocative Chinese descriptive designations of glazes, the appearance is called "partridge feather" or "hare's fur." The glaze of the three-color bowl with splotches (No. 8), an 18th century work in T'ang Dynasty style, is termed "egg and spinach" or "tiger-skin."

In Japan, the dripping dark-brown ash glaze of Seto ware (No. 17) has an engaging, spontaneous informality, a quality echoed even more emphatically in the uneven surfaces of bowls of *raku* ware (No. 20), modeled by hand, rough and asymmetrical, prized by the masters of the tea ceremony as much for their suitability for use as for their patent esthetic appeal.[4] A streakiness akin to both Chinese and Japanese wares is evident in 18th century English Staffordshire pottery, particularly of Whieldon type (No. 11), and in 19th century American Bennington objects (No. 32): all of them are usually designated by the generic term, "tortoise-shell."

Webs of crackle, observable in both Chinese and Japanese wares (No. 17-19) as either background or sole decoration, were originally accidental, the result of differing rates of contraction of the clay body and its glaze during firing and subsequent cooling.[5] Hobson posited the addition of a powdered stone, possibly steatite, a *sui yu*, or crackle glaze, to produce crazing of the sort sometimes seen in dishes after long use.[6]

There is some visual similarity between the mottling of pottery and the marbling of paper, mentioned as early as 905 A.D. in the *Shoku kokin wakashu* (Anthology of Ancient and Modern Japanese Verse Continued), the technique being "*sumi nagashi* (ink floating), by which ink dropped on water is stirred to make a random pattern, and then paper is laid over it to absorb this design."[7] In its incarnation beginning in the early 16th century, "marbling is known as 'cloud art', *ebru* in Turkey, *abri* in Persia, and *abar* in India."[8] While marbling appears in Japanese 12th century books as background for pages of calligraphy, in Deccan (southern India) paintings of the mid-17th century it defines and comprises the figural subjects, most often through the method of stenciling (No. 5). Modern marbling has generally been used for papers for book-binding (since the late 18th century), gift-wrapping, and decorative screens, but in the Maurers' book *Dinosaurs Dining* (No. 106) the creatures themselves are composed of marbling in the Indian way. In his prints of figures of 1961 and 1962, Dubuffet formed their likenesses from details of natural textures found in graphics of his *Phenomena* series (No. 215, 220).

In contrast, two sheets of abstract marbling provide the illustrations of the "'motley emblem of my work'" in editions of Laurence Sterne's *Tristam Shandy*, 1768, 1788, and 1794.[9] In Italian Renaissance art, painted simulacra of the random natural veining of marble are seen in architectural details of works by such artists as Giotto, Mantegna, Crivelli, and Giovanni Bellini. Trained from 1899 to 1900 in the craft of decorative painting, Braque could adeptly reproduce marble table-tops in still-life canvases of 1925 and 1930.

Use of actual marble slices as art is exemplified by the unadorned panels of the "Four Seasons" of 18th century China (Fig. 3), and a school of North Italian or southern German masters of the 17th - 18th century, who adapted the veining as landscape settings, adding painted figures. Rocks, regarded by the Chinese as the bones of earth and as symbols of immortality, concentrations of natural energy, were arranged within their gardens and often depicted in their paintings. Miniature rocks, on a lesser scale resembling mountains, were collected for use as inkstones, brushrests, incense burners, and ornamental sculpture, much as automata and bronze figures furnished grace notes in European Renaissance connoisseurs' studies. Mountains, frequently wreathed in mist or rising from regions of waterspray, were sometimes deemed cloudlike in China, in a stage of change of vital energy, *qi*,[10] effected by water, in which rock was transformed into earth. Here (No. 7), the rock is, indeed, cloudlike, and its mineral content, malachite, was supposed by 5th century Chinese alchemists to be transmutable into cinnabar, one of the most familiar elixirs of immortality.[11] "A term for painting itself, established during the period when color was at the very heart of its being, was *danqing* ('cinnabar and malachite')."[12]

More diffuse than running pottery glazes but equally random, the decoration of Japanese lacquer wares (No. 4, 9, 29) involves a technique called *makie* ("sprinkled design"), in which powdered gold or silver is distributed by shaking from a tube over wet lacquer. The surface pattern, in its simplest flat form, *hiramakie*, is then lacquered and polished, providing a shining background of myriad dots.

Before the advent chiefly in 18th century England of the use of suggestive puddled washes on paper, Oriental painters, among them the Chinese Yun Shou-p'ing (No. 6) and the Japanese Kano Tanyu (No. 3), wielded the brush with calligraphic fluency in utter freedom to indicate impressionistically the character of forms. The fabled Oriental reverence for the accomplishments of predecessors often led to the emulation of bygone styles, but in such latter-day re-creations originality of manner was not wholly forfeited in favor of sedulous imitation.[13]

While Gainsborough (No. 14, 15, 22) and Romney (No. 16) were contemporaries of Alexander Cozens, there does not seem to have been a direct relationship among them. Often their drawings have a quality of randomness without apparent conscious intent akin to Cozens's blots, but they did not trace their initial sketches as Cozens advocated to provide foundations for finished works.[14]

Onetime drawing master at Christ's Hospital and Eton College, Alexander Cozens (1717-1786), who was described by his friend and pupil William Beckford, in 1781, as "almost as full of Systems as the Universe,"[15] paradoxically devoted his methodizing to advocating means of enabling the artist to devise landscape compositions in the freest and most accidental ways possible. His early publications on trees, clouds (in Part III, No. 178), which Constable copied, and on *Various Species of Composition in Nature* (see Constable's reproduction of one, No. 27) presented schematic renderings of their subjects, useful as guides for painters. Cozens's last, culminating publication, *A New Method of assisting the Invention of Drawing Original Compositions of Landscape*, 1785, codified his blotting system, an aid to the imagination. "An artificial blot," Cozens wrote in his introduction, "is a production of chance, with a small degree of design … The blot is not a drawing, but an assemblage of accidental shapes, from which a drawing may be made."[16] Cozens's own sequence is illustrated by No. 24 a, b and 25 a, b, with the prints of the blots accompanied by some of those of the subsequent drawings. Although Leonardo, Piero di Cosimo, and Botticelli noted the provocative aspect of random stains on walls, suggesting the forms of real objects, Cozens rightly lamented their scarcity, and his method produced a ready supply of equally suggestive blots, which could be made even more accidental by crumpling the paper before dropping ink upon it. He helpfully contrasted his procedure with the more usual practice of detailed drawing:

> To sketch in the common way, is to transfer ideas from the mind to the paper, or canvas, in outlines, in the slightest manner. To blot, is to make varied spots and shapes with ink on paper, producing accidental forms without lines, from which ideas are presented to the mind. This is conformable to nature: for in nature, forms are not distinguished by lines, but by shade and colour. To sketch, is to delineate ideas; blotting suggests them.[17]

Cozens's third rule in his New Method includes the admonition, upon beginning blotting, to "Possess your mind strongly with a subject," and his treatise concludes with a list of sixteen representative "Descriptions of the various Kinds of Composition of Landscape," generalities so unspecific, however, that they would not inhibit the freedom of the artist.

Although John Constable spoke of his abiding regard for the manner in which Rembrandt, Claude Lorrain, and Gainsborough executed their views of nature and often, for his self-instruction, copied prints after their works (and those of others, like Cozens), he nonetheless approached landscape freshly, sketching outdoors the details of scenes that particularly appealed to him. These have a notable spontaneity, as in No. 179, somewhat muted later in the relatively more finished paintings of the same subjects he completed in his London studio. To him, the homely aspects his familiar countryside afforded had great pictorial significance: "'He would also stand gazing at the bottom of a ditch, and declare he could see the finest subjects for painting.'"[18] Constable's affection was for the transient in his world: "… the sound of water escaping from Mill dams, so do Willows, Old rotten Banks, slimy posts, and brickwork. I love such things … "[19] From his close observations of these changing phenomena (including weather, especially clouds, see Section III) Constable fashioned his romantic, atmospheric art. In tune with Wordsworth —"The ordinary things should be presented to the mind in an unusual aspect" (Preface to *Lyrical Ballads*, 2nd ed., 1800) — he celebrated the affecting commonplaces of nature.

With the onset of the modern era, the processes and changeableness of the environment tended to be less often the subject of art (with such obvious exceptions as the Impressionists' devotion to study of transformations by light, and as modern-day photorealism and adaptation of bygone styles). Rather the effects of chance and natural change have been absorbed into the working techniques of artists, often in the service of non-objective content, producing a new, no less romantic reality, as varied in range as nature itself.

As random as the formation of waves in the water or the flicker of sunlight upon them, the disposition of elements over the surface of a picture can, in the absence of a naturally prescriptive model, be determined by unconscious selection, "automatism," or the direction of chance. Often the result of such unpremeditated placement of many constituents is an all-over patterning, an expression of *horror vacui* (seen here in the work of Cage, Conner, Miró, and Tobey, No. 107, 55, 37, 44). The early 20th century European art movements of Dada (itself so titled by a fortuitous finding in a dictionary) and its successor Surrealism both sought to establish a viewpoint, beyond and superior to that of the rational realm. In this new world view, the unpredictable reigned, as it can be observed doing in these random compositions.

Closely related to them are the comprising elements themselves, equally the products of chance: the skeins of whirling lines by Hayter (No. 46) and Pollock (No. 42) sometimes coalescing in near-recognizable forms; the concatenations of strokes achieved by the dynamic gesturings of Conner, Tobey, Nancy Graves, Joan Mitchell, Steir, and Yunkers (No. 55, 44, 81, 88, 82, 84-5); the expressive recordings of their pictorializing movements by

Dine, Hartung, LeWitt, Pollock, and Yektai (No. 86, 43, 77, 40-1, 48).

Jackson Pollock's essentially calligraphic black and white early style, interlocking lines and nodes (No. 40, 41), recalls, on a greater scale, the blots of Alexander Cozens. Undoubtedly it stemmed from Pollock's brief experimentation, in 1944-5, with intaglio graphics at Hayter's New York Atelier 17. There, in association with Hayter himself and with the emigres Masson and Miró, all of the Surrealist automatist bent, he explored the possibilities of unconsciously impelled, freely meandering linearity, within a shallowly defined depth that Greenberg relates to the flat planes of the Analytical Cubism of Picasso and Braque in 1912-1913 (No. 42).[20] The drips of Pollock's celebrated paintings in color, from enamel drizzled from cans or basters on to canvases spread on the floor, Danto regards as "monuments to accident, spontaneity, giving the paint its own life,"[21] as the artist had allowed the graver to assume its own orbit in his graphics.

The device of the dropped cord, coiling as it may upon impact, was first employed by Marcel Duchamp to form his *3 Standard Stoppages*, 1913: three one-meter threads were allowed to fall from a height of one meter, and the resultant curved profiles, traced on wood strips, were cut out and stored in a croquet box as templates of units of measurement, "canned chance,"[22] ready to shape lines in other works, such as *The Large Glass*. Hans Arp made more studied use of the method in his string reliefs of 1923-4 and 1929, and Ernst, in his series of "Hordes" paintings of 1927, made rubbings over twine. In the spirit of Duchamp, Douglass Morse Howell, the virtuoso artificer of handmade paper, with the aid of pulp beaters designed by himself and an encyclopedic knowledge of physics and historical lore absorbed into his processes, produced "synchronic drawings." These sheets, one embodying an actual string (No. 59) and the other shreds of dyed pulp (No. 60), are the culmination of a dance-like controlled accident, evidences of exquisite timing. Yunkers's *Les Pendus* suite appears to capture gravity acting on suspended lines (No. 84).

The respective natural properties of actual materials are otherwise demonstrated here in such examples as the spreading ink blot of Wally Depew's book (No. 83), the drips and splashes of Ernst's lithographs (No. 65), the poured pigments of Jenkins's painting and print (No. 61, 66), the aleatory assemblage of Landweber's photographed pills (No. 80), the liquid circles of Nicht's cliché-verre (No. 93), the pressed-out traces of Petrini's decalcomania (No. 67), the flowing syrup of Smith's photograph (No. 39), Sommer's spoors of smoke (No. 58), and Welling's camera views of clotted gelatin (No. 100).

The pictograms of Penck (No. 90) and the invented scripts of Snyder, Twombly, and Zazeela (No. 73, 64, 69) in their calligraphic abandon have the plausibility of parsable languages beyond the visual appeal of their linear vitality. *Frottages* — rubbings on paper or canvas of such textured objects as the grain of wood, the surface of stones, patterns embossed on cloths — transfer to a flat plane the designed or haphazard circumstances of their three-dimensional prototypes. Ernst, Miró, Motherwell, Rauschenberg, and Segal have all exploited the resources of this reservoir of motifs from found or manipulated objects (No. 36, 47, 56, 54, 79). Trevor Jones assembled actual leather fragments for binding a Joyce volume he regarded as a literary equivalent of collage (No. 76), and Charlesworth, in her Tartan sets (No. 102) and Stokes and Douglas, in their book *Mim* (No. 105), all focused on the pattern details of existing materials.

Mottled textures, recalling those of Japanese lacquer and woodblocks and Impressionist pointillism, all composed of an infinity of dots, were realized by Toulouse-Lautrec by flicking ink from a toothbrush on to his lithographic stones (No. 35), obtaining areas of *crachis* (spattering) in a fashion first wielded by Chéret. Lautrec's friend Charles Maurin discovered about 1893 that with a vaporizer he could invest his painted landscapes, aquatic and telluric, with misty atmosphere (No. 34), making an "art of exhalation … 'untouched by human hands.'"[23] Contemporary American graphics that partake of a similar pervasive evanescence, which is the whole content as well, are instances by Cage (No. 107) and Olitski (No. 71).

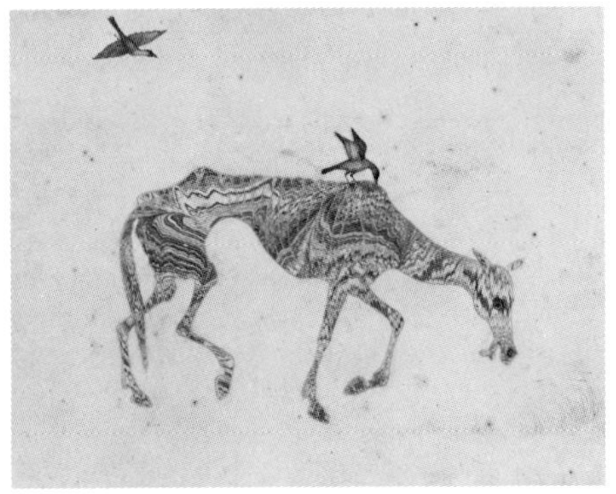

5. Unknown Deccan artist, about 1625

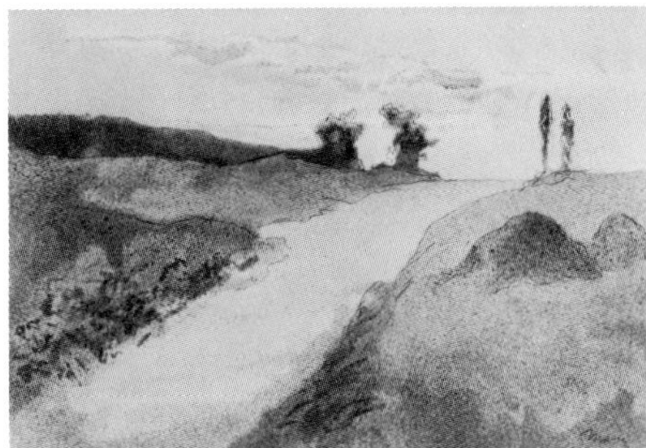

34. Charles Maurin, 1895

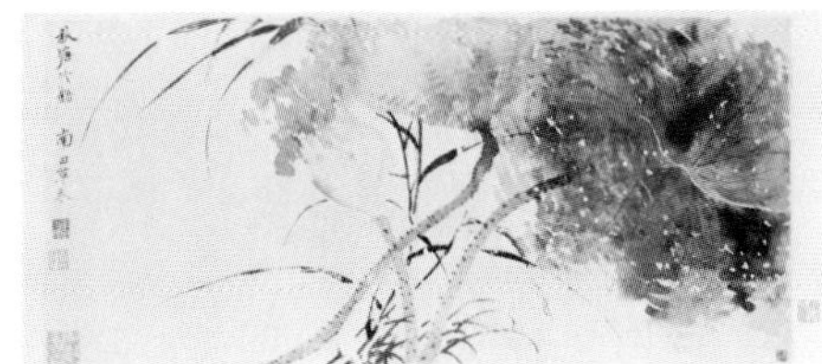

6. Yün Shou-p'ing, 1674

1. Jar with lid
Chinese, T'ang Dynasty (618-906)
Pottery, marbled ware, 2-1/2" (64 mm) high
Collection: The Nelson-Atkins Museum of Art, Purchase,
    Nelson Fund

The forerunner of English agate ware

2. Bowl
Chinese, Sung Dynasty (960-1279)
Pottery, Chien ware
3-3/8" (86 mm) high, 5-7/8" (155 mm) diameter
Collection: The Nelson-Atkins Museum of Art, Purchase,
    Nelson Fund

Streaming blue-black glaze with brown flecks

3. Kano Tanyu
Japanese, 1601-1674
Great Waves Below the Rising Moon
Hanging scroll, ink on paper
10" x 23" (254 x 584 mm)
Collection: The Nelson-Atkins Museum of Art, Bequest of
    Mrs. George H. Bunting, Jr.

The extreme spontaneity of the wave form is that of the
"flying white" stroke (*hihakutai*) in calligraphy, leaving
uninked areas from the impress of a split, nearly dry
brush tip.

4. Lid of writing box *(suzuribako)*
Japanese, Edo Period (1615-1867)
Lacquer
7-3/4" x 9-1/2" x 1-7/8" (197 x 242 x 48 mm)
Collection: The Nelson-Atkins Museum of Art, Bequest of
    Joseph H. Heil

5. Unknown artist
Deccan, southern India, Bijapur
Birds Attack a Dying Nag (Weimann 3)
About 1625
Marbled painting on paper, from one stencil: tarakli-ebru
5-3/8" x 6-9/16" (132 x 166 mm)
Collection: Arthur M. Sackler Museum, Harvard
    University, Cambridge, Massachusetts, Private
    Collection

Tarakli-ebru is the Turkish term for "combed" marbling,
produced by dragging through the colors a comb-like
device of wires protruding from a wood block.

6. Yün Shou-p'ing
Chinese, 1633-1690
Two of eight leaves of painting in the album *Landscapes,
    Flowers, and Vegetables*, 1674
a. Leaf c: "Cloudy Mountains," ink on paper
b. Leaf g: "Lotus," ink and color on paper
Each leaf, 10-1/8" x 23-3/8" (264 x 594 mm)
Collection: The Art Museum, Princeton University, Gift of
    David L. Elliott

Yün Shou-p'ing, who called himself "The Recluse of Nan-
t'ien," painted landscapes throughout his career in the
manner of masters of the Sung and Yuan dynasties. His
mountain scene is executed in the style of the Sung
painters Mi Fu (1052-1107) and Mi Yu-jen (1072-1151),
using their manner of splashing ink wash in dots to form
mountain and trees when, as Yün inscribed on the
painting, "Clouds pass, and lines on the trees blur…" and
"Following my impulses, I casually smeared on ink,
intending to make something resembling the Mi-style
cloudy mountains. The ink dripped and soaked in as the
brush raced around, producing this result" (Quoted and
translated by Julia K. Murray, "An Album of Paintings by
Yun Shou-p'ing, the Recluse of Nan-t'ien", p. 11). In his
later life, Yün made many paintings of flowers, in
the so-called "boneless" mode, disposing delicate
color washes to form shapes of blossoms and foliage
without previously outlining them in ink. As he notes in
his inscription on the previous leaf of peonies, Yün was
"sketching the idea" (*Ibid.*, p. 16) of the flower in the
manner of Hsu Ch'ung-ssu (11th century), and the
"Lotus" is close to paintings of the same subject by Ch'en
Shun (1483-1544), one of them in the Nelson-Atkins
Museum collection (reproduced, *ibid.*, Fig. 5, p. 18). The
dark strokes in the lotus are now accompanied by random
white dots resulting from loss of paint.

7. Malachite object
Chinese, 18th century
Inscribed: This stone was obtained at the slope of the
    White Mountain, north of Tali in Yunnan Province. Its
    color and shape are natural. Noted by Wu Liang in the
    10th year of the Chien-lung era [1745]. (Translation by
    Wai-kam Ho)
4-1/2" (114 mm) high, 3-1/2" (89 mm) wide; 7-1/2" (191
    mm) high with fitted wood stand
Collection: The Nelson-Atkins Museum of Art, Bequest of

Laurence Sickman

According to Mr. Ho, the engravings on the front of the rock—an elephant, horse, bird, and rose—are probably much later than the inscription.

8. Bowl
Chinese, 18th century
Pottery, three-color glazed ware, Ch'eng-hua mark on base
4-3/4" (121 mm) diameter
Collection: The Nelson-Atkins Museum of Art, Anonymous gift

Mottled polychrome glaze in T'ang style

9. Bottom portion of cosmetic box
Japanese lacquer, 18th century, Edo Period (1615-1867)
1/2" (38 mm) high, 4-1/2" (114 mm.) diameter
Collection: The Nelson-Atkins Museum of Art, Gift of Mrs. Jacob L. Loose

10. Plate
English, Staffordshire, dated 1746 (Burnap Cat. 388)
Agate ware pottery in blue, brown, and cream
11-1/2" dia. (292 mm)
Collection: The Nelson-Atkins Museum of Art, Gift of Frank P. and Harriet C. Burnap

The random veining of solid agate ware is obtained from the repeated superimposition of variously colored bats of clay beaten, rolled, and sliced to form a layered mass which is pressed into molds.

11. Teapot
English, Staffordshire, about 1755-1760 (Burnap Cat. No. 434)
Whieldon-type pottery ware, 4-1/8" high (105 mm)
Collection: The Nelson-Atkins Museum of Art, Gift of Frank P. and Harriet C. Burnap

The streaked blue and brown decoration is typical of the tortoise-shell glaze used on wares produced by the firm headed by Thomas Whieldon (1719-1795).

12. Teapot
English, Staffordshire, about 1755-1760 (Burnap Cat. No. 237)
Saltglaze pottery
4-1/4" high (108 mm)
Collection: The Nelson-Atkins Museum of Art, Gift of Frank P. and Harriet C. Burnap

The unusual decoration emulates the natural appearance of limestone strata bearing fossil forms.

13. Vase
English, Staffordshire, about 1769-1780 (Burnap Cat. No. 569)
Marbled pottery ware made by Josiah Wedgwood and Thomas Bentley at the Etruria factory
9-1/4" high (235 mm)
Collection: The Nelson-Atkins Museum of Art, Gift of Frank P. and Harriet C. Burnap

Wedgwood's version of agate ware is here a combination of randomly swirling color glazes.

14. Thomas Gainsborough
English, 1727-1788
Shepherd among Trees (Hayes 291)
Late 1760s
Brown wash over an offset outline
7-5/16" x 10-1/8" (186 x 257 mm)
Collection: The Nelson-Atkins Museum of Art, Bequest of Milton McGreevy

The wash is laid over a vestigial outline (visible along the back of the shepherd and the central sheep and on some of the tree forms). Such outlines in Gainsborough's drawings are believed to have been transferred by offset from wet oil colors, a process begun by Castiglione in the 17th century. "[P]ossibly it was the uncertainty of the effects that would result that he relished, a stimulus to his imagination akin to 'blotting'" (Hayes, *The Drawings of Thomas Gainsborough*, I, 25).

15. Thomas Gainsborough
English, 1727-1788
Study for "Repose" (Hayes 402)
Mid-1770s
Black and white chalk with touches of pink, ocher, and beige chalk on blue paper
11" x 12-9/16" (279 x 319 mm)
Collection: The Nelson-Atkins Museum of Art, Gift of Thomas Agnew and Sons

This study for the Museum's painting, *Repose*, about 1777-8, has a pentimento of a standing figure above the sleeping herdsman. The latter is so shown reclining in the canvas, but the earlier upright version may have been in the now vanished etching of the scene known only from a description in *The Illustrated London News*, July 25, 1846, p. 55 (Hayes, *Gainsborough as Printmaker*, No. 22). Black chalk is strongly employed throughout, modulated and accented with white chalk in the "moppings" of the clouds, and Hayes finds that "His animals are modelled in a welter of almost random touches" (Hayes, *The Drawings of Thomas Gainsborough*, 1, 44).

16. George Romney
English, 1734-1802
Rape of the Sabines, 1773-5
Pen and wash in brown ink
4-3/4" x 9-1/16" (121 x 230 mm)
Collection: The Nelson-Atkins Museum of Art, Gift of Mr. and Mrs. Robert L. Bloch

Fluidly and dashingly drawn, this "blottesque" sketch of a familiar classical subject may have been executed during the artist's stay in Italy studying the Old Masters. In its loosely defined manner, it appears to echo Alexander Cozens's precept: "... the idea or conception of any subject, in any branch of the art, may be first formed into a blot. Even the historical, which is the noblest branch of painting, may be assisted by it; because it is the speediest and the surest means of fixing a rude whole of the most transient and complicated image of any subject in the painter's mind" (from *The New Method*, in Oppé, *Alexander & John Robert Cozens*, p. 171).

17. Wine bottle
Japanese, about 1780
Pottery, Seto ware, made in Owari province
6-7/8" (175 mm) high, 4-3/4" (121 mm) diameter
Collection: The Nelson-Atkins Museum of Art, Purchase, Nelson Fund

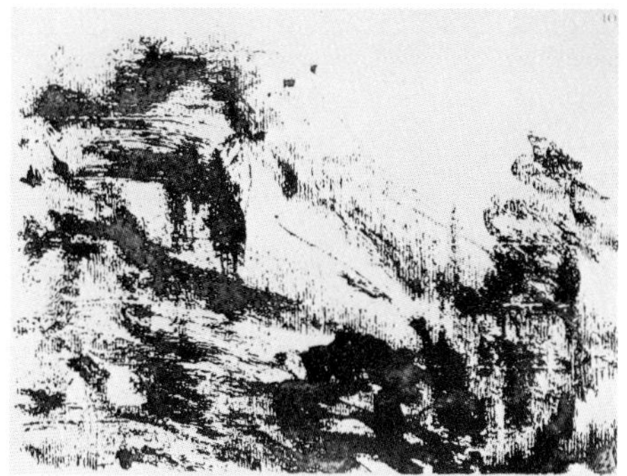
24a.   Alexander Cozens, about 1785

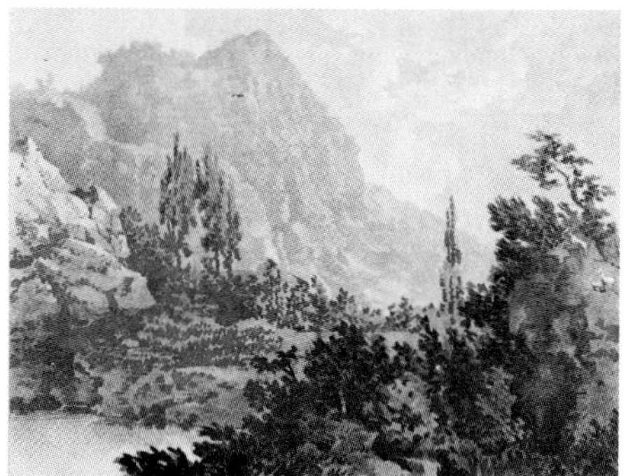
24b.   Alexander Cozens, about 1785

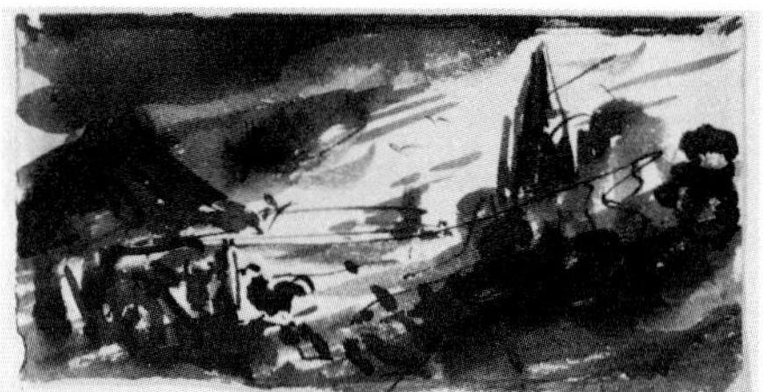
28.   John Constable, 1833

Crackle ware with dark brown glaze running unevenly from mouth down over the shoulders

18. Wine bottle
Japanese, about 1780
Pottery, Awata ware, made in Kyoto
7-3/4" (197 mm) high, 3-3/4" (96 mm) diameter
Collection: The Nelson-Atkins Museum of Art, Purchase, Nelson Fund

Fine crackle ware with irregular, brown-toned washes and a landscape and poem in blue glaze

19. Bottle
Japanese, about 1780
Pottery, Nabeshima ware, made in Hizen province
8-7/8" (226 mm) high, 5-3/4" (146 mm) diameter
Collection: The Nelson-Atkins Museum of Art, Purchase, Nelson Fund

Indented ovoid form with pale celadon glaze in large crackle

20. Tea bowl
Japanese, late 17th - early 18th century
Ichinyu (Raku IV) ware, Kyoto, copy of Koyetsu
2-3/4" (70 mm) high, 4-1/4" (109 mm) diameter
Oval-shaped form in black and red glaze
Collection: The Nelson-Atkins Museum of Art, Purchase, Nelson Fund

21. Tea bowl
Japanese, about 1810
Imbe ware, Bizen province
3-1/4" (83 mm) high, 5-1/4" (134 mm) diameter
Bowl coated with iron-rust glaze and clusters of white glaze in the interior
Collection: The Nelson-Atkins Museum of Art, Purchase, Nelson Fund

22. Thomas Gainsborough
English, 1727-1788
Landscape with Ruin and Shepherds (Hayes 742)
Mid- to later 1780s
Water color, white and black chalk
8-1/2" x 12" (216 x 305 mm)
Collection: The Nelson-Atkins Museum of Art, Bequest of Milton McGreevy

Large compositional masses appear to have been applied by "mopping" with bits of sponge. The broad washes thus obtained are detailed with brush strokes and with touches of black and white chalk. Trees, rocks, animals, and people alike are dashed in freely, providing an impressionist effect, recalling Cozens's suggestive blots.

23. Alexander Cozens
English, 1717-1786
Blots: prints in the publication *A New Method of assisting the Invention in Drawing Original Compositions of Landscape,* after drawings; about 1785 (Wilton 39, 40, 41)
Three aquatints, each 9-7/16" x 12-3/8" (240 x 315 mm)
Collection: Davison Art Center, Wesleyan University
The identification of the blots corresponds with the categories listed in Cozens's publication *Various Species of Composition in Nature,* which are shorter versions of the descriptions on Pages 32-33 of *A New Method*:
a. Plate 14: "A close or confined scene, with little or no sky."
b. Plate 15: "A landscape of a moderate extent between the right and left hand, the objects or groups placed irregularly, and no one predominant. The horizon above the bottom of the view."
c. Plate 16: "An extensive country, with no predominant part or object. The horizon above the bottom of the view."

The illustrations are exemplary of the "various Kinds of Composition of Landscape" (*A New Method*, p. 32) which the student or artist might have generally in mind when preparing blots true to those types as titled. The suggestive contents of blots, not considered the wholly accidental stains Leonardo, in his *Treatise on Painting*, cited as offering pictorial potential, Cozens believed should be guided by a preconceived notion. "The presence of an initial idea is the first and chief requisite of Cozens' blots… When he comes in the second part of the pamphlet to formulating his instructions for blotting, the first rule to be followed after the materials have been assembled is to *possess your mind strongly with a subject.*" (Oppé, *Alexander & John Robert Cozens,* p. 59).

24. Alexander Cozens
English, 1717-1786
A blot and a print from *A New Method…,* about 1785 (Wilton 65, 67)
One aquatint and one aquatint and mezzotint
Each, 9-7/16" x 12-3/8" (240 x 315 mm)
a. Plate 25 (inscribed "40"): blot

b. Plate 27 (inscribed "42"): print of the second of three
drawings made from the preceding blot; the mezzotint
was applied by William Pether (1731-1795).
Collection: Davison Art Center, Wesleyan University

25. Alexander Cozens
English, 1717-1786
A blot and a print, from *A New Method...*, about 1785
(Wilton 62, 63)
Two aquatints, each 9-7/16" x 12-3/8" (240 x 315 mm)
Collection: Davison Art Center, Wesleyan University
a. Plate 22 (inscribed "37"): blot
b. Plate 23 (inscribed "38"): print showing a brush
drawing made from the preceding blot

26. Bowl
English, Staffordshire, about 1810-1815 (Burnap Cat. No.
690)
Pottery, moonlight or marbled pink luster ware made by
Josiah Wedgwood II
3-1/4" high (83 mm), 6" dia. (105.3 mm)
Collection: The Nelson-Atkins Museum of Art, Gift of
Frank P. and Harriet C. Burnap

Gold salts applied over a white pottery body produce
pink luster, as marbled and variegated as agate ware.

27. John Constable
English, 1776-1837
A Spacious or Extensive Landscape, after Alexander Cozens
(Reynolds 23.54), 1823
Pen and brown ink, over faint pencil, with gray wash
4-1/2" x 7-3/8" (115 x 186 mm)
Collection: Fogg Art Museum, Harvard University,
Cambridge, Massachusetts, Transferred from the Fine
Arts Department

Constable made pen and wash copies of the sixteen
etchings in Cozens's publication *Various Species of
Composition in Nature* (all of the drawings but this one—
the sixteenth and last—are in the Oppé collection in
England). Each is inscribed at the top with the original
title, a shortened version of that which appears in the
"Descriptions" at the end of *A New Method*. While the
drawings generally correspond with the illustrative
aquatint blots, in this instance Constable's drawn copy
(like Cozens's own etching, in the collection of the Yale
Center for British Art, after his finished drawing in the
Oppé collection, Oppé, *Alexander & John Robert Cozens*, Pl.
4(b)) lacks the tall mountain of the background in the blot
(No. 23c), thus harmonizing more accurately with
Cozens's unabridged title "An extensive country, with no
predominant part or object" (*Ibid.*, p. 185). According to
Oppé (p. 70), "Where the etchings differ from the blots,
the variation is not more than might be expected from
Cozens's constantly changing mind or than was
permissible in converting the blot into a sketch." At any
rate, Constable's copying the works of Cozens would
seem to indicate the regard by one artist for another who
was committed to studying nature as closely as he, in a
syntax simultaneously both more loose and more
systematic.

28. John Constable
English, 1776-1837

Landscape, Dawn (Reynolds 33.46), 1833
Pen and ink and wash
2-1/4" x 4-3/8" (56 x 112 mm)
Collection: Yale Center for British Art, Paul Mellon
Collection

This is one of a small number of wash drawings, most of
them executed on drafts of letters, that are closest in
technique to Alexander Cozens's blots. The freedom and
spontaneity of the work did not preclude the dashing-in
of a recognizable church steeple, evidencing Cozens's
doctrine that the blotting artist should have a general
composition in mind, which the masses of dark and light
tend to adumbrate.

29. Top of mirror case, from a set of 19 boxes and accessories for a lady's toilette
Japanese, early to mid-19th century, Edo Period (1615-
1867)
Lacquer, 10-1/8" (263 mm) diameter, 14-5/8" (372 mm)
long
Collection: The Nelson-Atkins Museum of Art, Gift of Dr.
and Mrs. George Colom

All three of the Japanese lacquer objects (No. 4, 9, 29) have
backgrounds executed in *hiramaki-e* (flat sprinkled
design), obtained by dusting powdered gold over lacquer
that was still damp, producing a cloud of brilliant,
random dots.

30. Wine bottle
Japanese, about 1839
Pottery, Ofuke ware, made in Owari province
8-1/4" (210 mm) high, 5" (127 mm) diameter
Collection: The Nelson-Atkins Museum of Art, Purchase,
Nelson Fund

In bluish-brown fine crackle ware with irregular greenish
and iron-rust glazes, the bottle represents in the Tempo
period (1830-1843) a revival of the Seto-type Temmoku
surface treatment.

31. Joseph Mallord William Turner
English, 1755-1851
Lausanne and the Lake of Geneva, 1842?
Sepia wash and graphite
15-5/8" x 23-3/8" (397 x 595 mm)
Collection: The Nelson-Atkins Museum of Art, Purchase,
Nelson Fund

Once in the possession of members of the family of the
engraver John Landseer, the drawing bears on the reverse
an inscription in iron gall ink, "Lausanne," and another in
pencil with the title and date, on the mount. The dark
foreground areas of the water color have a distinctly
blottesque character, and the sweeping washes forming
the sky are overlaid by graphite strokes summarily
indicating cloud forms. In general treatment, the drawing
is akin to those Turner prepared for the prints for his *Liber
Studiorum*, some thirty years before. The sky has an
undramatic, cursory appearance unlike that of the
polychrome sketches (a few years later than the *Liber*
drawings), which Hawes feels are "as though Turner
viewed the sky as a sort of infinite colour-light organ"
(Hawes, "Constable's Sky Sketches," p. 356). Those seem
to anticipate Rothko.

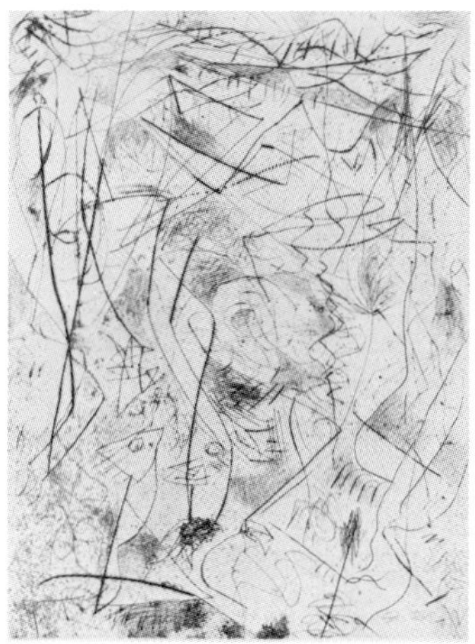

42a. Jackson Pollock, about 1944-5

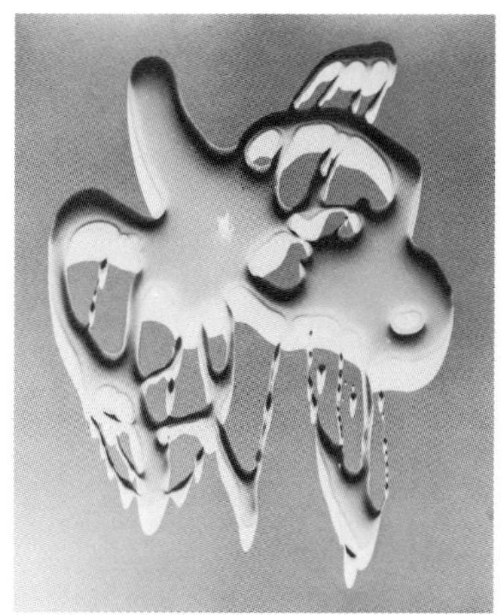

39. Henry Holmes Smith, 1950

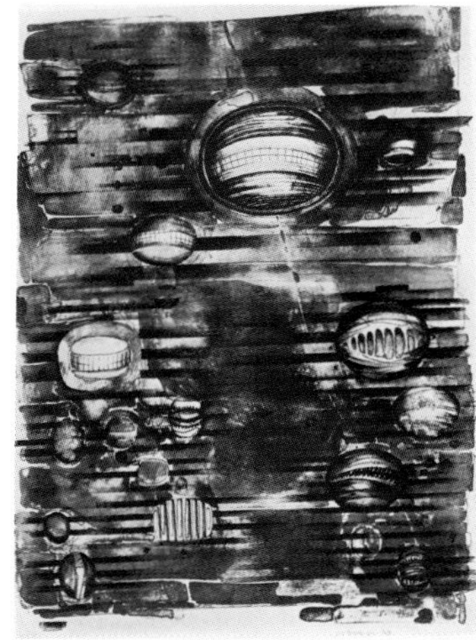

51. Lee Bontecou, 1963

32. Figure of poodle bearing basket of fruit

Made at the United States Pottery Company, Bennington, Vermont, about 1850
Pottery with flint enamel glaze, 8-1/2" (216 mm) high
Collection: The Nelson-Atkins Museum of Art, Gift of Frank P. and Harriet C. Burnap

Small bits of clay—so-called "cole slaw"—were applied at random in areas where it was necessary to represent hair. In contrast, the smooth, trimmed surface of the dog's body is glazed with flint enamels in powder form sprinkled from a perforated box on to a transparent glaze with which they fused, assuming a mottled appearance from flowing during firing.

33. Paul Gauguin

French, 1851-1903
Les Drames de la Mer: Une Descente dans Le Maelstrom, 1889 (Guérin 8)
Zincograph, 6-13/16" x 10-5/8" (173 x 270 mm)
Collection: Marion Koogler McNay Art Museum, Gift of Alice M. Hanszen

The second of Gauguin's lithographs on zinc of the same basic title and the eighth in his album of prints issued at the Cafe Volpini exhibition on the grounds of the Exposition Universelle, Paris, the picture alludes to a story by Poe in his *Histoires Extraordinaires*, translated by Baudelaire, concerning three fishermen engulfed during a storm in a whirlpool off the coast of Norway. It depicts a sailor vainly attempting to rescue his drowning brother before he himself is captured by the torrent. Encompassed within a fan format, the extraordinary span of tones hectically disposed gives a wildly dynamic decorativeness to the watery setting of this tragic scene.

34. Charles Maurin

French, 1856-1914
Landscape, after 1893
Sprayed pigment and pencil
12-1/2" x 18-7/8" (317 x 480 mm)
Collection: The Jane Voorhees Zimmerli Art Museum, Rutgers - The State University of New Jersey, Given in memory of Doris E. Brown (1914-1984), *The Home News* arts writer, by *The Home News*, colleagues, and friends

Spray-painted in yellow, orange, lavender, and purple, the picture demonstrates the early mechanization of mistiness, an "art of exhalation" (Eisler, *Charles Maurin: The Vaporizer Watercolors*, n.p.), a technique as random in effect as that of the nature it portrays.

35. Henri de Toulouse-Lautrec

French, 1864-1901
The Chap Book, 1896 (D. 362, A. 189, W. P18), II/II
Color lithograph, 16" x 23-3/8" (407 x 594 mm)
Collection: The Nelson-Atkins Museum of Art, Gift - Purchased through the Roy S. Odell Memorial Fund

The *crachis*—areas of randomly spattered colors—are supposed to have been applied by the artist with a toothbrush.

36. Max Ernst

German, 1891-1976
Death is something like Cousin Cynthia, Plate IV of nineteen *cliché-verre* illustrations to René Crevel, *Mr. Knife Miss Fork* (Paris: Black Sun Press, 1931)
This impression is from the separate edition issued with *Le Livre d'Art International* by *Arts et Metiers Graphiques*, Paris, 1931. (Glassman and Symmes, *Cliché-verre…*, No. 89)
Photogram on textured, photo-sensitized paper
6-15/16" x 4-7/16" (177 x 113 mm) mounted (as issued) on gray sheet 12-1/16" x 9-1/8" (307 x 232 mm)
Collection: Private

Ernst's original *frottage* (rubbing) drawings were executed on thin, translucent paper so that they served as negatives which were contact-printed on light-sensitive paper, producing white on black images, evocative of the dream-like theme of the Surrealist writer's text associating death and desire.

37. Joan Miró

Spanish, 1893-1983
Black and Red, 1938, 8/30, (Dupin 37)
Color drypoint
1 of a series of 8 drypoints executed in the studio of Louis Marcoussis; publ. by Pierre Loeb, Paris, and Pierre Matisse, New York: printed by Imprimerie Lacourière, Paris
6-11/16" x 10-1/8" (170 x 257 mm) on Arches vellum 11-3/8" x 15" (289 x 80 mm)

Collection: The Nelson-Atkins Museum of Art, Purchase

The turbulent composition has an automatist randomness, involving figures, both human and monstrous, perhaps related to the contemporaneous horrors of the Spanish Civil War. In the upper right is a circular being with waving appendages, suggesting the form of the Eskimo masks with which the artist first became familiar in the mid-1920s (Elizabeth Cowling, "The Eskimo, the American Indian, and the Surrealists," p. 489).

38. Hans Namuth
American, Germany, 1915
Jackson Pollock Painting "One," and Lee Krasner, Springs, 1950
Gelatin silver print, 1950
Collection: Albright-Knox Art Gallery, Gift of Seymour H. Knox

39. Henry Holmes Smith
American, 1909-1986
Pseudoform, 1950
Silver, cameraless print, syrup directly on paper
11" x 9-3/16" (279 x 232 mm)
Collection: Sheldon Memorial Art Gallery, University of Nebraska - Lincoln, F. M. Hall Collection

40. Jackson Pollock
American, 1912-1956
No. 6, 1952, 1952 (O'Connor and Thaw 350)
Oil on canvas, 55-7/8" x 47" (1420 x 1194 mm)
Collection: The Nelson-Atkins Museum of Art, Gift of the Friends of Art

41. Jackson Pollock
American, 1912-1956
Reproductions of two 1951 paintings from a portfolio of six, 41/50, printed 1964
Silkscreens: a. 23" x 29" (585 x 737 mm): b. 29" x 23" (737 x 585 mm)
Collection: The High Museum of Art, Atlanta, Georgia, Purchase with a gift from Atlanta Wire Works and Museum funds, 74-25
a. *Number 8, 1951/"Black Flowing"* (O'Connor and Thaw 1090 - P28)
b. *Number 19, 1951* (O'Connor and Thaw 1094 - P30)

Their original paintings likened by Fairfield Porter to "enormous blotters—not old ones, but some that have been used to dry a drawing" ("Reviews and Previews," *Art News*, December, 1951, p. 48), these sheets are among Pollock's only ventures into photographic reproductive printmaking, in a sense blotting on a smaller scale.

42. Jackson Pollock
American, 1912-1956
Two engravings with drypoint, printed 1967, in editions of fifty each, by Emiliano Sorini
Collection: The Minneapolis Institute of Arts, The Christina N. and Swan J. Turnblad Memorial Fund, 1978
a. *Untitled 6, 1944-5* (O'Connor & Thaw 1081-P18), 11-13/16" x 8-15/16" (300 x 227 mm)
b. *Untitled 7, 1945* (O'Connor & Thaw 1082-P19), 15-3/4" x 23-3/4" (400 x 603 mm)

Executed in Stanley William Hayter's Atelier 17 in New York, these two of Pollock's ten intaglio prints reveal the concentration on automatist line espoused by Hayter since his association with the Surrealists in Paris and shared by Masson and Miró. The "powerful urge to make a latent image visible" (Hayter, *New Ways of Gravure*, p. 270) is evident and operative in the skein of linear swirls enveloping nodes of often cryptic imagery. In *Untitled 6*, Fichner-Rathus discerns in the crossing of the darker coalesced bodies by meandering lines a lack of cohesiveness, while in the more sweeping diffuse expanse of *Untitled 7* the "behavior of line is a first step in the evolution of the linear drip, which ultimately doubled back on itself repeatedly, recoiling from the static perimeters of the canvas" (Fichner-Rathus, "Pollock at Atelier 17," p. 165). Pollock's brief experimentation with intaglio printmaking in the sympathetic atmosphere of Hayter's atelier had a salutary progenitive impact on the direction of his later linear painting style.

43. Hans Hartung
German, born 1904
Composition, 1957, 7/75
Color intaglio, 15-1/2" x 30-3/4" (396 x 527 mm) on sheet 19-3/4" x 25-3/4" (503 x 658 mm)
Collection: The Nelson-Atkins Museum of Art, Gift of Jane Wade in memory of Curt Valentin

44. Mark Tobey
American, 1890-1976
Space Ritual No. 6, 1957
Sumi ink drawing, 44-1/2" x 35" (1131 x 890 mm)
Collection: The Nelson-Atkins Museum of Art, Gift of the Friends of Art

45. Norman Bluhm
American, born 1920
No. 14, 1958
Water color, ink, and gouache, 39-7/8" x 26" (1001.3 x 661 mm)
Collection: The Nelson-Atkins Museum of Art, Gift of Jane Wade in memory of Curt Valentin

46. Stanley William Hayter
English, 1901-1988
Witches Sabbath, 1958, 16/50
Color etching and aquatint
19-1/2" x 28-1/8" (495 x 638 mm) on paper 26-3/8" x 32-3/4" (670 x 833 mm)
Collection: Solomon R. Guggenheim Museum

From his association with the Surrealists in Paris, Hayter adopted the automatist approach, evident in the random, swirling linearism that defines images. The artist stated in a letter to Davis S. Rubin (quoted in Konheim, *Prints from the Guggenheim Museum Collection*, p. 21) that after successive engravings the plate was thrice covered with texture and then subjected to bitings of the acid. "The final work consisted of widening some of the initially engraved lines which in printing were carefully cleaned and so appear as white in the final print."

47. Joan Miró
Spanish, 1893-1983

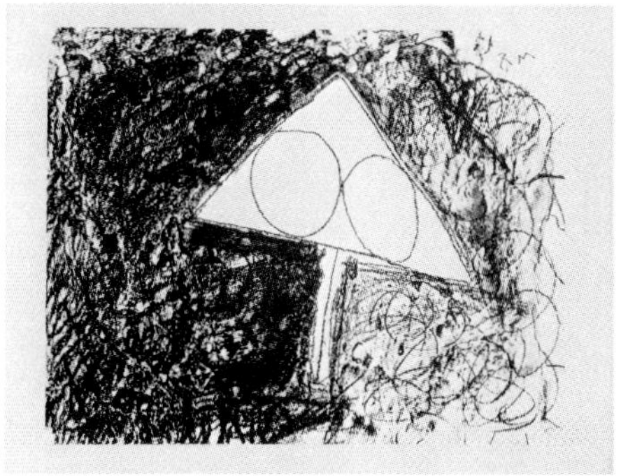

57. Robert Motherwell, about 1965-8

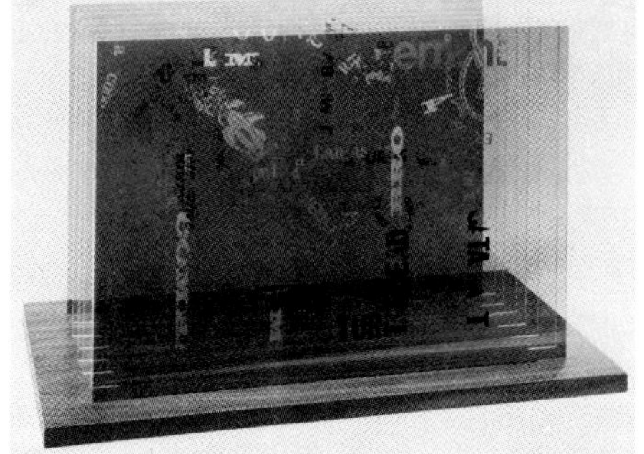

62. John Cage, 1969

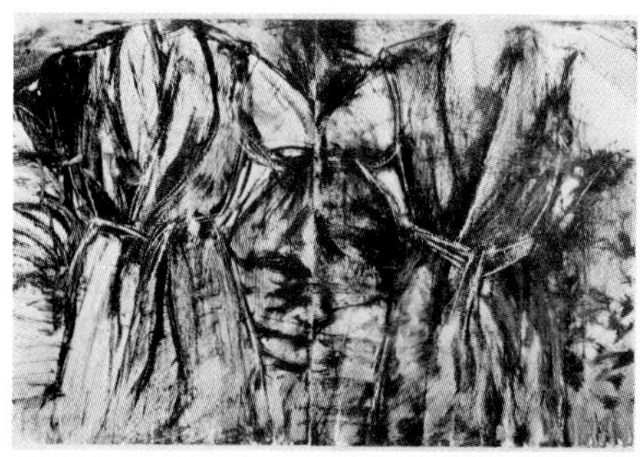

86. Jim Dine, 1980-3

Woodcut illustrations to Paul Eluard, *A Toute Epreuve*, (Dupin 161-234)
New York: George Braziller, 1984. First facsimile edition: after No. 75 of the original edition published in Geneva, 1958, by Gérald Cramer
104 pp.; 12-5/8" x 9-3/4" (321 x 248 mm)
Collection: Private

Made between 1948 and 1958, the 233 wood blocks which form the pictures vary in texture and the ability to hold ink. The incisions and holes added by the artist produce "in the impression clouds of uneven color, white flecks, even what could be trails of moving objects. In any two copies of the same print, the effects differ. Like the surrealists, Miró was intrigued by the rôle chance may play in works of art. His exploitation of wood's primitive texture was related [to] his ideas about 'l'imprévu,' the unexpected or accidental, which he termed 'an enticement'; when chance events occur in printing, he said, "the more there are, the more excited I get.' The entirely different effects he creates with worked and unworked wood, and with smooth and rough textures, correspond to contrasts between man and woman, dream and reality, inner and outer worlds, subjects all found in the poems" (Anne Hyde Greet, "The Making of the Book," p. 12, in introductory pamphlet to *A Toute Epreuve*).

48. Manoucher Yektai
American, born 1921
Spanish Bull Game, 1958
Charcoal and red crayon, 11" x 15" (279 x 381 mm)
Collection: The Nelson-Atkins Museum of Art, Gift of Jane Wade in memory of Curt Valentin

49. Sam (Samuel Lewis) Francis
American, born 1923
Composition No. 3, 1959
Water color and ink, 17" x 20" (432 x 508 mm)
Collection: The Nelson-Atkins Museum of Art, Gift of the Friends of Art Memorial Fund

50. Tancredi Parmeggiani
Italian, 1927-1964
Daybreak in Venice
Oil on canvas, 42-1/2" x 54-5/8" (1008 x 1308.8 mm)
Collection: The Nelson-Atkins Museum of Art, Gift of Miss Peggy Guggenheim

51. Lee Bontecou
American, born 1931
Fourth Stone, 1963, 1/19 (Field 4)
Published by ULAE
Lithograph, 37-15/16" x 29-5/16" (964 x 745 mm) on sheet 41-3/8" x 29-11/16" (1051 x 754 mm)
Collection: The Museum of Modern Art, New York, Gift of the Celeste and Armand Bartos Foundation. 492.63

Executed on the same cracked stone later used by Rauschenberg for *Breakthrough I* and *II* (Foster, *Robert Rauschenberg: Prints 1948/1970*, No. 26, 27), the print utilizes the narrow fissure as the downward orbit of the largest of the planetary toothed objects that populate the striated void. The horizontal bands which cross the space "were created by pressing tape onto the stone, and using the residue of glue as the 'drawing' when the stone was etched" (Castleman, *American Impressions*, No. 67). Describing this barred background, the artist said, "It's like a prison, a jail..." (quoted in Towle, "Two Conversations with Lee Bontecou," p. 27).

52. Jean Dubuffet
French, 1901-1985
La Lunette Farcie, 34/50
Alès and Paris: PAB, 1963
Page size, 17-1/8" x 15" (435 x 381 mm)
Collection: The Toledo Museum of Art; Gift of Molly and Walter Bareiss

53. Sam (Samuel Lewis) Francis
American, born 1923
Blue - Violet, 1963, AP (Kornfeld and Klipstein 1)
Printed by Robert Gardner at Tamarind
Color lithograph, 22-1/8" x 30" (565 x 760 mm)
Collection: The Nelson-Atkins Museum of Art, Gift of Mr. and Mrs. lrving Groupp

Francis "perceives the stone as an animated substance with unique physical properties—'you breathe on it and it shows'" (Einstein, "The Prints of Sam Francis" in Selz, *Sam Francis*, p. 251). The artist sees himself as a vehicle for "a stone spirit. Thus, he acknowledges a mysterious element which remains partially beyond his control and which causes the image to rise out of the stone. When he comments, 'A dream is the way I work on stone—not something I think about or formulate in my mind,' he does not diminish his own creative rôle, but, on the contrary, professes that he is the unique medium through which these images can be revealed and preserved" (*Loc. cit.*).

54. Robert Rauschenberg
American, born 1925
Canto XXXI: The Central Pit of Malebolge, The Giants, from *XXXIV Drawings for Dante's Inferno*, 1964, 25/300
Published by Harry N. Abrams, Inc.
Color half-tone facsimile of drawing in solvent transfer, red pencil, gouache, and pencil
14-7/16" x 11-7/16" (367 x 291 mm)
Collection: The Nelson-Atkins Museum of Art, Gift of Mr. and Mrs. Sidney B. Lurie

Using his version of *frottage*—rubbing the backs of half-tone pictures from magazines and newspapers with the nib of an empty ballpoint pen to transfer the images to paper moistened with lighter fluid—Rauschenberg makes evidence of the scribbling process visible. The collaged results, illustrating with modern details a Renaissance classic, here liken titans to Olympian-sized athletes: the fanfare with which Dante and Virgil enter the central pit is symbolized by the trumpet; the fragment of a massive chain evokes power and confinement. " 'The Jack-the-Giant Killer' literalism here is in keeping with Dante's own lapse into churlish prejudice. Dante seems to shrink from the giants more from their freakish grossness than for any legitimate crime on their part" (Dore Ashton, *Commentary* p. 30). The artist's very choice of subject for a drawing cycle is believed to have been entirely random (Tomkins, *Off the Wall*, p. 157, and *The Bride and the Bachelors*, p. 224).

55. Bruce Conner
American, born 1933
Black Drawing, 1965
Ink and graphite on paper, 20" (508 mm) square
Collection: The Nelson-Atkins Museum of Art, Gift of Jane Wade in memory of Curt Valentin

56. Robert Motherwell
American, born 1915
Automatism B, 1965-6 (Belknap 7)
Printed and published by Irwin Hollander Workshop
Lithograph on Rives BFK paper from one zinc plate
30" x 20-3/4" (762 x 527 mm)
Collection: University Art Museum, University of New Mexico, Gift of Irwin Hollander

The vigor of the artist's brush charged with tusche is evident in the forceful calligraphy and splashings: "He's seeing differently. There are a lot of surprises. The way he made his marks, moved his brush—it was *strong*" (Irwin Hollander, interview with Stephanie Terenzio, *The Painter and the Printer: Robert Motherwell's Graphics 1943-1980*, p. 28).

57. Robert Motherwell
American, born 1915
Untitled, from the *Madrid Suite*, 1965-6, 1/100 (Belknap 11)
Printed and published by Irwin Hollander Workshop
Lithograph, composition irreg., 19-13/16" x 25-3/4" (503 x 654 mm)
Collection: The Museum of Modern Art, New York, Gift of the artist. 1016.65.3

Reprised from a series of graphite and conté drawings made by rubbing on paper taped on the walls of a hotel room in Madrid, where the artist was honeymooning with Helen Frankenthaler, in 1958, the ten prints in the suite were later similarly executed by rubbing with lithographic crayons over French transfer paper on the roughly spackled walls of Hollander's Tenth Street studio, in New York. The richly black, grainily textured designs approximated those of the original Madrid drawings: "It was just like play. They have to be looked at and spoken about very differently—that's the essence of them. Here is the simple language of Motherwell, coming from the hand, the wrist, very freely, innocently, seeing the surface of the wall, not imposing his own will..." (Irwin Hollander, interview with Stephanie Terenzio, *The Painter and the Printer: Robert Motherwell's Graphics 1943-1980*, p. 33).

58. Frederick Sommer
American, born Italy, 1905
Smoke on Glass, 1965
Silver print, 13-5/8" x 10-1/2" (340 x 267 mm)
Collection: Nebraska Art Association Collection with the aid of the National Endowment for the Arts. Courtesy of Sheldon Memorial Art Gallery, University of Nebraska - Lincoln

Much of the artist's work after 1962 was focused on non-objective *cliché-verre* pictures from negatives consisting of greased glass plates bearing transferred impressions of Sommer's drawings on aluminum foil later blackened by soot from candle smoke (Symmes, *Cliché-verre*, p. 172). Such prints have diffuse images, dramatically suggestive of the flames (the white areas, where the soot was most dense on the glass) that enveloped the original tracery of the drawing on the foil.

59. Douglass Morse Howell
American, born 1906
Black String - Intense, 1966
Synchronic drawing: handmade paper
16" x 20" (406 x 508 mm)
Collection: The artist

"Synchronic drawings are formed in the papermaker's vat while making handmade paper. Black string, twine, yarn are used, and a length is dropped—in a sort of movement of the dance of the hands—onto a freshly made sheet of paper, formed in the mold from wet pulp made from clean linen or cotton rags. ... These synchronic drawings are, in part, a controlled accident. To the emotions are left the decision of the length of black string, its arrangement on the fingers of the hand, and the movement of the hands, except at the very last moment, or movement, when the intellect supervenes to say NOW, and in that fraction of an instant the pattern or drawing is made" ("Douglass Howell: Poet in Pulp and Rag," p. 30). While the choreography shaping the dropping of the string is entirely subject to chance (guided, however, by the vast experience of the artist, which also dictates the second of release), the optimum condition of the receiving material—the pulp—is determined by the long and technically sophisticated labor of beating the chosen ingredients of the paper-to-be.

60. Douglass Morse Howell
American, born 1906
Red and Gold, 1966

Synchronic drawing: handmade paper
16" x 20" (406 x 508 mm)
Collection: The artist

This polychrome work was made from linens previously vat-dyed. "[It] was accomplished using four Vats, each with its own prepared material (papermaker's stuff), and the skill was to go from Vat to Vat, with the mould (for forming sheets), without disturbing what had just been done previously" (Letter from the artist to George McKenna, July 24, 1988). "Lastly, the pattern formed is of a nature akin to that of cloud formations, in which each discovers his own meaning while gazing" ("Douglass Howell: Poet in Pulp and Rag," p. 30).

61. Paul Jenkins
American, born 1923
Moving Mantle, 1967
Oil on canvas, 78" x 51-1/2" (1982 x 1308 mm)
Collection: The Nelson-Atkins Museum of Art, Gift of Mr. David Kluger

62. John Cage (in collaboration with Calvin Sumsion)
American, born 1912
Plexigram I from "Not Wanting to Say Anything about Marcel," 1969, 21/125
Silkscreen on eight plexiglas panels, 14" x 20" (356 x 509 mm)
Collection: The High Museum of Art, Atlanta, Georgia, Gift of Graphics International, Ltd., 73.78a

The first of a set of four, the construction disposes letters and alphabetical fragments at random, the perceptual sensation of images floating free within a pellucid atmosphere being enhanced by the real transparency and physical separation of the plastic sheets.

63. John Cage (in collaboration with Calvin Sumsion)
American, born 1912
Not Wanting to Say Anything about Marcel, 1969
Lithograph on black paper
27-5/8" x 39-3/8" (702 x 1001 mm)
Collection: The High Museum of Art, Atlanta, Georgia, Museum purchase with funds from the Members Guild, 74.26

Aleatorily arranged, this first graphic by Cage, like the four associated plexigrams of the same title (No. 62), is a tribute to Marcel Duchamp, without any direct reference to the artist. "[Cage] is asking what happens when one avoids something deliberately. Among the things he is trying to avoid are conscious choice, taste, harmony, and quality as deliberately imposed elements" (Barbara Rose, essay on the portfolio copyrighted by EYE Editions, quoted in Kostelanetz, ed., *John Cage*, pp. 188-9). Visual flotsam and letters are used as objects, as "found" as any of Duchamp's readymades, shifting in a flecked, transparent sea, wordlessly poetic.

64. Cy Twombly
American, born 1929
Untitled II, 1967-74, 17/23 (Bastian 11)
Published by ULAE
Open-bite etching and aquatint printed in white and black ink, 23-5/8" x 28-1/8" (600 x 714 mm) on sheet 29" x 42" (737 x 1067 mm)

Collection: Yale University Art Gallery, J. Frederic Byers, III, B.A. 1962, Fund

The exquisitely scrawled zones fluidly and unstudiedly written in incised glyphs of an unknowable language have a sense of infinite extension, like a detail of a vast palimpsest. "In his own particular way, TW [Twombly] tells us that the essence of writing is neither form nor usage but simple gesture—the gesture that produces it *by allowing it to happen:* a garble, a smudge, a negligence" (Barthes, "Non Multa Sed Multum," p. 14). "In short, it's a form of writing of which the only thing that remains is the slant and the cursiveness" (*Ibid.*, p. 16).

65. Max Ernst
German, 1891-1976
Nous nous sommes portés à la rencontre des foulards, 1/70, illustration for René Char, *Dente Prompte*
Paris: Galerie Lucie Weill, 1969
Color lithograph, 18-3/8" x 15-5/16" (467 x 389 mm)
Collection: The Nelson-Atkins Museum of Art, Gift of Mrs. Louis Sosland

66. Paul Jenkins
American, born 1923
Untitled, 1969, 24/300
Published by Triton Press
Color lithograph, 35-1/4" x 26-1/4" (895 x 665 mm)
Collection: The Nelson-Atkins Museum of Art, Gift of Mr. and Mrs. Robert L. Bloch

67. Francesco Petrini
Italian, contemporary
0.01, 1969
Decalcomania, 6-7/16" x 9-7/16" (164 x 240 mm)
Collection: Private

Making decalcomanias, practiced by the Surrealist Oscar Dominguez (1906-1958) from about 1935, is a transfer process beginning with a sheet of paper on which gouache has been spread. A second sheet pressed over the matrix and peeled from it bears an impression, like a monotype, that often has an adventitious resemblance to a fantastic landscape, in this instance a mountain ridge with trees and waterfalls. André Breton described decalcomania: "What you have before you may be nothing but the paranoiac 'old wall' of Da Vinci, but it is that wall *carried to its perfection*" (Quoted in Rubin, *Dada and Surrealist Art*, p. 314).

68. Robert Stanley
American, born 1932
Paul's Mud, 1969
Printed by Domberger, Stuttgart
Color silkscreen, 30" x 37" (762 x 940 mm)
Collection: The artist

Absorbed by ecological concerns, the artist made a number of prints illustrating the unpredictable and unanticipated inroads of pollution on nature. "This print is based on a photograph I took in the winter of 1968 in Stonington, Conn., a photo of the glitterings of light on the mud flats oozing into Long Island Sound" (Letter from the artist to the curator, December 2, 1987).

69. Marian Zazeela
American, contemporary

Calligraphy about 1969, from *Aspen*, 9 (Winter Spring 1970)
Lithograph, 9-1/16" x 11-15/16" (230 x 330 mm)
Collection: Private

In addition to working in inked, invented scripts, the artist has collaborated with the composer LaMonte Young, producing for the continuing major sound-light project "The Tortoise, His Dreams, and Journeys" visual phenomena called "Ornamental Light Years Tracery," involving the shadows cast by illumining suspended objects creating a sort of calligraphic dance. Excerpts from their joint project were exhibited, in 1970, at the Gallery of the Institute for the Arts, Rice University, Houston.

70. Joan Miró
Spanish, 1893-1983
Avent Lettre, 1970, 120/200
Color lithograph
22-1/2" x 19-1/2" (568 x 493 mm) on sheet 29-7/8"x 21-7/8" (757 x 555 mm)
Collection: Spencer Museum of Art, The University of Kansas, Gift of Dr. and Mrs. Richard Cummings

The automatist-driven skein of swirling lines coalesces in liquid nodes, the whole calligraphic sweep moving within an astrally dotted expanse.

71. Jules Olitski
American, born Russia, 1922
Untitled, 1970, 80/150
Published by Leslie Waddington Prints, London
Color screenprint, 25-5/16" x 34-15/16" (660 x 888 mm)
Collection: The Nelson-Atkins Museum of Art, Gift of Mr. Robert W. Carlson

72. James Rosenquist
American, born 1933
Bunraku, 1970 (Varyan 18, Tucker 27)
Published by Castelli Graphics and Hollander Workshop
Lithograph, 32-1/2" x 23-1/2" (825 x 597 mm)
Collection: Milwaukee Art Museum, Gift of Quad/Graphics, Inc. with National Endowment for the Arts Matching Funds

The fruit-like balloon forms (untethered creatures of the Bunraku, or Japanese puppet theater?), seen also in the contemporary painting *Flamingo Capsule*, bob gently forward from a ground of random sketchy calligraphy as dynamically tangled as a patch of grass. The partly transparent ovoids bear an adventitious resemblance, here and there, to Brancusi's portrait of Mlle. Pogany.

73. Don Snyder
American, contemporary
Goeralegan, written and illuminated calligraphy, about 1970, from *Aspen*, 9 (Winter Spring 1970)
Lithograph, 14-11/16" x 12-1/4" (373 x 311 mm)
Collection: Private

74. John Cage
American, born 1912
30 *Drawings by Thoreau*, from *A Portfolio of Seven Prints Recording Collaborations with the Merce Cunningham Dance Company*, 1974, AP 21/30
Color serigraph, 30" x 20" (763 x 508 mm)

Collection: The Whitney Museum of American Art, New York; Gift of Calvin Tomkins. 80.34.1

After 1850, Henry David Thoreau (1817-1862) included some 700 drawings in his *Journal*. These thumb-nail sketches, most of them of natural objects but including also Indian-made artifacts, Cage photographed from the 1963 Dover edition, from 1967 on using them as components, arrayed by chance determined through computerized I Ching tables, of his assembled pictures and musical scores. The variously enlarged drawings have a delicate linearity, and it and their arrangement recall the illustrations in the albums of Hokusai's *Manga*.

75. Jim Dine
American, born 1935
Piranesi's 24 Colored Marks (Krens 211), 1974-6, 30/30
Etching with hand coloring, 25-3/4" x 23-3/4" (654 x 603 mm) on sheet 39-1/2" x 27-1/2" (1003 x 701 mm)
Collection: Marion Koogler McNay Art Museum, Museum Purchase made possible by a grant from the National Endowment for the Arts, and funds provided by the Ruth and Vernon Taylor Foundation, the Roy W. and Ellen S. Quillin Foundation, Mr. and Mrs. Eugene Ames, Walter Mathis, Mrs. Donald Saunders, Robert Tobin, and C. Thomas Wright

Published by Petersburg Press, New York, this is the culmination of the artist's early series of tool icons of the 1960s and 1970s, a subject not to be resumed until 1984 in Paris (see No. 92). This and two other images were reworked from the plate of *Wrench in Nature* (1973, Krens, 147). In addition to the free scrawls and spots, the picture includes an impression of a glove "obtained by pressing [it] into the heated hard ground on the plate surface, thereby removing some of the ground and exposing the copper to the action of the acid" (Krens, *Jim Dine Prints: 1970-1977*, p. 114). In this most populated of Dine's tool views, likened to "monumental, Piranesian architecture" (D'Oench, "Jim Dine, Portrait of a Printmaker," in *Jim Dine Prints 1977-1985*, p. 5), the likeness of an electric die-grinder, a device newly manipulated by Dine to produce some of the smudging effects, stands imposingly at the right margin. The spectrum of water-color dashes at the bottom (not to be approximated again until the sampling of washes in Dine's lithograph *Two Robes with Water Color*, 1983, No. 86) seems to invite the viewer's imagination to distribute hues appropriately, as marks might be added to an unpunctuated manuscript.

76. Trevor Jones
English, contemporary
Book by James Joyce
Tales Told of Shem and Shaun. Three Fragments from Work in Progress.
Paris. The Black Sun Press, 1929.
One of 550 copies on Holland Van Gelder Zonen paper of an edition of 650
Binding by Trevor Jones, 1975
8-1/16" x 6-9/16" x 5/8" (205 x 167 x 17 mm)
Collection: The Lilly Library, Indiana University

This, the second binding produced by Trevor Jones for a copy of the Joyce text, is bound in mid-gray Nigerian goatskin, with inlaid panels, on obverse and reverse, of assemblages of jetsam and found leather. "It seemed to me that this reuse, and refashioning, of fragments of discarded artefacts was a reasonable parallel to the way Joyce was reshaping language in these chapters of what was to become *Finnegans Wake*. ... I have always visualized Joyce's experiments in literature in terms of the work of those artists of the period who were using collage; making fine art from commonplace or discarded materials (Trevor Jones, "The Featured Bookbinding," p. 119).

77. Sol LeWitt
American, born 1928
Lines & Color
Zurich: Annemarie Vera; Bari: Marilena Bonomo; and
    Basel: Rolf Preisig, 1975
72 pp., 8" square (202 mm)
Collection: Private

Aside from the straight lines, all are of aleatory composition. Each page, whose stripe is the color of the ground of the adjoining page, is reflected in its adjacent companion, giving rise to secondary hues whose intensity is in direct ratio to the acuteness of the angle with which the book is held.

78. Arnulf Rainer
Austrian, born 1929
Self Portrait, about 1975, 39/50
Photogravure, etching, and crayon
21-1/8" x 15" (527 x 381 mm)
Collection: Yale University Art Gallery, Gift of the
    Cosmopolitan Arts Foundation

"In the autoportraits, Rainer plays the fool in opposition to all dominant institutions and their moral and aesthetic views" (Courtney, "The Autoportraits of Arnulf Rainer," p. 80). In Rainer's role as a jester, the photograph of himself in the expressive grimacings of accesses of simulated emotions the artist overscores with opaque strokes, causing the means and thrust of obliteration to be the theme (*Ibid.*, p. 81). This overlaying is entirely spontaneous and may be accomplished by "'rapidity and closing one's eyes (blind drawing)[which] is not artistic but merely a way to obtain unpremeditated forms of expression'" (the artist, quoted by Courtney, *loc. cit.*). While Kozloff sees Rainer's activity as "defacing photographs" in his "*Facefarces*, he calls them" (Kozloff, "Pygmalion Reversed," p. 33), Rainer, in his once-removed version of bodyworks, did not mutilate himself in the fashion of the self-Pygmalions but ravaged only his representation, achieving with the camera-shot surrogate a vaster scope of unique statement.

79. George Segal
American, born 1924
*Three Figures in Red Shirts: Two Front, One Back, from Blue
    Jeans* Series, 1975
Published by 2RC Editrice
Color etching and aquatint
38-5/8" x 77-15/16" (981 x 1979 mm) on sheet 45" x 85-
    5/8" (1144 x 2175 mm)
Collection: The Museum of Modern Art, New York,
    Purchase, John B. Turner Fund. 565.76

Segal's familiar white plaster casts of human beings are here supplanted by flat impressions made on sensitized plates by bodies partly clad in denim, a polychrome variation on Yves Klein's canvases which received the likenesses of nude women smeared with blue pigment —the living being as brush and subject—and on Rauschenberg's cyanotype of Pat Pearman. The images transferred are unpredictable in each instance.

80. Victor Landweber
American, born 1943
Half a Million Tiny Time Pills, 1976
Grid of 100 Polacolor prints
40" x 50" (1016 x 1270 mm)
Collection: The artist

The limitless colorful concatenation of cold capsules, randomly disposed, evokes in the viewer a host of associations with, among them, landscape from an aerial vantage, a starry firmament, a view through a microscope. A hundred compartments suggest the infinitude of the prospect; the title identifies the prosaic reality. This is the artlessness of art brut.

81. Nancy Graves
American, born 1940
Ruis, 1977, ed. 33 (Tyler 207:NG6)
Printed by Rodney Konopaki at Tyler Graphics Ltd.
Etching, aquatint, engraving, solidified paint stick on
    paper
31-1/2" x 35-1/4" (800 x 892 mm)
Collection: Walker Art Center, Minneapolis; Tyler
    Graphics Archive, 1984

This is the sixth, least colored, and most linearly full of the six etchings the artist made between January and August, 1977 at Tyler Graphics. All of the set are closely related to her paintings of the time: "It is interesting that the titles of these works—words like Pia, Nervia, Straeo— also function as gesture, sign, and symbol, acquiring their 'meaning' not through verbal definition, but through their auditory and visual aspects." (Heinemann, "Nancy Graves: The Painting Seen," p. 140). In an elegant language expressive solely of itself, *Ruis* shares with its five predecessors a layering of colored marks completed by the artist's finally drawing directly with pastel on the image after it was printed.

82. Pat Steir (Iris Sukoneck)
American, born 1938
Time Line in Time, 1977, 101/102 (Broun 7)
Published by The Print Collectors of the Friends of Art,
    Kansas City, Missouri
Printed at Crown Point Press by Patrick Foy
Color drypoint and etching on Rives BFK paper
13-3/4" x 13-9/16" (350 x 345 mm) on sheet 19" x 18-1/4"
    (482 x 464 mm)
Collection: The Nelson-Atkins Museum of Art, Gift of The
    Print Collectors

"I don't choose the grid. I just arbitrarily throw one on," said the artist (in interview with Elizabeth Broun, *Form Illusion Myth*, p. 34). Within this randomly chosen framework, a square is sited at each corner, each centering another square, bordered or unbordered, thickly or thinly hatched, in one instance composed of letters and words. All the squares refer to the passage of time expressed by the surge of the linear markings. Speaking of the work of the two years previous to this print, Steir stated, "I wanted to purify and find the range of the language, starting from the simplest mark—dot, smudge, straight line; circle, square, diamond; border, frame" (*Ibid.*, p. 21). "I kept thinking that the line is an image—an image of a figure. Or it might not be a figure, just a collection of lines" (Ratcliff, interview with Pat Steir, *Pat Steir Paintings*, p. 36).

83. Wally Depew, ed.
American, contemporary
PN2 experiment - Book 25: The Five Cent Scarlet Ink Book 3
Sacramento: Wally & Linda Depew, 197?
40 pp.; 3-5/8" x 4-1/4" (91 x 109 mm
Collection: Private

Colored at its center by an injection through a hole, each page bears a blot successively larger.

84. Adja Yunkers
American, born 1900
Les Pendus II, 1980, ed. 40
Intaglio, 30" x 22" (762 x 559 mm)
Published by Vermillion Editions Ltd., Minneapolis
Collection: Vermillion Editions

85. Adja Yunkers
American, born 1900
Untitled IV, 1980
Intaglio and screenprint, 30" x 22" (762 x 559 mm)
Published by Vermillion Editions Ltd., Minneapolis
Collection: Vermillion Editions

86. Jim Dine
American, born 1935
Two Robes with Water Color (D'Oench and Feinberg 150), 1980-3, 6/9
Lithograph with water color
37-3/4" x 58-3/4" (961 x 1493 mm)
Collection: The Nelson-Atkins Museum of Art, Gift of The Guild of the Friends of Art

87. Nancy Graves
American, born 1940
Approaches the Limit of II, 1981, ed. 30 (Tyler 209:NG8)
Color lithograph and engraving
47-7/8" x 31-5/8" (1216 x 803 mm)
Collection: Walker Art Center, Minneapolis; Tyler Graphics Archive, 1984

In 1981, during her second foray into printmaking at Tyler Graphics, the artist executed this, two other intaglios, and thirty-one monotypes. More overtly colorful and calligraphic than her 1977 work (No. 81), the picture shows the bunchy floral forms and floating metallic ribbons reminiscent of her sculpture, producing a stronger, emphatic, yet lyrical statement.

88. Joan Mitchell
American, born 1926
Flower III, from the *Bedford Series*, 1981, ed. 70 (Tyler 371:JM9)
Color lithograph, 42" x 32-3/4" (1080 x 830 mm)
Collection: Walker Art Center, Minneapolis; Tyler Graphics Archive, 1984

This is the most complex of the three flower themes among the eleven lithographs the artist completed at Tyler Graphics in 1981. Her feeling for and of landscape is translated into a freely brushed combination of a blooming upper form over a zone of grasslike stems.

89. John Cage
American, born 1912
Déreau, 1982, #35 from a series of 38 related images in 2 impressions each
Published by Crown Point Press
Photo-etching, engraving, drypoint, aquatint
18" x 24" (457 x 610 mm)
Collection: Crown Point Press

Déreau (derived from "decor" and "Thoreau") makes further use of photographs of the author's sketches in his *Journal*, some of which appear in Cage's *30 Drawings by Thoreau* (No. 74). While the siting of the photo images of the actual drawings remains constant throughout the series, those drawings that were not used are represented, in varying positions, by an outlined circle, a horizon line, heavy drypointed bars, and curves from yard-long strings dropped on to plates having the same size and shape as the Kodalith films of the unshown drawings. "Thus the Thoreau drawings are a kind of stage set or 'decor' for the other elements" (Lilah Toland, "Déreau, 1982" in Brown, ed., *John Cage Etchings 1978-1982*, p. 21). Five different palettes were employed, which "appear alone or in combination with one of forty-five colors in chance-determined percentages with or without white" (Cage quoted, *loc. cit.*).

90. A. R. Penck (Ralf Winkler)
German, born 1939
Night Vision, 1982, from Portfolio I
Published by Multiples/Marian Goodman
Woodcut, 39-3/8" x 31-1/2" (1001 x 801 mm)
Collection: The Toledo Museum of Art; Gift of Edward Drummond Libbey

Penck's cryptic pictograms and stick figures revert to cave painting in forming a modern language-landscape of signs, almost as dense as Pollock's all-over patternings, but, in woodcut, awkwardly rigid: "… the resistance of the material almost forces the shape on the artist" (Dietrich, "A Talk with A. R. Penck," p. 94).

91. Robert Motherwell
American, born 1915
Illustration for Rafael Alberti's poem, *El Negro Motherwell* (Motherwell's Black), 23/51, 1983: "Elegy black black/ Black with blood coagulated black/ With the white lime of bones outlining forms"
Printed and published by Tyler Graphics Ltd.
Lithograph, 1 of 19 in book 17" x 16-5/8" (432 x 422 mm)
Collection: Dr. James N. Hueser

92. Jim Dine
American, born 1935
The New French Tools—For Pep (D'Oench and Finberg 173), 1984
Etching, aquatint, and electric tools
23-3/4" x 19-5/8" (604 x 499 mm) on sheet 42-3/8" x 30-1/8" (1076 x 765 mm)

Collection: Museum of Fine Arts, Boston, Gift of the
   Artist, 1984.272

The "Pep" in the title is the nickname of the wife of Aldo
Crommelynck, who printed the suite of five tool prints the
artist made in Paris. The print manifests many scratchings
obtained with electric instruments and a myriad of
random aquatint blots.

93. Sandra K. Nicht
American, contemporary
Another Green World/Sunrise, 1984
Cliché-verre C-print
15-3/4" x 14-7/8" (400 x 378 mm) on sheet 19-15/16" x 15-
   15/16" (507 x 405 mm)
Collection: Private

94. Diane Philipoff Maurer
American, contemporary
Page of miniature stone marbling, 1989
Gouache colors, 17" x 10-3/16" (432 x 258 mm)
Collection: The Nelson-Atkins Museum of Art, Gift of the
   artist

95. Diane Philipoff Maurer
American, contemporary
Page of marbling with multiple images, 1989
Gouache colors, 15-5/8" x 11-1/16" (397 x 281 mm)
Collection: The Nelson-Atkins Museum of Art, Gift of the
   artist

96. Paul Maurer
American, contemporary
Page of Persian stone marbling, 1988
Gouache and drawing ink colors
11-7/8" x 17-13/16" (301 x 452 mm)
Collection: The Nelson-Atkins Museum of Art, Gift of the
   artist

97. Paul Maurer
American, contemporary
Page of marbling in *sumi nagashi* technique, 1988
Sumi ink and dye colors
17-7/8" x 11-13/16" (429 x 284 mm)
Collection: The Nelson-Atkins Museum of Art, Gift of the
   artist

98. George Wightman and Abdullah al-Udhrai (transl.)
Poems by Majnun Laila, a Seventh Century Arab Poet, 1985
Published by the Red Gull Press, Hitchin, Herts, England
   and Twinrocker Handmade Paper, Brookston, Indiana
24 pp.; 1 of 75 copies on decorated paper of abaca fiber
9-5/8" x 6-11/16" (245 x 170 mm)
Collection: The publishers

A chance meeting, in Minneapolis, in 1984, between
Michael Gullick and Kathryn and Howard Clark of
Twinrocker Handmade Paper led to the publication of this
work. Natural flecks in the long-fiber abaca pulp were
retained to harmonize with the spirit and locus of the
poems, and the irregular green wash on the upper part of
both sides of the sheets provides a dreamy contrast with
the formal rigidity of the sans-serif typography. Written
by Qais Ibn-al-Mulawwah, known as Majnun (Madman),
the poems deal with the author's unrequited love for his
cousin Laila, whom he sought vainly while insane after
her family forbade their marriage.

99. Iris Nevins
American, contemporary
Traditional Marbling, 316/500
Sussex, New Jersey: I. Nevins, 1985
44 pp.; 10-3/16" x 7-15/16" (259 x 199 mm)
Collection: Private

In addition to instructional material, the book contains
fourteen full-color tipped-in plates illustrating types of
marbling.

100. James Welling
American, contemporary
Gelatin Photographs 1-12, ed. 400
Buffalo: CEPA, 1985
12 pp.; 7-3/4" x 9-15/16" (197 x 253 mm)
Collection: Private

The size and form of these white-flecked, indefinably
menacing black images seem entirely determined by
chance.

101. John Cage
American, born 1912
Eninka, 1986, #7 from a series of 50 monotypes
Published by Crown Point Press
Monoprint: 24-1/2" x 18-1/2" (622 x 470 mm)
Collection: Crown Point Press

"The title encapsulates the process, for apparently 'en'
means circle, 'in' means stamp, and 'ka' fire in Buddhist
incantations" ("Prints & Photographs Published," *The
Print Collector's Newsletter*, Vol. XVII, No. 2, May-June,
1986, p. 59). In that process, according to the *Newsletter*,
wet gampi paper is placed over newspapers blazing on a
press, and, after being rolled through, the gampi bears
impress of both the flame and the inked patterns of the
newsprint. "It was then bonded to handmade Farnsworth
paper and branded with a metal circle from a ship's chain
hoist" (*Loc. cit.*). Variabilities of time and placement were
determined by reference to the I Ching.

102. Sarah Charlesworth
American, born 1947
Tartan Sets
   a. *Dress MacLeod*
   b. *MacGregor*
   c. *Black Stewart*
Three color photolithographs printed by Maurice Sanchez
   at Derrière L'Etoile Studios, New York, 1986
Each, 32" x 24" (813 x 610 mm)
Collection: Editions Ilene Kurtz

Printed from hand-cut stencils determined by computer
analysis of color separations obtained by laser-scanning of
Charlesworth's photographs, the plaids incorporate all of
the patterning beyond the simple rectilinear grid of
threads. Heartney sees the chosen cruciform format as
"making a reference to the religious aspirations of
modernist abstraction" (Heartney, "Sarah Charlesworth
Tartan Sets," p. 135), and Cohen ("New Abstraction V," p.
11) celebrates their uniqueness as pure color images and
considers the prints as part of the artist's "ongoing

examination of the language of representation." In the current mode of appropriation-simulation, these works afford a striking concentration on the infinite subtleties and usually unremarked visual power of the commonplace.

103. Chris Costan
American, contemporary
You're Just a Pack of Cards, 1986, 50/75
Published by Martin Hason/Avenue B Gallery
Color lithograph, 43-1/2" x 28-1/2" (1105 x 724 mm) on sheet 48" x 31-3/4" (1125 x 807 mm)
Collection: The Nelson-Atkins Museum of Art, Anonymous Gift

Combining abstract and representational themes, the picture contains recognizable forms of an egg and of dishes (the latter found in Canal Street discount bins), suspended from a spring. These, partly overlaid by circles, float in conjunction with red cardlike shapes, all against a setting of randomly applied blue and green streaks over black.

104. Robin Heyeck
American, contemporary
Marbling at the Heyeck Press, 145/150
Woodside, Calif: The Heyeck Press, 1986
66 pp.; 11-1/4" x 8-1/4" (286 x 210 mm)
Collection: The artist

The book recounts the author's experiences with marbling and presents examples of projects which she has completed.

105. Telfer Stokes and Helen Douglas
Contemporary
Mim
Deuchar Mill, Yarrow, Scotland: Weproductions, 1986
120 pp.; 7-1/2" x 5-3/16" (190 x 130 mm)
Collection: Private

A collection of real, patterned papers and photographs of other, actual and simulated patterns, all texturally striking.

106. Diane Philipoff Maurer and Paul Maurer
American, contemporary
Dinosaurs Dining
Centre Hall, Pa: The Maurers' Hand-Marbled Papers, 1986
20 pp.; 11" x 8-7/16" (279 x 215 mm)
Collection: Private

The illustrations by Paul Maurer are reproductions of collaged black-and-white marbled papers.

107. John Cage
American, born 1912
Where There Is Where There, 1987, 1 of a set of 38
Monoprint: smoke resist flatbite
22-3/4" x 29-15/16" (578 x 761 mm)
Collection: Hallmark Collections

108. John Cage
American, born 1912
Déka, 1987, #4 from a series of 35 related images, each impression unique
Published by Crown Point Press
Monoprint: 11" x 14-3/4" (284 x 375 mm) on sheet 15-3/4" x 19" (400 x 483 mm)
Collection: Crown Point Press

From a fire built with newspapers soaked with asphaltum, oily smoke rose to create an acid resist on the copperplate. The period of time the plate was held over the fire was defined by consulting the I Ching. "Each print used three to five of these plates, inked with one of 17 randomly selected earth pigments. Along the lower edge of each was printed a narrow band, and it is this band that makes *Déka* (décor plus fire) such an interesting variation on the theme, for it creates an effect of three-dimensional space, suggesting an atmospheric setting" ("Prints & Photographs Published," *The Print Collector's Newsletter*, Vol. XVIII, No. 2, May-June, 1987, p. 64).

109. Ten artists: Roger Brown, Art Green, Philip Hanson, Gladys Nilsson, Jim Nutt, Ed Paschke, Christina Ramberg, Suellen Rocca, Barbara Rossi, Karl Wirsum
American, contemporary
The Chicago Imagist Print, 1987
Published by The David and Alfred Smart Gallery, University of Chicago
Color photolithographic poster: *cadavre exquis* (exquisite corpse)
38-1/2" x 25" (978 x 635 mm)
Collection: Private

Derived from an old parlor game which involved the addition of words to a piece of paper folded before being passed to each successive writing player, producing a sentence that was a verbal collage, the technique about 1927 was adapted by the Surrealists to visual means that ended in a collective image of notable discontinuity, the *cadavre exquis*. One of the first verbal accomplishments in the genre was the sentence *"Le cadavre exquis boira le vin nouveau"* (The exquisite corpse will drink the young wine, Rubin, *Dada and Surrealist Art*, p. 278). The graphic shown here resulted from the action of each of ten artists making individual additions to a schematic diagram of a standing human figure without having seen the contributions of any of the collaborators.

110. Rosalind Kimball Moulton
American, born 1941
Untitled (Self Portrait)
Photogram, 22" x 13-7/8" (559 x 353 mm)
Collection: Hallmark Collections

According to Keith F. Davis, curator of the lender's fine arts holdings, in a letter of August 31, 1987 to George McKenna, the image is "a unique photogram created by 'drawing' with a thin beam of light in the darkroom on two sheets of photographic paper. Of course, she could not see what she had until the paper was developed, and the image captures this sense of spontaneity and chance."

111. Gunnar A. Kaldewey
Contemporary, born in Germany
Clouds/Wolken, 1982, 1 of an edition of 35

Printed and published by the Kaldewey Press, Poestenkill,
  New York
Book: 26 pages on aluminum sheets printed in blue
  letterpress on black offset background, each page
  sprayed to suggest cloud formation; bound in
  aluminum by Christian Zwang, Hamburg, Germany
6-5/16" x 17-1/8" (160 x 430 mm)
Collection: The artist

The text of this book was reprinted on broadsides which
were dropped from helicopters at the premiere of *Cloud II*,
a musical composition by Bun-ching Lam, performed in
the final act of "The Floating Opera: A Treading of Steps"
on the shores of Puget Sound, Seattle, Washington,
September 20, 1987, as a part of Performa '87, a three-
month-long festival of new works sponsored by the King
County Arts Commission.

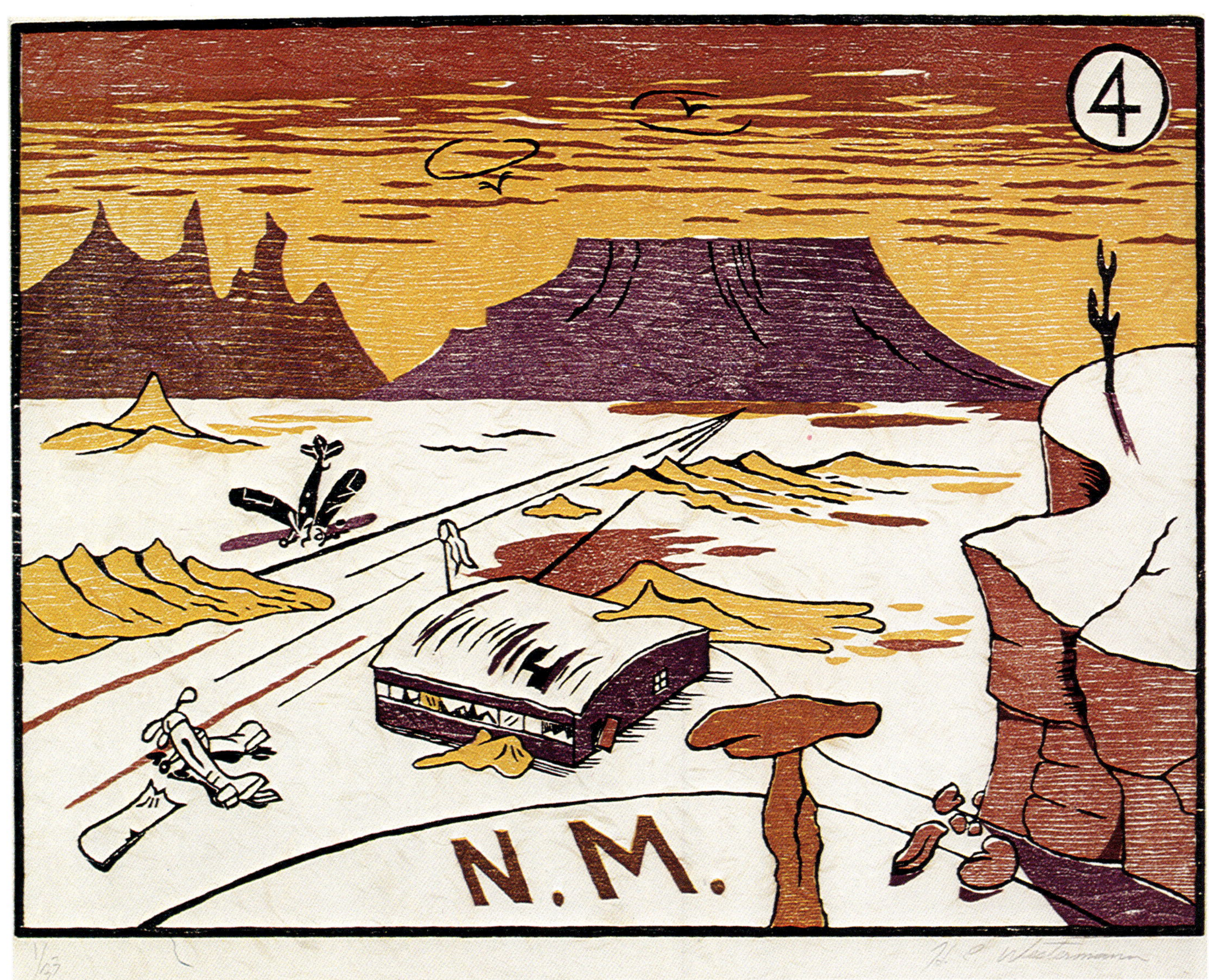

170. Horace Clifford Westermann
American, 1922-1981
No. 4, from *The Connecticut Ballroom*, 1976, 1/33
Color woodcut
Collection: The Nelson-Atkins Museum of Art, Gift of Mrs. Jean S. Lighton

II. Dreams, Miracles, Disasters, and Coincidences

In this section of the exhibition, the unforeseeable as theme rather than an adjunct of technique is considered. Real, devised, or imagined, the mysteries and vicissitudes of life furnish limitless sources for art. The effort to account for the vagaries of existence led to the devising of mythologies that might serve to explain the natural forces which impacted, often disastrously, on humankind. To suggest familiar forms for such impersonal forces, endowing them with human failings and emotions, made them analogously understandable. Illustration made them visible.

In the guise of animals, persons, or objects, furnished with appropriate attributes, the gods became recognizable, to be worshipped, propitiated, evaded. More exotic entities—monsters, specters—inconceivable wholly as earthly creatures—allowed the artist more originality of depiction, although they, too, most often are imaginative distortions of known beings. Han Fei, a Chinese artist (d. 233 B.C.) said: "Everyone is acquainted with dogs and horses since they are seen daily. To reproduce their likenesses is very difficult. On the other hand, since demons and spiritual beings have no definite form and since no one has ever seen them, they are easy to execute."[24]

When artists depicted Biblical themes, the unseen single, but triune God, who, according to Christian theology, created humanity in His image, was appropriately represented as a man (the Father sometimes only as a hand from heaven, while the Holy Ghost materialized as another of God's familiar creatures, a dove). To stiffen the resolve of the faithful, the saints were often portrayed in the throes of martyrdom and the afflicted were shown as the beneficiaries of miracles. The figures were frequently depicted in garments of the artist's time and in actual settings, much as, about 1500-1506, Girolamo Mocetto situated his engraving of the scene of the classical allegory of *The Calumny of Apelles* in the campo of SS. Giovanni e Paolo, in Venice. Of course, as early as the late 15th century in Europe[25] and the beginning of the 16th century in China,[26] illustrated printed books, or drawing manuals, had been published, furnishing guides for artists to methods of rendering objects, as well as models for proper personifications of abstract ideas. In addition, ecclesiastical, as well as royal, patrons were not averse to specifying the details of art works commissioned for them. None of these guidelines could, however, wholly circumscribe artistic spontaneity, particularly in the act of rendering the imaginary visible.

In the ages before photography, untoward newsworthy occurrences—wars (No. 133), fires, the beaching of a whale, the drowning of a rhinoceros (see Dürer, No. 319)—were, for public consumption, represented in prints, perhaps prepared as eyewitness testimony, but more usually sight unseen, from secondhand reports or pure invention. In the latter instances, the pictures, though essentially informative, are as contrived as illustrations of myths. They manifest the same immediacy, a plausibility possibly more dependent on the convincing qualities of artists' pictorializing abilities than on observers' necessarily unquestioning credulity.

When commonly known subjects are treated—

plants and flowers, trees and rocks, fish and animals—their characteristic lineaments can be illusionistically represented in a variety of ways. Some may be so factually and physically sketchy that the viewers' expectations and experience are summoned to complete the images for themselves. "'There are things which ten hundred brushstrokes cannot depict but which can be captured by a few simple strokes if they are right. That is truly giving expression to the invisible.' The maxim into which these observations were condensed might serve as a motto of this chapter: *i tao pi pu tao*—idea present, brush may be spared performance.'"[27] This rule might give comfort to the conceptualist artists of recent times, but when the artist's purpose is visual precision rather than suggestion (even given painstaking verbal descriptions on the order of those by such a *nouvelle vague* author as Alain Robbe-Grillet), bodying forth the particularity of details of nature requires close observation and reproduction. Attention to veracity of seeing can be noted in the floral borders of Springinklee's engraving, 1518 (No. 116)(recalling those of medieval Books of Hours), and in a number of 16th-17th century drawn designs for decorative uses (No. 119, 125, 134). While alluding to architectural ornamentation of some centuries earlier, De Coulon's statement would seem applicable, also, to these equally anonymous Renaissance drawings for embellished constructions shown in the exhibition: "The leaves, flowers, and tendrils of Rheims and Southwell, which, in the later twelfth century, break through the frozen crust of monastic fear, have the clarity of newly created things. Their very literalness and lack of selection is a proof that they have been seen for the first time."[28]

Leaving aside the studied prodigies of perception and rendition of nature represented by printed herbals, bestiaries, ornithologies, and other illustrative compendia, the camera studies by Karl Blossfeldt (No. 159)—magnified views of individual plants—bring most freshly to our notice salient forms of growth that have their counterparts in art. "Here can be observed the delicacy of a Rococo ornament, the severity of a Renaissance chandelier, the mystically tangled scrollwork of flamboyant Gothic, domes, towers, and the noble shafts of columns—a whole exotic language of architecture ... all these man-made forms find their original form in the world of plants."[29] In the hands of Barker, Singley, Preston, and Genthe, photography functions with equally stunning fidelity in the role of recording the dismaying aftermaths of natural cataclysms: the Johnstown flood (No. 158), the Galveston hurricane (No. 160), and the San Francisco earthquake (No. 161, 162).

Adaptations (like Warhol's series of variously colored silkscreened replicas of photographs of the results of automobile crashes) and coincidences, fortuitous or intended, are widespread in art. Hockney's series on Los Angeles weather (No. 167) derives from details of Hiroshige's woodblocks (No. 149, 150, 157), and Shimomura's silkscreen (No. 169) revises a Hokusai precedent (No. 156). Man Ray's pair of lover's lips floating in the sky (No. 165), suggesting the age-old discernments of shapes in clouds, is close to Minor White's low-horizon photographs of rural scenes (No. 166). The triple coincidence of a 5th century Coptic textile (No. 112) and contemporary prints by Kushner (No. 173) and Tanaka (No. 174), all showing rows of faces, demonstrates the antiquity and longevity of serial imagery, often employed by Warhol. One cannot infer any direct relation among these farflung artists, although Kushner is known to have traveled to Iran and to have interest in the patterns of Near Eastern fabrics.[30]

On the general subject of tradition tending to direct the artist's vision, it is helpful to recall the propensity of Chinese painters to emulate, with personal variations, the styles of bygone masters and to cite the well-known proclivity of observers of nature to gauge its accuracy in terms of its approximation to pictures of the same sort of subject which they have seen exhibited. John Constable, speaking of familiar Suffolk scenery, said, "It is a delightful landscape for a painter. I fancy I see Gainsborough in every hedge and hollow tree."[31] Gombrich traces Gainsborough's source, in turn, to Ruysdael,[32] and we cannot forget that Constable learned, also, from Alexander Cozens, whose preceptor in landscape depiction was Claude Lorrain.

There is some validity in T. S. Kuhn's assertion, in *The Structure of Scientific Revolutions*, 1970: "I suspect, for example, that some of the notorious difficulties surrounding the notion of style in the arts may vanish if paintings can be seen to be modelled on one another rather than produced in conformity to some abstract canons of style."[33] It is, however, debatable if Rupert Sheldrake's theory of morphic resonance—inherent universal memory, over past space and time, of 'formative causal influences'—can be applied to the stylistic inclination of artists. It may be correct that "the appearance of new variations on basic themes tends to become less frequent as time goes by: the number of possible variant forms may be finite. As new versions appear and either die out or become increasingly habitual, there are progressively fewer remaining potentialities that have not already been explored."[34] At this point of reduced possibilities, Kuhn, Monod, Sheldrake, and others propose the spontaneous creative generation of new paradigms, or archetypes: "We also know, since the shift into Modernism, that progress is not made, as was once thought, by the accumulation of knowledge within existing categories: it is made by leaps into new categories or systems. Art is not a descriptive statement about the world as it is, it is a recommendation that the world ought to be looked at in a given way"[35] and "Chance *alone* is at the source of every innovation …"[36]

———————

112. Photographic color print of detail of Coptic textile
Textile, 5th century A.D.
Wool and linen, 56-1/2" x 79" (1435 x 2007 mm)
Print, 20" x 16" (508 x 406 mm)
Collection: The Nelson-Atkins Museum of Art, Purchase, Nelson Fund

The tapestry-weave fabric, with heads and confronted birds in a design possibly of Sasanian origin, was most likely a funerary hanging. The works by Kushner (No. 173) and Tanaka (No. 174) bear resemblance to its succession of faces in rows.

113. Albrecht Dürer
German, 1471-1528
St. Eustace, about 1500-01 (Meder 60 d of k), watermark M. 158, Briquet 12494
Engraving, 14-3/16" x 10-1/4" (360 x 261 mm)
Collection: The Nelson-Atkins Museum of Art, Gift of Mr. Robert B. Fizzell

According to legend, the Roman pagan Placidus, captain of the guards for the Emperor Hadrian, was converted to Christianity when he beheld, while hunting, a stag bearing a luminous representation of Christ's crucifixion between his horns. Known after his conversion as Eustace, he later suffered martyrdom. A similar tale is recounted of St. Hubert. Usually the two are distinguished by their apparel: Eustace in armor, Hubert in hunting garb.

114. Albrecht Dürer
German, 1471-1528
The Opening of the Fifth and Sixth Seals (from the Apocalypse, Revelation of St. John, VI, 9-15) (Meder 168, Strauss 51)
Page from the second (Latin) edition, 1511
Woodcut, 15-1/2" x 11-1/8" (393 x 282 mm)
Collection: The Nelson-Atkins Museum, Gift from the Collection of Anne Foster Kriehn - 1962

In the illustration of St. John's fantastic vision, the sequelae of the opening of the two seals are shown, culminating in the eclipses of the black sun and the bloody moon, the shrinking of the sky in upon itself (indicated by the scalloped edges of the elliptical heaven), a shower of stars in rhomboid form (symbolic of the continents), and an earthquake. An angel at the top, behind the altar, distributes white robes to the martyrs crying for vengeance against their slayers; the innocent are ranged at the lower left corner and the guilty cower opposite them at the right (Strauss, *The Wood Cuts and Wood Blocks of Albrecht Dürer*, p. 189).

115. Ugo da Carpi
Italian, about 1480 - about 1532
The Death of Ananias, after Raphael, 1518 (B. II, 27)
Chiaroscuro woodcut from four blocks
9-5/8" x 14-3/4" (245 x 375 mm)
Collection: The Nelson-Atkins Museum of Art, Purchase, Nelson Gallery Foundation Funds

Illustrated is the Biblical account, in Acts of the Apostles, V, 1-10, of St. Peter's condemnation and punishment of Ananias, a member of the first Christian community, for having falsely asserted that he had yielded up to the church all of the proceeds from selling some land for its benefit.

116. Hans Springinklee
German, about 1490/95 - about 1540
The Holy Trinity, 1518 (Bartsch 59)
Illustration from second set of *Hortulus animae*, printed for J. Koberger by F. Peypus, Nuremberg
4-7/8" x 3-3/8" (123 x 86 mm)
Collection: The Nelson-Atkins Museum of Art, Purchase, Nelson Fund

Plant forms abound in the border.

117. Agostino de Musi, called Veneziano
Italian, 1490-1540
The Death of Ananias, after Raphael (B. XIV, 42, Passavant VI, 52.161)
Engraving, 10" x 15-11/16" (254 x 399 mm)
Collection: The Nelson-Atkins Museum of Art, Purchase, Nelson Fund

118. Hans Baldung Grien
German, 1476-1545
Bewitched Groom, about 1544 (B. VIII, p. 470, no. 15 - as Hans Brosamer; G. 122, H. 237, Nat. Gall. 87)
Woodcut, 13-1/2" x 7-7/8" (342 x 200 mm)
Collection: The Nelson-Atkins Museum of Art, Purchase, Nelson Fund

A definite interpretation of the subject has not been attained. Whatever the cause of the man's state of possession, it would seem to be related to the menacing presence of the torch-wielding crone.

119. Artist unknown
German, 16th century
Design for an Ecclesiastical Candleholder, 1559
Pen and black ink
25-5/8" x 10-3/8" (651 x 264 mm)
Collection: The Nelson-Atkins Museum of Art, Gift of Mr. Milton McGreevy

120. Giorgio Ghisi
Italian, 1520-1587
Raphael's Dream (Allegory of Life), 1561 (Bartsch 67, Boorsch - Lewis 28)
Engraving, 14-15/16" x 21-1/4" (380 x 540 mm)
Collection: The Art Museum, Princeton University, Museum purchase, by exchange, Caroline G. Mather Fund

With a male figure derived from a Raphael drawing and a female figure from a medal by Leone Leoni, this mysterious composition supposedly of Raphael's invention has a puzzling content, probably alchemical in origin. "At a glance, Ghisi's print can be seen to unite, as it were, the pairs of opposites male and female, young and old, barren and fruitful, winter and summer, storm and calm, mountains and plain, night and day" (Boorsch and Lewis, *The Engravings of Giorgio Ghisi*, n. 13, p. 120). The fantastic crepuscular landscape crowded with living creatures and vibrant with imaginative decorative forms has all the plausible, detailed immediacy of a vision, whoever its author.

121. Federico Barocci
Italian, about 1535-1612
The Vision of St. Francis, 1581 (Bartsch 4, Richards 73)
Etching and engraving
21-1/16" x 12-5/8" (525 x 320 mm)
Collection: Yale University Art Gallery, Everett V. Meeks, B.A. 1901, Fund

In an intensely varied repertoire of intaglio lines and dots, the artist brought to new life in black and white his polychrome altar painting in the church of San Francesco in Urbino. As A. Hyatt Mayor noted, "So long as the earth seemed but a shadow cast by heaven, the medieval artist found it simple to represent visions, but when science began to make the earth more real than heaven, the artist had to choose which world to emphasize. If a picture combined the ever more irreconcilable realms of the vision and the visionary, the artist ... might demonstrate that the vision, although violating natural law, was really factual, by focusing a sharp light on every fold of cloth and eyelash..." (Mayor, *Prints and People*, 436).

122. Hendrick Goltzius
Dutch, 1558-1616
The Dragon Devouring the Fellows of Cadmus, after Cornelis Cornelisz van Haarlem, 1588, III/IV (Hollstein 310, Bartsch 262)
Engraving, 9-9/16" x 12-7/16" (243 x 317 mm)
Collection: Private

According to legend, Cadmus, preparing to sacrifice to Athena the cow who had as the oracle at Delphi prophesied led him to the site where he founded the Greek city of Thebes, in Boeotia, sent some of his companions to fetch water from a nearby well owned by Ares and guarded by a dragon, one of Ares's sons. The dragon slew Cadmus's men, and Cadmus killed the dragon, later planting its teeth, as he was advised by Athena, and harvesting a group of armed men, the Sparti, or the Sown. Speaking of inculcating the Greeks with certain 'salutary' beliefs, "After all, says Plato, this is not too difficult: people who can believe in Cadmus and the dragon's teeth will believe anything" (Dodds, *The Greeks and the Irrational*, p. 212).

123. Horazio Farinati
Italian, 1559 - after 1616
The Crossing of the Red Sea, 1599, after Paolo Farinati (B. XVI, 1, 168)
Etching, 14-3/16" x 22-1/8" (361 x 563 mm)
Collection: Fogg Art Museum, Harvard University, Cambridge, Massachusetts, Gift of Ian Woodner

124. Unknown Flemish artist after Martin de Vos
Late 16th century, published by member of the Sadeler family
Burning of Troy
Engraving, 7-11/16" x 10-5/8" (195 x 270 mm)
Collection: Museum of Art and Archaeology, University of Missouri - Columbia, Gift of Mrs. Barbara Stratton Bolling and Mrs. Deborah S. Booker in memory of Arthur Hills Stratton

125. Artist unknown
Italian, 16th - 17th century
Arabesque Decorations
Pen and bistre and wash
16-7/8" x 4-3/16" (429 x 106 mm)
Collection: The Nelson-Atkins Museum of Art, Gift of Mr. Paul Gardner

126. Ludolph Büsinck
German, about 1599/1602-1669
Aeneas Saving His Father Anchises from Troy, about 1628-30, after Georges Lallemand (About 1575 - about 1640) (Stechow, Hollstein 22, Strauss 94, LeBlanc 20, Nagler 8)
Chiaroscuro woodcut, 13-5/8" x 8-9/16" (346 x 218 mm)
Collection: The Nelson-Atkins Museum of Art, Purchase, Nelson Gallery Foundation Funds

127. Jacques Callot
French, 1592-1635
Punishment by Hanging and *Punishment by Shooting*, from the series *Les Grandes Misères et Les Malheurs de la Guerre*, 1633, II/III, (Lieure 1349, 1350; Meaume 574, 575)
Etchings, pl., each 3-1/4" x 7-3/8" (83 x 187 mm)
Collection: The Nelson-Atkins Museum of Art, Gift of Mr. Robert B. Fizzell

128. Rembrandt van Rijn
Dutch, 1606-1669
The Hundred Guilder Print (Christ Healing the Sick), about 1639-1643, II/II (B. 74, H. 236)
Etching, 11" x 15-9/16" (281 x 395 mm) on sheet 11-7/8" x 16-3/8" (301 x 416 mm)
Ex Coll.: Yeger Mackowsky, Moscow; Hermitage, Leningrad
Collection: The Nelson-Atkins Museum of Art, Purchase, Nelson Fund

Known from the price it brought as early as the artist's lifetime, the print depicts the several episodes in the Biblical book of St. Matthew, Chapter 19: Christ healing the sick, receiving the children, disputing with the Pharisees, and conversing with St. Peter. The miraculous

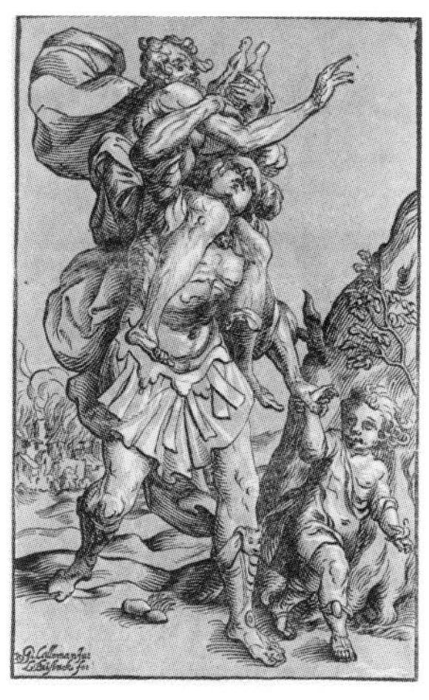

126.   Ludolph Büsinck, ca. 1628-30

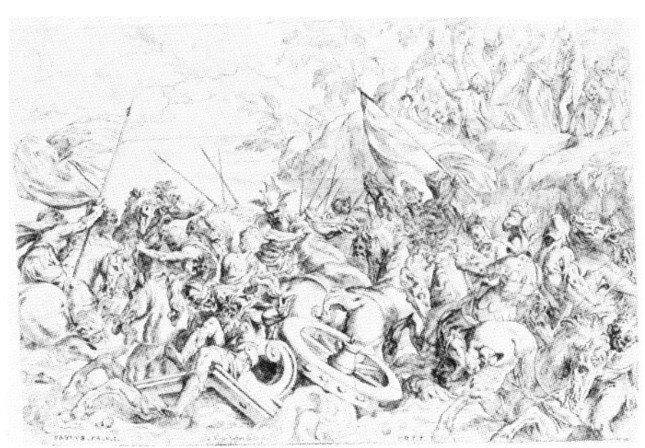

123.   Horazio Farinati, 1599

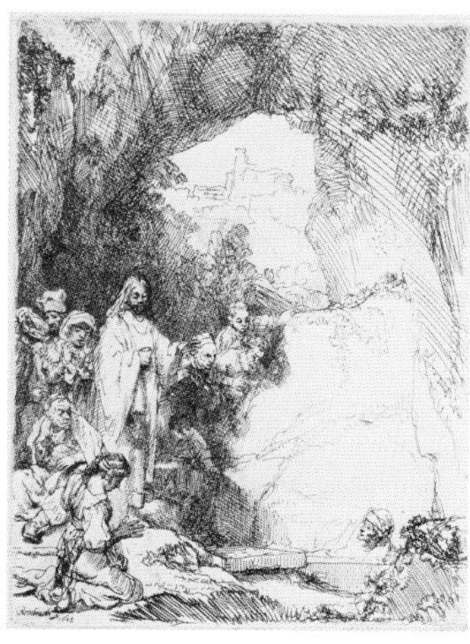

129.   Rembrandt van Rijn, 1642

curing of the ill has no higher pictorial priority than the other activities; all are depicted and encompassed within the group of persons clustering around Christ.

Rembrandt is not known to have signed or dated impressions of this print, but this example bears the ink-written artist's name.

129. Rembrandt van Rijn
Dutch, 1606-1669
The Raising of Lazarus, small plate, 1642 (H. 198, B. 72)
Etching, 6" x 4-5/8" (153 x 118 mm)
Collection: Yale University Art Gallery, Everett V. Meeks, B.A. 1901, Fund

130. Claude Mellan
French, 1598-1688
The Sudarium, 1649
Engraving, 16-3/4" x 12-3/8" (425 x 315 mm) on sheet 18" x 13-1/2" (457 x 343 mm)
Collection: Yale University Art Gallery, Bequest of Ralph Kirkpatrick, Hon. M.A., 1965

The theme of Christ's face miraculously impressed on the napkin proffered by St. Veronica to the suffering Lord bearing the cross on His way to crucifixion was executed in a prodigious feat using a single continuous spiral centered on the nose. "(When Christ impressed his features on Veronica's veil he sanctified picture printing by making the first monotype)" (Mayor, *Prints and People*, 8).

131. Rembrandt van Rijn
Dutch, 1606-1669
Faust, about 1652, II/II (H. 260, B. 270)
Etching on Japan paper
8-1/4" x 6-5/16" (209 x 160 mm)
Collection: The Art Institute of Chicago, Clarence Buckingham Collection, 1938.1757

Titled as "A Practicing Alchemist" in the 1679 inventory of Clement de Jonghe's possessions, the subject became known as Faust in the 18th century, and Rembrandt's etching was copied for the first edition of Goethe's *Faust* in 1790. The learned scholar is seen to be confronted by a disc-headed apparition with the INRI monogram of Christ at its center, encircled by an enigmatic text on the two

surrounding annuli. This anagram has been variously interpreted and seems to refer to "divine love" (Rosenberg, *Rembrandt*, Vol. I, pp. 158-9). Van de Waal relates the picture to the Christian sect of the Mennonites, in Holland, whose founder was Faustus [!] Socinus, suggesting that they may have commissioned the print and caused their leader to be portrayed as the beneficiary of the mysterious vision (Kok, *Rembrandt etchings and drawings in the Rembrandt House*, p. 140).

132. Salvator Rosa
Italian, 1615-1673
The Dream of Aeneas, about 1663-4 (Bartsch 23, Wallace 117)
Etching with drypoint, only state
13-3/4" x 9-5/16" (349 x 237 mm)
Collection: The Art Institute of Chicago, William Reed Memorial Fund, 1976.659

The sleeping Aeneas is advised on his future by the god of the river Tiber. Wallace finds in the print "a kind of shifting, insubstantial, crepuscular tonality that is wonderfully evocative of the world of dreams" (Wallace, *The Etchings of Salvator Rosa*, pp. 103-104).

133. Romeyn de Hooghe
Dutch, 1645-1708
The French Reign of Terror in the Dutch Villages Bodegraven and Zwammerdam, 1673, 1 of 7 plates in the series (Hollstein 90-96)
Etching, 7-13/16" x 12-1/8" (199 x 308 mm)
Collection: The Nelson-Atkins Museum of Art, Gift of Mr. Laurence Sickman

134. Artist unknown
Italian, 17th century
Design for a Baroque Monument
Pen and bistre ink, gray wash
17" x 10-3/8" (432 x 264 mm)
Collection: The Nelson-Atkins Museum of Art, Gift of Mr. Milton McGreevy

135. Bernard Picart
French, 1673-1733
Convoi Funêbre d'un Grand de la Chine, 1729 (Orange, *The Chater Collection*, p. 459, No. 15)

Engraving, 12-7/8" x 16-3/16" (336 x 412 mm)
Collection: The Nelson-Atkins Museum of Art, Gift of Mr.
    Laurence Sickman

At the right, figures release flares or fireworks that soar
overhead.

136. Anne Claude Philippe de Tubières, Comte de Caylus
French, 1692-1765
and Nicolas de Le Sueur
French, 1691-1764
La Chute de Phaeton, after drawing by Giuseppe Cesari,
    called Cavaliere d'Arpino (1568-1640), Pl. 90 from
    Crozat's *Recueil d'estampes d'après les plus beaux Tableaux
    et … dessins qui sont en France dans le Cabinet du
    Roy, dans celuy du Duc d'Orleans et dans d'autres
    Cabinets,* 2 vol., 1729 (Nagler, XVII, 56, 22: Le Blanc II,
    543, 24)
Etching by Caylus printed in black; two wood blocks by
    Le Sueur printed in brown and green
17-1/8" x 10-11/16" (435 x 268 mm) on sheet 21-1/8" x 15-
    5/16" (537 x 389 mm)
Collection: Private

Phaeton, "the shining," the scion of the sun god Helios, or
Hyperion, was allowed one day to pilot the chariot of the
sun on its quotidian course across the heavens, but, too
weak to rein in the steeds when they approached the earth
almost close enough to ignite it, he was killed by Zeus
with a bolt of lightning, causing him to fall into the river
Eridanus, or the Po. (Phaeton's sisters, who had yoked up
the horses, were transformed into poplars and their tears
into amber.) The mythological flight of the horses was
first mentioned by Homer.

137. Matthäus Merian the Elder
Swiss, 1621-1687
Death of the Painter (Hans Hug Klauber), Pl. 79 in *Dance of
    Death*
Basel: Jean Rodolphe Imhof, 1744, 3rd ed.
Engraving, 4-5/8" x 4" (118 x 102 mm)
The plates designed by Merian were executed by Jacques-
    Antony Chovin (Chauvin)(1720-1776).
Collection: The Nelson-Atkins Museum of Art, Gift of Mr.
    Laurence Sickman

138. Giovanni Domenico Tiepolo
Italian, 1727-1804, after Giovanni Battista Tiepolo, 1696-
    1770
St. Paulinus Exorcising a Possessed Boy, after 1747 (Rizzi 106
    II/II - as "St. Patrick Cures a Cripple")
Etching, 20-5/16" x 10" (516 x 253 mm) on sheet 28-3/4" x
    21-3/16" (731 x 539 mm)
Collection: The Art Museum, Princeton University, Gift of
    Prof. and Mrs. Felton L. Gibbons

139. Giovanni Elia or Gionaella Morghen
Italian, 1721 – active about 1789
Apotheosis (Allegory on the Death) of Lorenzo de' Medici
Engraving after painting by Francesco Furini (1604-1646),
    completed by Giovanni da San Giovanni (Mannozzi or
    Mannori) (1596-1656)
25-3/8" x 16-1/16" (645 x 407 mm) on sheet 27-15/16" x
    17-1/16" (710 x 434 mm)

Collection: The Nelson-Atkins Museum of Art, Gift of Mr.
    John Donnelly

After a fresco in the Sala degli Argenti, Palazzo Pitti, the
print bears an inscription translatable as: "The thread of
life of the magnificent Lorenzo having been cut short by
Fate, the swan Phoebus takes away from the surge of the
river Lethe that by which it is saddened, the portrait of
himself expressed in a medal; Virtue full of sorrow,
running here and there, sees Justice, Peace, and Fame
return to dwell in Heaven; and the Earth in Tumult, in
which menacing Mars suddenly descends."

140. Francisco José de Goya y Lucientes
Spanish, 1746-1828
It is Time, Pl. 80 from the series *Los Caprichos,* 1st ed., publ.
    1799 (Harris 115)
Etching, burnished aquatint, drypoint, and burin
Pl., 8-7/16" x 5-7/8" (215 x 150 mm)
Collection: The Nelson-Atkins Museum of Art, Purchase,
    Nelson Fund

The final plate of the series shows a quartet of fantastic
creatures, one with a group of human figures suspended
from his waist like a bunch of keys, awakening to vanish
into the dawn. As Goya commented, "As soon as day
breaks, they fly each one his own way, the witches, the
hobgoblins, the visions, and the phantoms. It is a good
thing these people show themselves only by night and in
the dark. No one has ever been able to find out where
they hide and lock themselves up during daytime…"
(Lopez-Rey, *Goya's Caprichos,* p. 212). These are images
dreamed by man that are vanquished by the daylight of
reason.

141. Francisco José de Goya y Lucientes
Spanish, 1746-1828
The sleep of reason produces monsters, Pl. 43 from the series
    Los Caprichos, 1st ed., publ. 1799 (Harris 78)
Etching and aquatint: pl., 8-3/8" x 5-13/16" (213 x 148
    mm)
Collection: The Nelson-Atkins Museum of Art, Purchase,
    Nelson Fund

In his effort to combat the follies and superstitions of the
day with the weapon of truth, Goya equated them with
the caprices of dreams. Here, in a print which proclaims
the artist's theme, he shows himself besieged in sleep by
embodiments of the evils that infest the unreasoning mind.

142. Giovanni Battista Piranesi
Italian, 1720-1778
Prisoners on a Projecting Platform, Pl. X from the *Carceri*
    series, V/VI (Hind 10, Robison 36)
In First Paris Edition, 1800-1809, Vol. 7 of 23 volumes
Etching, engraving, sulphur tint or open bite, burnishing:
    pl., 16-7/16" x 21-3/4" (417 x 553 mm)
Collection: The Nelson-Atkins Museum of Art, Gift of Mr.
    John H. Bender

The capricious inventions of fantastic architecture in the
Prisons series are shown by Robison (*Piranesi, Early
Architectural Fantasies,* pp. 37-42) to derive some of their
features from the artist's earlier works, the *Prima Parte,
Grotteschi,* and single plates, all showing buildings, ruins,
and constructions in the Roman spirit. These, with their

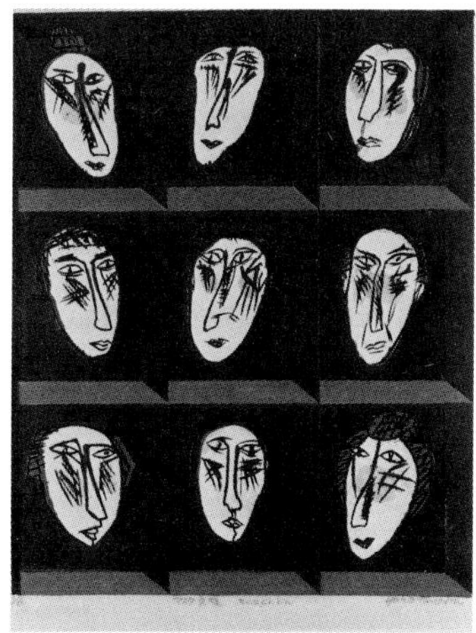

174. Yoko Tanaka, 1988

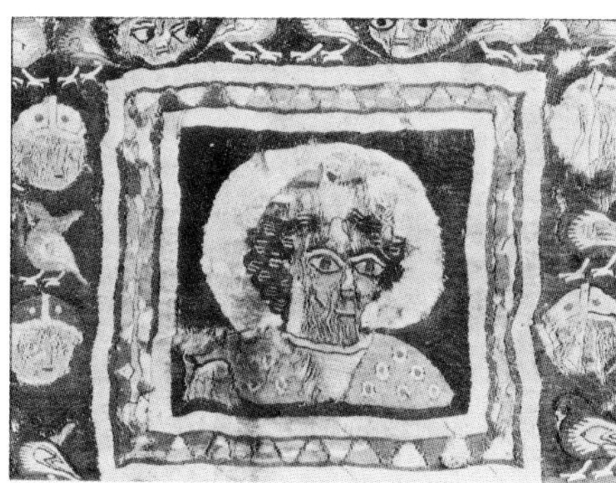

112. Detail of Coptic textile, 5th century A.D.

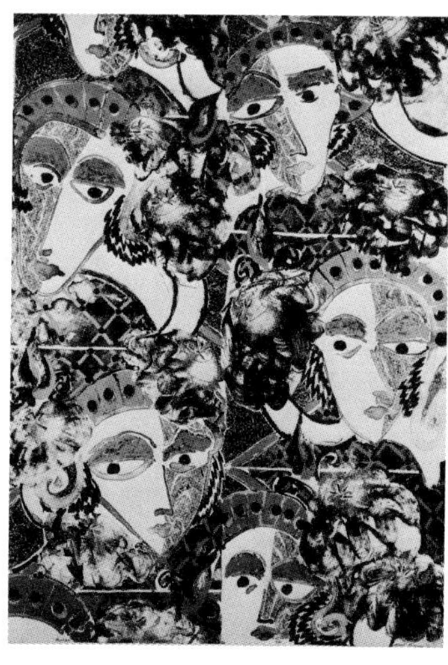

173. Robert Kushner, 1980

swirls of smoke, are no less imaginative and magnificent than the enigmatic prisons to which Piranesi imparted a nightmarish reality. In 1912, Arthur Samuel could write somewhat hectically: "Piranesi, full of the nightmare, slashed away with his needle, heedless of ocular digestion, architectural coherence, or structural correctness" (*Piranesi*, p. 111). Detailed meaningful niceties of joinery may cavalierly have been ignored in the pursuit of grandiloquence, but the general, overwhelming effect of the vision is plausible. A. Hyatt Mayor has stated a view more palatable to present-day taste (and most relevant to our exhibition theme): "The *Prisons* fascinate because their abstract patterns are like clouds, or ink blots, or the cracks and stains on a wall, in which each man sees the projection of his deepest disturbances. They are Piranesi's only landscapes of the mind" (*Giovanni Battista Piranesi*, pp. 29-30).

143. George Cruikshank
English, 1792-1878
Boney Hatching a Bulletin, or Snug Winter Quarters!!!, December, 1812 (Cohn 940)
Hand-colored etching: pl., 9-1/2" x 12-3/4" (242 x 324 mm) on sheet 9-13/16" x 13-1/4" (249 x 337 mm)
Contained in Vol. VI of *Essays on the Genius of George Cruikshank by Christopher North, W. M. Thackeray, Cuthbert Bede, etc.* 6 vol. London: Strand Magazine, n.d. [1889]
Collection: The Nelson-Atkins Museum of Art, Oak Hall Collection

A favorite target of Cruikshank's cartoons, Napoleon Bonaparte is shown here with his army on the retreat from Russia.

144. Francisco José de Goya y Lucientes
Spanish, 1746-1828
Dreadful events in the front row of the ring at Madrid and death of the mayor of Torrejon, Plate 21 from the series *Tauromaquia,* 1st ed., 1816 (Harris 224)
Etching, burnished aquatint, lavis, drypoint, and burin
9-9/16" x 12-1/2" (243 x 317 mm) on sheet 13-3/4" x 18" (350 x 457 mm)
Collection: The Nelson-Atkins Museum of Art, Purchase, Nelson Fund

The artist's title for the picture of the disastrous occurrence is translated as: "The bull jumped into the bleachers and killed two. I saw it." (Sayre, *The Changing Image: Prints by Francisco Goya,* p. 231). The incident may have happened on June 15, 1801 (Holo, *La Tauromaquia: Goya, Picasso, and the Bullfight,* p. 24).

145. William Blake
English, 1757-1827
With Dreams upon my bed thou scarest me & affrightest me with Visions, Pl. XI in the series *Illustrations of the Book of Job,* 1825, V/V (Binyon 116)
Engraving: Image, 7-11/16" x 5-7/8" (196 x 150 mm); plate, 8-7/16" x 6-11/16" (215 x 170 mm); sheet, 16-3/16" x 12-3/8" (412 x 315 mm)
Collection: The Nelson-Atkins Museum of Art, Purchase, Nelson Fund

At the turning point of his life, Job is confronted in his dreams by the apparition of the God of worldly justice he created, the image of self-righteousness, his mirror-imaged counterpart, the cloven-hoofed Satan entwined with the serpent of Materialism.

146. Ferdinand Victor Eugène Delacroix
French, 1798-1863
Mephistopheles Appearing to Faust, 1828 (D. 62), early state between III and V
Lithograph, 10-1/4" x 8-1/4" (261 x 209 mm)
Collection: Des Moines Art Center, Rose F. Rosenfield Graphic Arts Purchase Fund

147. Ferdinand Victor Eugène Delacroix
French, 1798-1863
The Ghost of Marguerite Appears to Faust, 1828-9 (D. 72)
Lithograph, 10-7/16" x 14-1/8" (267 x 359 mm) on sheet 12-3/4" x 18-5/16" (324 x 466 mm)
Collection: The University Art Museum, University of New Mexico, Albuquerque

148. Ferdinand Victor Eugène Delacroix
French, 1798-1863
Lioness Ripping Open the Chest of an Arab, 1849 (Delteil 25, Moreau 17), II/III
Soft-ground etching printed in sanguine

5-7/8" x 10-5/8" (150 x 273 mm) on sheet 6-5/8" x 11-1/8"
(167 x 283 mm)
Collection: The Nelson-Atkins Museum of Art, Gift of Mr.
John Donnelly

149. Ando Hiroshige
Japanese, 1797-1859
Taisha Shrine, Isumo Province, 1853, from *Views of Famous
Places in the Sixty-Odd Provinces*
Color woodcut
14-3/16" x 9-1/2" (361 x 242 mm)
Collection: The Nelson-Atkins Museum of Art, Purchase,
Nelson Fund

The receding line of trees resembles that of the palms in
Hockney's *Mist* (No. 167d).

150. Ando Hiroshige
Japanese, 1797-1859
Snow, Yabukoji at Atagoshita, 1857, from *Hundred Views of
Yedo*
Color woodcut
14-1/4" x 9-1/2" (362 x 242 mm)
Collection: The Nelson-Atkins Museum of Art, Purchase,
Nelson Fund

The snow-laden branches at the top right are repeated in
Hockney's winter scene (No. 167a).

151. Francisco José de Goya y Lucientes
Spanish, 1746-1828
Bury Them and Keep Quiet, Pl. 18 from the series *Los
Desastres de la Guerra*, 1st ed., publ. 1863 (Harris 138, III,
1a, 1 of 500)
Etching, burnished lavis, drypoint, and burin
Pl., 6-1/4" x 9-1/8" (160 x 232 mm)
Collection: The Nelson-Atkins Museum of Art, Purchase,
Nelson Fund

The accumulation of corpses could have ensued after the
French invaders' sieges of Zaragoza in 1808 and 1809 or
after the mass execution in Chinchon in 1808. The
despairing search of the survivors is accentuated
by silhouetting them against a threatening, cloudy sky.

152. Charles Meryon
French, 1821-1868
Le Ministère de la Marine, 1865-6 (DW 45, Burke 81)
Etching and drypoint, V/VI
6-5/8" x 5-3/4" (168 x 148 mm)
Collection: The Art Institute of Chicago, Clarence
Buckingham Collection, 1938.1628

In his last view of a Parisian theme, the artist felt
compelled to add to the sky the apparitions of birds,
horses, flying fish, and other imagined creatures.

153. W. M. Hooper
English, 1834-1912
The Dream of King Pharamond, after Burne-Jones, for "Love
is Enough," the Kelmscott Press, 1897
Engraving on vellum, 10-3/4" x 7-5/8" (273 x 193 mm) on
sheet 11-1/8" x 8-3/16" (283 x 207 mm)
Collection: The Nelson-Atkins Museum of Art, Gift of Mr.
Milton McGreevy

154. James Ensor
Belgian, 1860-1949
The Vengeance of Hop-Frog, 1898 (Croquez 111, Delteil 112),
II/II
Etching hand-colored by the artist
13-3/16" x 9-3/4" (335 x 248 mm) on sheet 15-1/2" x 11-
1/8" (394 x 283 mm)
Collection: The Nelson-Atkins Museum of Art, Purchase,
Nelson Fund

Derived from a story by Edgar Allan Poe, the print shows
a king and his seven councilors, covered with tar and
flax, secured in chains, and hoisted aloft on a chandelier,
being burned by the court jester, the dwarf, Hop-Frog,
who tricked them into attiring themselves as orangutans
at a fête. He thus exacted revenge for the insults the
eight nobles had inflicted on him and his dwarf lover,
Tripetta.

155. Francisco José de Goya y Lucientes
Spanish, 1746-1828
Al Toro y al Aire Daries Calle (Make way for bulls and
wind), 1st ed., 1877 (Harris 269), III/III, one of
additional plates for the *Proverbios* series
Etching and aquatint, 8-1/4" x 12-3/4" (210 x 323 mm) on
sheet 11-9/16" x 17-1/8" (293 x 435 mm)
Collection: The Nelson-Atkins Museum of Art, Purchase,
Nelson Fund

Known also as "The Rain of Bulls" and the series as
"Disparates," or follies, the enigmatic scene with its dark
background has the mysterious reality of a dream. In the
weightiness of its pictured descent it has been contrasted
with the airiness of the levitating winged men in another
plate of the series, "Where there's a will there's a way," or
"a way of flying."

156. Katsushika Hokusai
Japanese, 1760-1849
The Waterfall of Kirifuri, at Mt. Kurokami, Shimozuke
Province
Color woodcut, 14-5/8" x 9-5/8" (372 x 250 mm)
Collection: The Nelson-Atkins Museum of Art, Purchase,
Nelson Fund

157. Ando Hiroshige
Japanese, 1797-1859
Rain at Yamabashi-dani, Mimasaku Province, from *Views of
Famous Places in the Sixty-Odd Provinces*
Color woodcut
14-1/2" x 9-11/16" (370 x 246 mm)
Collection: The Nelson-Atkins Museum of Art, Purchase,
Nelson Fund

Hockney's lithograph has similar swirling lines of rain
gusts (No. 167c).

158. George Barker
American, 19th century
Johnstown Calamity—Wreck of the Day Express (Johnstown
Flood), 1889
Published by Underwood and Underwood
Stereograph, 3-1/2" x 7" (89 x 178 mm)
Collection: Private

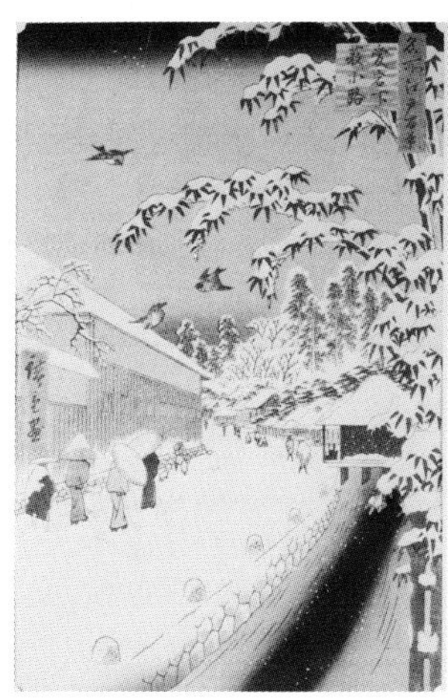

150.   Ando Hiroshige, 1857

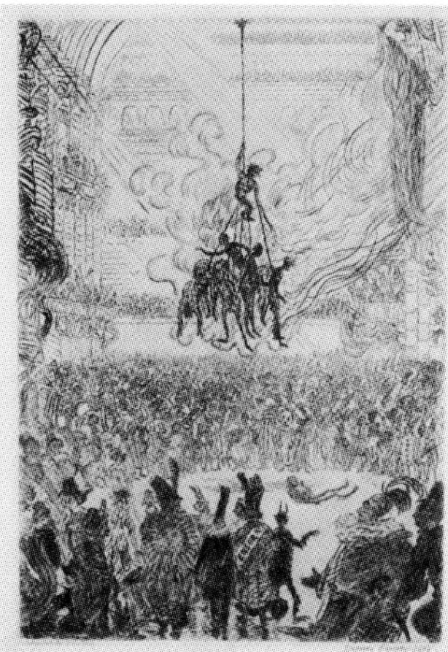

154.   James Ensor, 1898

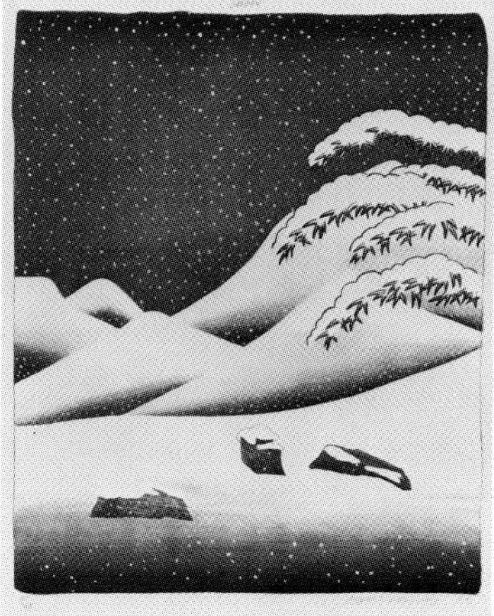

167a.   David Hockney, 1973

159. Karl Blossfeldt
German, 1865-1932
Portfolio of twelve prints
1975 gelatin silver prints after 1900-28 negatives
10-3/16" x 8" (259 x 203 mm) on sheets 16-3/4" x 12-3/4"
  (428 x 325 mm)
Collection: University Art Museum, University of New
  Mexico, Albuquerque, Gift of the Friends of Art

a. Aesculus parviflora. Small-flowered American horse-
   chestnut
b. Allium Ostrowskianum. Garlic
c. Cucurbita. Pumpkin
d. Papaver. Poppy
e. Aristolochia. Birthwort
f. Dipsacus laciniatus. Teasel, thistle, "Venus's Bason"
g. Blumenbachia Hieronymi. Geoffnete Samenkapsel
h. Blumenbachia Hieronymi. Geschlossene Samenkapsel
i. Papaver orientale. Oriental poppy
j. Impatiens glandulifera. Gland-bearing Balsam
k. Acanthus mollis. Artist's, Common, or Soft-leaved
   Bear's-Breech
l. Sesseli gummiferum

The artist's photographs of plant forms enlarged,
intended as models for his sculpture, as aids in his
teaching, and as illustrations for his books, seem in their
imposing reality to be the very archetypes of their
subjects. These are shapes that engender the shock of
recognition, showing us the originals from which familiar
styles in art and architecture have been derived. Natural
types, largely unvarying through the centuries, have a
second life in their adaptations in art. Blossfeldt's pictures
reveal "the unity of the creative will in nature and art"
(Nierendorf, intro., Blossfeldt, *Art Forms in the Plant World*,
n. p.). A few accompanying drawings and a print from the
Museum collection exhibit motifs of the sort one can
associate with those in these photographs.

160. B. L. Singley
American, 19th-20th century
Searching for the Dead among the Ruins, Galveston, Texas,
  (Galveston Flood), 1900
Published by the Keystone View Company

Stereograph, 3-1/2" x 7" (89 x 178 mm)
Collection: Private

161. Preston
American, 20th century
Post Street, North of Kearney, San Francisco, (San Francisco
  Earthquake), 1906
Photographic print, 5-7/8" x 7-15/16" (149 x 202 mm)
Collection: Private

162. Arnold Genthe
American, born Germany, 1869-1942
*Emergency Feeding of Homeless People after the San Francisco
  Earthquake,* 1906
Gelatin silver print
Collection: Gernsheim Collection, Harry Ransom
  Humanities Research Center, The University of Texas at
  Austin

163. Käthe Kollwitz
German, 1867-1945
Run Over, 1910 (Zigrosser 26, Lipstein 104d)
Soft-ground etching
9-7/8" x 12-9/16" (252 x 322 mm) on sheet 14" x 19-1/4"
  (355 x 491 mm)
Collection: The Nelson-Atkins Museum of Art, Purchase-
  Gift of the Richard Shields Fund

164. Otto Dix
German, 1891-1969
Corpses before Burial at Tahure, 48/70, from the series *Der
  Krieg* (War), 1924 (Karshan 119)
Etching with drypoint and aquatint
7-9/16" x 10" (192 x 252 mm) on sheet 13-7/8" x 18-3/4"
  (353 x 475 mm)
Collection: The Nelson-Atkins Museum of Art, Gift of Mr.
  Laurence Sickman

165. Man Ray
American, 1890-1976
A l'heure de l'observatoire—les amoreux (Observatory
  Time—The Lovers), 1968, 44/150
Serigraph, 26-1/2" x 40-3/4" (673 x 1036 mm)

Collection: Albright-Knox Art Gallery, Gift of Wade
   Stevenson, 1983

The print, like the painting of the same title completed in
1934, shows a pair of lips that seem to have the reclining
shapes of two embracing lovers. The image floating in the
sky has the plausibility of a dream or of a photograph of
clouds by Minor White.

166. Minor White
American, 1908-1976
Two Barns, Danville, New York, 1955
Gelatin silver print, 9-3/8" x 11-7/8" (238 x 302 mm)
Collection: Hallmark Collections

Compare with Man Ray, *A l'heure de l'observatoire—les
amoreux*, No. 165.

167. David Hockney
English, born 1937
Five prints from the *Weather* series, 1973
Color lithographs
a. *Snow*, 40" x 33-1/2" (1016 x 851 mm)
b. *Wind*, 40" x 31-1/8" (1020 x 791 mm)
c. *Rain*, 39" x 31-5/8" (991 x 830 mm)
d. *Mist*, 37-1/8" x 32" (943 x 813 mm)
e. *Lightning*, 39-3/8" x 31-5/8" (1000 x 803 mm)
Collection: National Gallery of Art, all except *Mist*, Gift of
   the Woodward Foundation, Washington, D. C. *Mist*,
   Gift of Gemini G.E.L.

168. Malcolm Morley
English, born 1931
Train Wreck, 1975, state 3, unique proof
Printed by Alan Koslin, Styria Studio, Inc., New York
Published by D'Arc Press, Inc., New York
Color etching and aquatint
32-3/4" x 43-5/8" (832 x 1108 mm) on sheet 35-13/16" x
   46-11/16" (910 x 1186 mm)
Collection: The Museum of Modern Art, New York, Mrs.
   John D. Rockefeller 3rd Fund. 236.84

A free copy in reverse after a painting of the same title
now in a museum in Vienna, the subject is "the carriages
of a model train, heaped up in a shallow box whose sides
appear in the picture, lettered in Chinese, Cyrillic and
Japanese scripts: 'catastrophe' and 'train wreck' "
(Compton, *Malcolm Morley Paintings 1965-82*, p. 13).

169. Roger Shimomura
American, born 1939
Oriental Masterprint #16, 1975
Silkscreen, 24" square (610 mm)
Collection: Hallmark Collections

This print, derived from Hokusai's *Waterfall of Kirifuri*
(No. 156), is from a series of such graphic adaptations
which revise and update their famous prototypes,
sometimes adding Occidental elements to them. *#16* is
one of the least Westernized of the group. It is shown here
as an instance of the pictorial embodiment of the
unpredictable flow of a watery cascade, made even more
fortuitous as a modification of an artistic precedent.

170. Horace Clifford Westermann
American, 1922-1981
No. 4 from *The Connecticut Ballroom* series, 1976, 1/33
Color woodcut, 17-15/16" x 23-7/8" (455 x 607 mm) on
   sheet 24" x 30" (608 x 760 mm)
Collection: The Nelson-Atkins Museum of Art, Gift of
   Mrs. Jean S. Lighton

The six woodcuts in this group have been described as
the artist's " 'letter to the world'—a suite of letters
sent back from a trip to the interior of his mind"
(Allan Frumkin Gallery, "Westermann Woodcuts," p. 3),
much like the drawing-letters which he mailed to his
friends during a journey across the country depicting
many of the obsessive images that were to populate his
later work.

171. Robert Cooney
American, contemporary
A.O.U.L.I.T.S. No. 1
New York: Robert Cooney, 1977
54 pp.; 11" x 8-1/2" (280 x 216 mm)
Collection: Private

"Cooney combines color xeroxes of a train disaster, quotes
from Jonathan Swift on the art of political lying, and news
captions from media controlled by Rupert Murdock. Two
tragedies are suggestively compared: a train wreck and
the social horror engendered by the propagandistic nature
of the media" (Nancy Princenthal, *Printed Matter
Catalogue 86/87*, p. 51).

172. Braco Dimitrijevic
Yugoslavian, contemporary
Tractatus Post Historicus
Tubingen, West Germany: Braco Dimitrijevic and Edition
   Dacic, 1977
66 pp.; 11-11/16" x 8-5/16" (297 x 210 mm)
Collection: Private

A treatise on history as an infinite number of
interpretations of events is contrasted with the history of
art as a series of accepted, repeated formal innovations
and illustrated with copies of pairs of photographs
seemingly taken by chance and yet demonstrative of the
author's anti-establishment thesis.

173. Robert Kushner
American, born 1949
Angelique, 1980
Lithograph with fabric, sequins, and acrylic
Sheet, 48-7/8" x 35-3/8" (1219 x 905 mm)
Collection: Milwaukee Art Museum, Gift of
   Quad/Graphics, Inc., Pewaukee, with National
   Endowment for the Arts Matching Funds, 1981

One of five lithographs published by the Barbara
Gladstone Gallery, this work seems closely akin to a
Coptic funeral hanging in the Nelson-Atkins Museum
collection (see enlarged panel in the exhibition, No. 112).
In its serial, grill format it recalls Warhol's printed and
painted rows of likenesses. A contemporary woodcut by
Yoko Tanaka (No. 174) continues in this vein of patterning
using human faces as the decorative components.

174. Yoko Tanaka
Japanese, contemporary
Yumemoyo (Dream Pattern), 1/60
Color woodblock print
21-1/8" x 16-1/4" (537 x 413 mm) on sheet 23-5/16" x 18-
  3/4" (592 x 476 mm)
Collection: Private

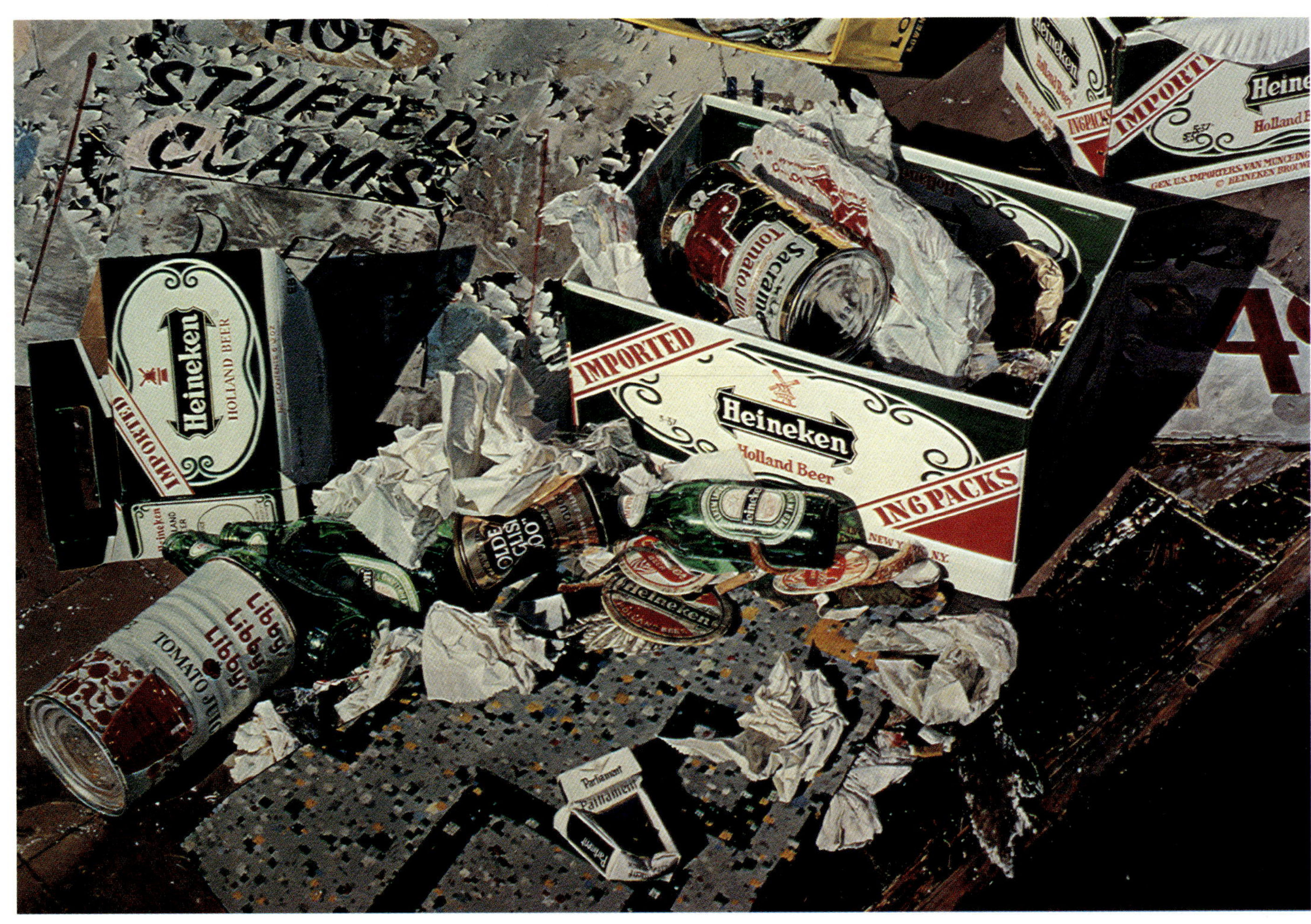

247.   Idelle Weber
       American, born 1932
       Heineken, 1976
       Oil on linen
       Collection: The Nelson-Atkins Museum of Art, Gift of Mr. and Mrs. Adam Aronson

III. Captured Transiences and Appearances of Spontaneity

Visual evidence of the close attention of artists to documenting the ephemeral, fixing an instant amid the flux of change, is found in pictures of the objective world showing both natural and manmade realities. The manner and the chosen content of their representation proceed from the individual's training and experience, the latter often causing direct observation of the subject to be shaped by pictorial traditions with which the artist is familiar and may, in revolutionary fervor, believe to be rejecting. In Plato's terms, what is being portrayed are shifting appearances, not unvarying eternal archetypes, although the artist may well launch his renderings of perceived reality by resorting to summary schemata of types, like Alexander Cozens's engravings of cloud forms (No. 178), which Constable once copied.

Conventional means of indicating denizens of the world and its overlords—children's stick figures, Cycladic flat idols, attenuated Etruscan bronzes, Egyptian effigies of gods, persons, and plants—are diagrammatic embodiments of the idea, if not the ideal or the actuality of their models. Among these stylized images in the exhibition are the 18th century rounded-staple forms of fountains at Versailles (No. 177), Jim Dine's snow, grass, and clouds in *Seven Days of Creation* (No. 222), the re-creations of waves by Bartlett (No. 255), and Jasper Johns's *Usuyuki* (No. 254), simultaneously symbolic of snow and reminiscent of an eccentric automobile paint job.

The ever-drifting amorphousness of clouds, like Alexander Cozens's blots and Leonardo's stains on walls, allows the imaginative observer to descry in them all manner of scenes and beings (as cited by Shakespeare in *Anthony and Cleopatra* and in *Hamlet*)—animals, human figures, landscapes, wheeling armies in combat, buildings, etc. But the study of the actual shifting structures of skies—as breeders of weather, major portions of our viewing of nature, and mood-inducing elements in landscape art—was undertaken most thoroughly by John Constable, sketching in oil colors on the scene, an unprecedented procedure (No. 179).[37] As early as the beginning 1790s, when the artist worked at his father's windmill, at East Bergholt, in Sussex, he had been sensitive to the vagaries of weather, drawing the forms of clouds, the first of many such sketches.[38] Constable would have agreed with Ruskin's assessment regarding the Romantic predilection for the expressive potential of nature: "So that, if a general and characteristic name were needed for modern landscape art, none better could be invented than 'the service of clouds.' "[39] In his concentration on commonplace themes, including ubiquitous but usually disregarded clouds, Constable, in the words of Peckham, "inspired I believe by Wordsworth, practically created modern painting by abandoning, as he put it, 'the plausible argument that subject makes the picture.' "[40]

Just thirty-four years later, in 1856, Gustave Le Gray (No. 182) photographed the sky and a seascape in a single negative. But it was not until the late 1920s that Stieglitz produced his *Equivalents,* (No. 189) camera studies of clouds, without an orienting ground line, of which he said: "My photographs are a picture of the chaos in the world, and of my relationship to that world. My prints show the world's constant upsetting of man's equilibrium, and his eternal battle to reestablish it."[41] Less loftily, Greenough has noted that "[the title *Equivalent*] emphatically stated that the clouds were not a symbol or a metaphor for his feelings, but their direct visualization; at that instant of time, these forms and tones were equivalent to his subjective state."[42] In their cloud photographs, Hyde (No. 242) and Minor White (No. 207) (whose series *Song Without Words* is titled after Stieglitz's *Songs of the Sky*, of 1923) seem, among others, most attuned to the abstract symbolism of Stieglitz. But Steiner (No. 273) actively solicited the metaphors which spectators felt were evoked in them by his photographs of clouds, and it must be admitted that Stieglitz's own inner state was not necessarily echoed in the perceptions by observers of his prints. In ink-printed graphics, the work of Schueler (No. 263-4) appears closest to the spirit of that of Stieglitz.

Beyond its vaporous state, the protean substance of water in fluid form could be as expressive a subject for artists. Whether in vast sparkling expanses, leaden sheets, or the ceaseless succession of breakers, bodies of water can be integral to landscape depiction, essential in establishing atmosphere, light, and emotion. In Vija Celmins's *Waves* (No. 231, 240), seen from the vantage of a gull or a sailor, the minutely serried plane immerses us in a sea of infinity. Seemingly realistic, it is an invented ocean, illustrating that "In a way, art is a theory about the way the world looks to human beings."[43] Edward Weston's Point Lobos tide pool and surf (No. 200, 199) which, though furnished with bits of shore and rocks, providing deceptive orientation, have a similar illimitableness, a fractal geometry in which the tiniest irregular fragments are an echo of the largest. Minor White's photograph of frost (No. 210) shares with Jim Dine's pool of water in *Seven Days of Creation* (No. 222) an inchoate, unscaled liquidity, a primordial stew suggestive of the site of origin of living organisms. Snow crystals, the most transient form of water other than rain (whose atmospheric and psychological effects have regularly been exploited in pictures), were studied as early as the 2nd century B.C. in China[44] and were recorded by Wilson Bentley, in Vermont, in many thousands of photomicrographs in the late 19th and early 20th century (No. 187). The (usually) hexagonal shape of these crystals, varying in accordance with temperature, gives them a visual appeal like that afforded by symmetrical patterns in textiles and glass.

A more solid, but no less varying, substance—earth—with the structures erected upon it, all subject to the inroads of weathering, is an inexhaustible source for artists. No one more than Dubuffet (No. 215, 218, 220) has explored the field more intensively:

> His fascination with the minutiae of nature is also indicated by his drawings of small patches of ground, areas of crumbling walls, or the scratches of time on doorways. It is not surprising that he should concern himself with the texture of nature, for this is the same artist who finds sculptured beauty in pieces of coal, clinkers, slag, sponges, and driftwood.[45]

For his vast multiple lithograph series *Phenomena*, the artist compiled a notebook reservoir of printed impressions of pictures of surface textures, in black and white and color, from whose plates he could select those for new combinations of pictorial effects. These illustrate different microcosms in whose terrestrial disorder he felt that a possible clue to deciphering the strangeness of existence might be manifested. Dubuffet believes that "... it is at the far end of strangeness that one has a chance to find the key to things."[46] An allied belief no doubt animates, among others, Robert Stanley's photo-derived *Paul's Mud* (No. 229), Jim Dine's *Earth* (No. 222), and photographs by Andreas Feininger of mud flakes (No. 209), by Aaron Siskind of rocks (No. 213), by Edward Weston of a juniper (No. 197), and by Minor White of stone strata (No. 221).

Turning from natural earthscapes to human-crafted environments, there is considerable visual capital in the unpredictable patterned effects of gradual disintegration of materials: peeling paint (Siskind, No. 205; White, No. 217b), weathered wood (Weston, No. 198), partially defaced walls (Nakahashi, No. 272; Siskind, No. 219, 224; Von Schaewen, No. 250), the rusting of automobiles (Evans, No. 194, Sheehan, No. 206). Concentration on the changes in appearance wrought by varying illumination is especially evident in Bartlett's seascape (No. 255), LeWitt's rough expanses of walls (No. 248, 249), Frecot's viaduct (No. 261), and Dieter Roth's book of illusionistically shadowed substances (No. 246). Our habituation to the mundane sights of our familiar daily round often inures us to their singularity, an unfocused presumptiveness that artists' emphasis acts to dispel. By isolating and highlighting them, elements of the world are brought to fresh notice. If, however, the manner of presentation itself becomes hackneyed the stage is set for a new, more stimulating mode of portrayal. "A style, like a culture or climate of opinion, sets up a horizon of expectation, a mental set, which registers deviations and modifications with exaggerated sensitivity."[47]

Within our experience perhaps nothing is more startling than exceptional conduct among our fellow beings. When individuals are caught in the act of surprising behavior, often apprehended by the lens of the cameraman at the propitious moment, as in many photographs in this section of the exhibition (by Cartier-Bresson, Doisneau, Erwitt, Gozu, Kertesz, Lartigue, Levitt, Nakahashi, Parks, Smith, Weegee, and Winogrand), the observer is delighted by the novelty. No matter that in some instances hours of waiting may have been required to be prepared to capture an image at the opportune instant: the process is the antithesis of staged action. These are arrested incidents as "found" as static, photographed objects—Callard's ailanthus (No. 251), Corman's intruding finger tips (No. 268), McGough's crocodile puddles (No. 270), MacWeeney's flies (No. 238), and Souza's "Death" signs (No. 244).

People in masses—crowds—as unpredictable in congregate action as they are in the movements of their component individuals, are best observed in bird's-eye views. Certainly a crowd's collective activity, haphazard growth, and eventual dissolution are most easily descried from above, despite the tapestry-like effect engendered by distance. Although the "view may be as accessible to the human eye as it is to the camera, the image received by the eye cannot be enlarged the way a negative is enlarged. This means that mass movements,

including war, constitute a form of human behavior which particularly favors mechanical equipment ... Mass reproduction is aided especially by the reproduction of masses."[48] Feininger's Coney Island beach scene (No. 227) demonstrates the cohesiveness of a crowd, while Genovés's *Many Men* (No. 234) shows its mysterious dispersal. Among non-human groups, Clift's photograph of a peaceful flock of sheep amid canyon rocks carved with petroglyphs (No. 241) contrasts with Crane's series of the apparently confused whirlings of urban pigeons (No. 245). Referring to the seemingly abrupt, concerted mass take-offs and banking of birds, Selous wrote "I ask how, without some process of thought transference so rapid as to amount practically to simultaneous collective thinking, are these things to be explained?"[49]

Panoramic series of photographs not only document their main subjects, the natural expanses and manmade constructions that flank their central track (all evidencing weather-induced modifications), but unavoidably often incorporate the chance traffic which can inhabit them: pedestrians and vehicles on streets, boats in water. Shear's record of both banks of the Hudson, may be, as the title page asserts, the first such riverine panorama (No. 183), but Ruscha's and Henderikse's complete views of city streets (No. 223, 267) have a precedent in *Avenida Central*, the collotype publication, in 1907, of photographs by Marc Ferrez of each structure erected on every block of a new street driven through an old quarter of Rio de Janeiro.[50]

---

175. Jacques Callot
French, 1594-1635
Fireworks on the Arno, plate in *Les Caprices*, second series, Nancy, 1622 (Lieure 472, Meaume 857), I/II
Etching, 2-1/16" x 3-1/16" (52 x 78 mm)
Collection: The Nelson-Atkins Museum of Art, Purchase, Nelson Fund

Two views of Versailles
176. Attributed to Adam Perelle
French, 1640-1695
Le Bassin d'Enclade, published about 1704
Hand-colored etching, 8" x 11-7/16" (203 x 291 mm) on sheet 8-9/16" x 11-15/16" (217 x 303 mm)

177. Antoine Aveline
French, 1691-1743
Veue et perspective de la Salle des Antiques

Hand-colored etching, 8-1/8" x 12-5/16" (205 x 313 mm) on sheet 8-1/4" x 12-7/16" (210 x 315 mm)
Collection: The Nelson-Atkins Museum of Art, Gift of Mrs. William H. Chapman

The jets of water are indicated by continuous vertical loops.

178. Alexander Cozens
English, 1717-1786
Clouds (Wilton 50, 56, 60)
About 1785
Line engravings, each approx. 4-3/8" x 6-5/16" (113 x 160 mm)(trimmed to edge of subject)
Collection: Davison Art Center, Wesleyan University, Middletown, Connecticut
Inscribed:
a. "25) The same as the last, but darker at the bottom than the top—" (The last is inscribed: "24) Half cloud half plain, the lights of the clouds lighter, and the shades

darker/ than the plain part and darker at the top than
the bottom—/ The Tint once over in the plain part, and
twice in the clouds.—")

   b. "31) The same as the last, but darker at the bottom than
the top—" (The last is inscribed: "30) All cloudy, except
one large opening, with others smaller, the lights of the
clouds lighter, & the shades/ darker than the plain part,
and darker at the top than the bottom.—/ The Tint once
over in the openings, and twice in the clouds.—")

   c. "35) All cloudy, except a narrow opening at the top of
the sky, with/others smaller, the clouds darker than the
plain part, & darker at the top than the bottom.—/The
Tint twice over.—"

These are three of the somewhat diagrammatic twenty
illustrations of cloud studies in Cozens's *A New Method*, of
which Constable made freely drawn copies. As Hawes
notes ("Constable's Sky Sketches," p. 350), the engravings
"appear to derive as much from memory as from
observation, falling roughly mid-way between 'schemata'
and empirical studies." Possibly the rigor of their
classification in terms of their light or dark quality may
have been instrumental in convincing Constable to
embark upon an intensive examination himself of the
varieties of clouds that might be incorporated in paintings
(No. 179). Not as suggestive as Cozens's landscape blots,
the engravings supply the skies which they lack, but thus
neither can approach the atmospheric interaction that
Constable deemed paramount in nature and art. But
Cozens was the first English artist to draw skies and to
engrave them, and his pictures are superior to the cloud
examples first published in 1803 by the pioneer
meteorologist Luke Howard, often adduced as influential
on Constable.

179. John Constable
English, 1776-1837
Study of Cumulus Clouds (Reynolds 22.16)
1822
Oil on paper laid on canvas
12" x 20" (305 x 508 mm)
Collection: Yale Center for British Art, Paul Mellon
   Collection

During an intensive bout of "skying," Constable
produced some fifty oil sketches of clouds from the
vantage of Hampstead Heath, unique in their close-up,
dramatic character. Many of these are accompanied by
precisely worded labels on the reverse, as in this instance,
recorded as "Augt 1. 1822 11 o clock A.M. very hot with
large climbing Clouds under the Sun. wind westerly."
This particularity accords well with the newly published
studies in then nascent metereology which provided the
designations we still use for clouds (cirrus, cumulus,
stratus, nimbus, etc.) and with the drawings made in 1823
by Constable (now in the Courtauld Institute) after
Alexander Cozens's schematic patterns of clouds in *A
New Method* (No. 178). The latter are concerned with the
relative lightness and darkness of the cloud forms
themselves, a concern for their illuminative impact on
landscapes Constable notes in his letter of October 23,
1821 to his friend Rev. John Fisher: "It will be difficult to
name a class of Landscape, in which the sky is not the *'key
note,' the standard of 'Scale,'* and the chief *'Organ of
sentiment'* ... The sky is the *'source of light'* in

nature—and governs everything. Even our common
observations on the weather of everyday are suggested by
them but it does not occur to us" (John Constable's
Correspondence, VI, 77).

180. William P. Blake
American, 1825-1910
Mirage on the Colorado Desert, 1853, Pl. XII, Vol. 5, *Reports
of Explorations and Surveys to Ascertain the Most
Practicable and Economic Route for a Railroad from the
Mississippi River to the Pacific Ocean*, 1856
Color lithograph, 5-11/16" x 8-11/16" (145 x 221 mm)
Collection: The Nelson-Atkins Museum of Art, Gift of Dr.
   and Mrs. Joseph F. Jacobs

Blake was the geologist for Lt. R. T. Williamson's
exploratory surveys of two possible routes in southern
California. While most of Blake's sketches dealt with his
specialty, a few, including this extraordinary vision, were
of more general pictorial interest (Taft, *Artists and
Illustrators of the Old West*, p. 257, n. 17).

181. Ando Hiroshige
Japanese, 1797-1859
Fireworks at Ryogoku, from *Famous Views of Yedo*
Color woodcut
14-7/8" x 5-1/16" (378 x 130 mm)
Collection: The Nelson-Atkins Museum of Art, Purchase,
   Nelson Fund

182. Gustave Le Gray
French, 1820-1862
Brig Upon the Water, 1856
Albumen print from wet collodion on glass negative
12-3/4" x 16-1/2" (324 x 419 mm)
Collection: Gernsheim Collection, Harry Ransom
   Humanities Research Center, The University of Texas at
   Austin

Such scenes as this, one of the first photographic
seascapes in which the sky and the water are printed from
a single negative made during one underexposure
(Gernsheim p. 264, Janis p. 73, Scharf p. 114), producing
an effect of moonlight, captured clouds with an accuracy
not attained in contemporary painting. The photograph
seems to forecast shoreside canvases by Courbet and by
the Impressionists.

183. G. Willard Shear
American, 19th-20th century
*Panorama of the Hudson Showing Both Sides of the River from
New York to Albany ... First Photo-Panorama of Any River
Ever Published*, 1902
Published by Bryant Literary Union, New York
50 pp.; 7-11/16" x 12-9/16" (196 x 319 mm)
Two horizontal half-tone labeled plates on each page
   show each shore; the bottom plates are printed upside
   down.
Collection: The Nelson-Atkins Museum of Art, Spencer
   Art Reference Library

184. Jacques Lartigue
French, 1896-1986
Cousin "Bichonade" in Flight, 1905
Gelatin silver print, 6-5/8" x 9-1/16" (169 x 230 mm)

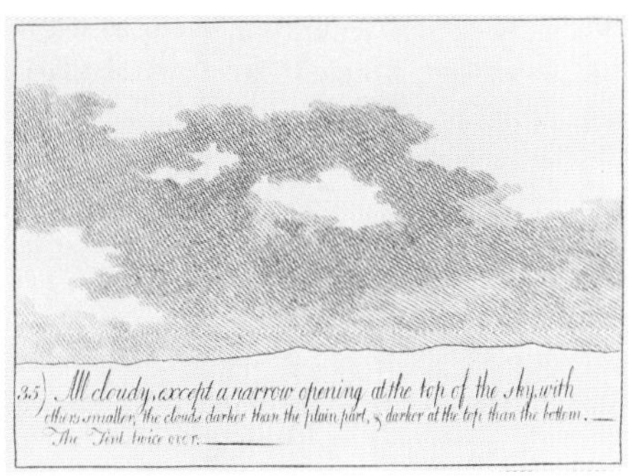

178c.   Alexander Cozens, about 1785

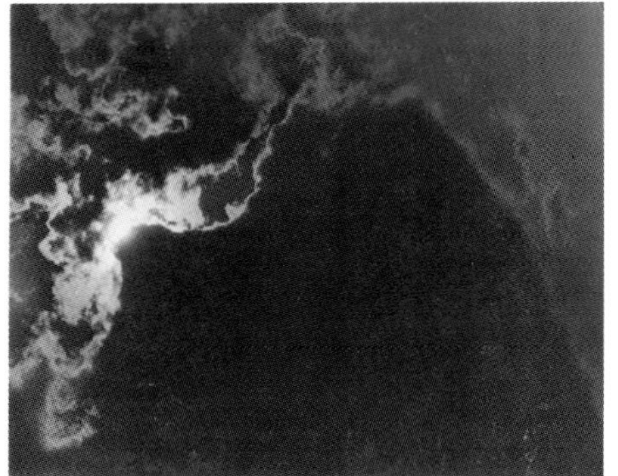

189e.   Alfred Stieglitz, 1927

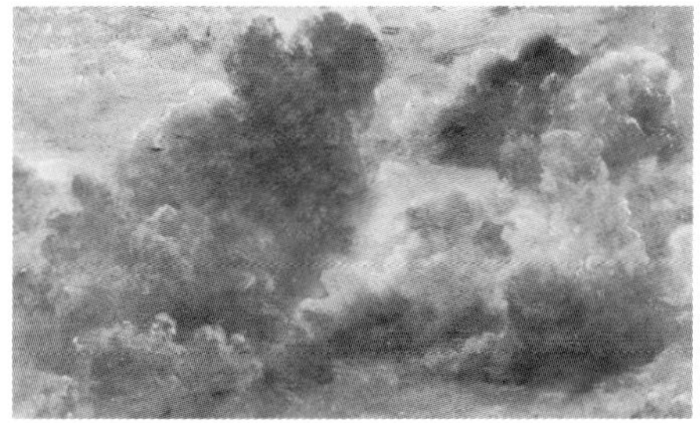

179.   John Constable, 1822

Collection: New Orleans Museum of Art, Ella West
Freeman Foundation Matching Fund

185. Jacques Lartigue
French, 1896-1986
Grand Prix of the Automobile Club of France, 1912
Gelatin silver print, 14-15/16" x 12-15/16" (380 x 329 mm)
Collection: New Orleans Museum of Art, Ella West
Freeman Foundation Matching Fund

186. Alfred Stieglitz
American, 1864-1946
The Steerage, 1915
Photogravure print, 13-1/8" x 10-3/4" (333 x 264 mm) on
sheet 18-5/16" x 12-1/16" (465 x 320 mm)
Collection: The Nelson-Atkins Museum of Art, Purchase-
Gift of the NBC and Anonymous Funds

This famous picture resulted from a serendipitous visit by
the artist to the bow of an ocean liner on which he was
traveling to Europe in 1907 amid a group of nouveaux
riches swells. On the lower deck of the ship he discerned
the abstract design and affecting humanity that combined
to make this photograph uniquely powerful; Stieglitz
recognized the affinity of the scene with the compassion
and chiaroscuro of the art of Rembrandt.

187. Wilson Alwyn Bentley and W. J. Humphreys
American, 19th century
a. *Snow Crystals*
New York: Dover Publications, Inc., 1962
227 pp., 10-3/16" x 8" (260 x 203 mm)
Collection: Private

This is a republication of the volume first published for
the American Meteorological Society by the McGraw-Hill
Book Company, Inc., in 1931. It contains 2453 illustrations
of snowflakes chosen from more than 5000
photomicrographic plates made by Bentley during a
period of nearly fifty years. Many of these had been
reproduced previously in issues of the *Monthly Weather
Review* from 1901 to 1927. The first known photographs of
snow crystals, they do not harbor among them a
duplicate, although recent research purports to have
discovered a pair of identical crystals, hardly an
unimaginable occurrence considering the infinitude of
possible specimens.

Drawings of snowflakes were first made by Olaus
Magnus, Archbishop of Uppsala, in 1555, and, in 1611,

Johannes Kepler first published an account of the relation
of the unvarying hexagonal form of the snowflake and the
symmetrical geometry of crystals (Mason, "On the Shapes
of Snow Crystals," in Kepler, *The Six-Cornered Snowflake,* p.
52). In his theories, Kepler had, however, been anticipated
by Thomas Herriott, who, "As early as 1599, … saw the
relationship between certain decorators' patterns and the
corpuscular theory of matter" (*Loc. cit*). It is of interest that
observations of both natural and artificial phenomena
could give rise to the same conclusions about the
symmetrical character of the structure of crystals. But not
until the 19th century was it recognized that "The
hexagonal symmetry of a snow crystal is a macroscopic,
outward manifestation of the internal arrangement of the
atoms in ice (*Ibid.,* p. 53). All the study of snowflakes had
begun in China about 135 B.C. when Han Ying in his book
Han Shih Wai Chuan (Moral Discourses Illustrating the
Han Text of the Book of Odes) wrote: " 'Flowers of plants
and trees are generally five-pointed, but those of snow are
always six-pointed' " (quoted in *Ibid.,* p. 48).

In more modern times, since 1932, the Japanese scientist
Ukichiro Nakaya and his colleagues have conducted
research into the formation of snowflakes. Kepler posited
a "formative faculty" which determines the shape of all
natural bodies (*The Six-Cornered Snowflake,* p. 33) and, in
orderliness, does not permit them "'to fall in an ugly and
immodest fashion'" (*Ibid.,* p. 35). The observation by
physicists of snowflakes has revealed that the hydrogen
atoms in the water that composes them are irregularly
distributed in crystals at normal temperatures, while the
oxygen portion remains constantly stable. "The visually
perfect hexagon starlet is the progeny of a union of order
and disorder" (Whyte, "Kepler's Unsolved Problem and
the *Facultas Formatrix,*" in Kepler, p. 61). What causes the
snowflake to take its particular form remains unknown
now, as it was to Kepler: "What in the ultimate laws
produces visually perfect patterns?" (*Ibid.,* p. 63).

b. Four etchings on glass after Bentley's negatives
20th century
3" dia. (76 mm)
Collection: Private

188. Eadweard Muybridge
American, born England, 1830-1904
*The Human Figure in Motion: An Electro-Photographic
Investigation of Consecutive Phases of Muscular Actions,*
5th ed.

London: Chapman and Hall, 1919
9-3/4" x 12" (248 x 305 mm)
Collection: Private

The first edition of this work was published in 1901, and it and the following reprints are republications on a reduced scale, with half-tone plates, of some of the collotypes in the 1887 *Animal Locomotion*. Subjects in *The Human Figure* were, in 1884, students and graduates from the University of Pennsylvania; the wild animals were photographed in the Philadelphia zoological gardens in 1885.

189. Alfred Stieglitz
American, 1864-1946
Five *Equivalents*
Gelatin silver prints
a. Equivalent - 1924, 4-5/8 "x 3-11/16" (118 x 93 mm)
b. Equivalent - 1925, 4-5/8" x 3-1/16" (118 x 90 mm)
c. Equivalent - 1926, 4-9/16" x 3-5/8" (117 x 92 mm)
d. Equivalent - 1926, 4-11/16" x 3-5/8" (119 x 92 mm)
e. Equivalent - 1927, 3-11/16" x 4-9/16" (93 x 116 mm)
Collection: The Art Museum, Princeton University, Museum purchase, Fowler McCormick, Class of 1921, Fund

190. André Kertesz
American, born 1894
Meudon, 1928
Gelatin silver print, 9-3/4" x 6-3/4" (248 x 172 mm)
Collection: Hallmark Collections

191. Laszlo Moholy-Nagy
American, born Hungary, 1895-1946
Marseilles, 1928
Gelatin silver print, 11-1/2" x 8-7/8" (292 x 226 mm)
Collection: Hallmark Collections

Varnedoe has noted painted precedents for such overhead views through balcony railings, in works of the 1880s by such artists as Caillebotte, Seurat, and Van Gogh (Varnedoe, *Gustave Caillebotte*, p. 154). Even earlier are the stereographs of street scenes by Hippolyte Jouvin, 1860-1865 (Scharf, *Art and Photography*, Pl. 113-115) and, for the foreground screening element, Hiroshige's *Moon Pine at Ueno*, of 1858 (Varnedoe, *op. cit.*, p. 154).

192. Henri Cartier-Bresson
French, born 1908
Behind the Gare St. Lazare, 1932
Gelatin silver print, 14-1/4" x 9-1/4" (362 x 240 mm)
Collection: Hallmark Collections

193. Helen Levitt
American, born 1918
New York, about 1942
Gelatin silver print, 10-3/8" x 6-7/8" (264 x 175 mm)
Collection: Hallmark Collections

194. Walker Evans
American, 1903-1975
Joe's Auto Graveyard, Pennsylvania, 1936, printed 1971
Gelatin silver print, 4-3/4" x 6-11/16" (121 x 170 mm)
Collection: Milwaukee Art Museum, Gift of Karen Johnson Boyd, Racine, Wisconsin

195. Arthur Rothstein
American, born 1915
Dust Storm, Cimarron County, Oklahoma, 1936
Gelatin silver print, 10-1/8" x 10" (257 x 254 mm)
Collection: Hallmark Collections

196. Edward Weston
American, 1886-1958
Clouds
Gelatin silver print, 7-9/16" x 9-9/16" (192 x 243 mm)
Collection: Sheldon Memorial Art Gallery, University of Nebraska - Lincoln, Allocation of the Works Progress Administration

197. Edward Weston
American, 1886-1958
Juniper, Lake Tenaya, 1937
Gelatin silver print
9-1/2" x 7-1/2" (241 x 191 mm)
Collection: The Nelson-Atkins Museum of Art, Gift of Mr. and Mrs. Milton McGreevy through the Mission Fund

198. Edward Weston
American, 1886-1958
Potato Cellar, Lake Tahoe, 1937
Gelatin silver print, 7-1/2" x 9-1/2" (190 x 242 mm)
Collection: The Nelson-Atkins Museum of Art, Gift of Mr. and Mrs. Milton McGreevy through the Mission Fund

On Saturday, September 18, 1937, in the town of Meyers, a pony express stop near Tahoe, Weston and Charis Wilson noticed: "At the end of the line of tall pine buildings was a little potato cellar, its snow-polished board front crisscrossed with rust tracks from the nails" (Charis Wilson, *California and the West*, p. 118).

199. Edward Weston
American, 1886-1958
Surf, Point Lobos, 1938
Gelatin silver print, 7-1/2" x 9-1/2" (191 x 241 mm)
Collection: The Nelson-Atkins Museum of Art, Gift of Mr. and Mrs. Milton McGreevy through the Mission Fund

200. Edward Weston
American, 1886-1958
Tide Pool, Point Lobos, 1938
Gelatin silver print, 7-1/2" x 9-1/2" (190 x 242 mm)
Collection: The Nelson-Atkins Museum of Art, Gift of Mr. and Mrs. Milton McGreevy through the Mission Fund

201. Weegee (Arthur H. Fellig)
American, born Poland, 1899-1969
The Critic, 1943
Gelatin silver print, 10-5/8" x 12-3/4" (270 x 324 mm)
Collection: New Orleans Museum of Art, Museum Purchase through Zemurray Foundation Fund

202. Minor White
American, 1908-1976
Fog Bank and Surf, San Mateo County, 1947, from *Song Without Words* portfolio, 1948
Photographic print, 4-5/8" x 3-5/8" (118 x 92 mm)
Collection: The Art Museum, Princeton University, Gift of F. Jeffris Elliott

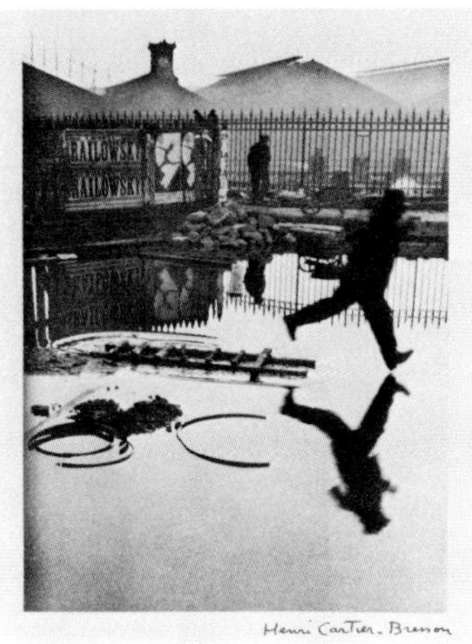

192. Henri Cartier-Bresson, 1932

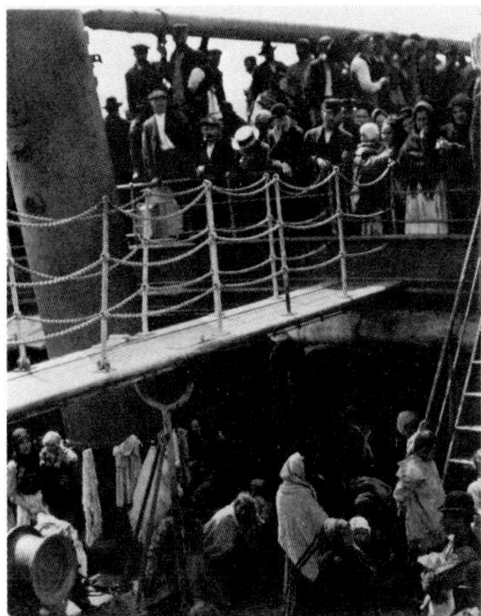

186. Alfred Stieglitz, 1915

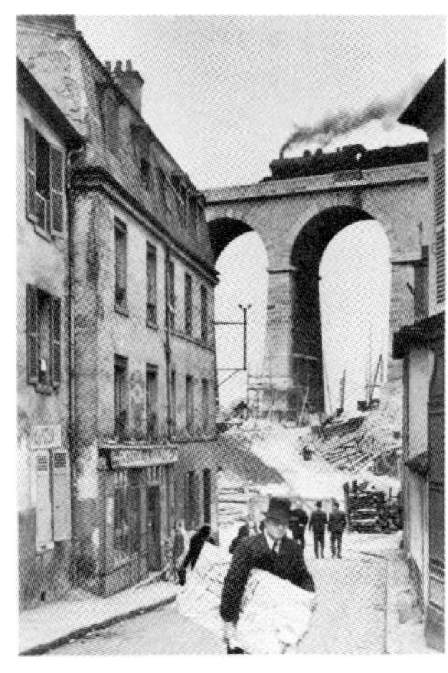

190. André Kertesz, 1928

203. Robert Doisneau
French, born 1912
La Dame Indignée, 1948, 72/100, in portfolio published by
    Hyperion Press, Ltd., 1979
Gelatin silver print
9-9/16" x 12-1/32" (242.5 x 305 mm) on sheet 11-15/16" x
    16" (303.5 x 406 mm)
Collection: The Nelson-Atkins Museum of Art, Gift of Dr.
    Carl W. Melcher

204. Robert Doisneau
French, born 1912
L'Innocent, 1949, 72/100, in portfolio published by
    Hyperion Press, Ltd., 1979
Gelatin silver print
11-5/16" x 9-19/32" (288 x 244 mm) on sheet 15-31/32" x
    11-7/8" (406 x 302.5 mm)
Collection: The Nelson-Atkins Museum of Art, Gift of Dr.
    Carl W. Melcher

205. Aaron Siskind
American, born 1903
Jerome, Arizona, 1949
Gelatin silver print, 19-1/2" x 14-1/4" (495 x 362 mm)
Collection: Hallmark Collections

206. Robert F. Sheehan
American, 1922-1969
Cars in a Wrecker's Yard, 1950
Cibachrome print, 11" x 14" (280 x 356 mm)
Collection: Davison Art Center, Wesleyan University,
    Middletown, Connecticut

207. Minor White
American, 1908-1976
Song Without Words No. 9, 1950s
Gelatin silver print, 3-7/16" x 4-1/2" (91 x 115 mm)
Collection: Hallmark Collections

208. Minor White
American, 1908-1976
Twisted Tree, Point Lobos, 1951
Gelatin silver print, 9-5/16" x 7" (237 x 177 mm)
Collection: University Art Museum, University of New

Mexico, Albuquerque, Gift of Laurie and Thomas
Barrow

209. Andreas Feininger
American, born 1906
Mud Flakes, New Mexico, 1952
Gelatin silver print, 13-7/16" x 11-5/8" (341 x 295 mm)
Collection: New Orleans Museum of Art, Museum
    Purchase through National Endowment for the Arts
    and Museum Funds

210. Minor White
American, 1908-1976
Beginnings, Rochester, New York, 1962
Gelatin silver print, 11-3/4" x 9" (298 x 229 mm)
Collection: Hallmark Collections

211. Gordon Parks
American, born 1912
Man Emerging, Harlem, 1952
Gelatin silver print, 19-3/16" x 29-5/8" (482 x 753 mm)
Collection: Edwin A. Ulrich Museum of Art, The Wichita
    State University Endowment Association Art
    Collection, Wichita, Kansas

212. Minor White
American, 1908-1976
Two Waves and Pitted Rock, 1952
Gelatin silver print, 8-5/8" x 11-1/16" (219 x 281 mm)
Collection: Yale University Art Gallery, S. Sidney Kahn,
    B.A., 1959, Fund

213. Aaron Siskind
American, born 1903
Martha's Vineyard, 1954
Gelatin silver print, 10-1/2" x 12-3/4" (262 x 324 mm)
Collection: Hallmark Collections

214. W. Eugene Smith
American, 1918-1978
Pittsburgh (Pride Street), 1955
Gelatin silver print, 13-1/2" x 9" (343 x 229 mm)
Collection: Hallmark Collections

215. Jean Dubuffet
French, 1901-1985
Fragilité (Fragility), August, 1959
Plate VI of ten lithographs, *Banalités* (Banalities), sixth
    album in color from series *Les Phénomènes* (Phenomena),
    January, 1961
Color lithograph, 17-5/8" x 14-5/8" (448 x 371 mm) on
    sheet 25" x 17-7/8" (635 x 454 mm)
Collection: Solomon R. Guggenheim Museum, New York,
    Gift, Mr. and Mrs. Ralph F. Colin, 1971

"Each printed sheet could serve as Leonardo's wall. ... As
a group, the *Phenomena* testify to Dubuffet's philosophy
that the world is incoherent, and that one should seriously
delight in it. In the ambiguity of their imagery and scale,
they underscore his belief that art should be a cryptogram
which cannot be deciphered, which cannot be explained,
but which can provide endless roads for every
imagination" (Johnson, "The Phenomena of Jean
Dubuffet," p. 27).

216. Daniel Farber
American, born 1906
Red Tug Boat (Reflection), 1959
Dye transfer print
12-3/4" x 18-3/4" (324 x 476 mm) on sheet 13-1/2" x 19-
    1/2" (343 x 495 mm)
Collection: The Nelson-Atkins Museum of Art, Gift of the
    artist

217. Minor White
American, 1908-1976
Two photographs from the *Jupiter* portfolio, 1975:
a. *Birdlime and Surf, Point Lobos, California*
b. *Peeled Paint, Rochester, New York*, 1959
Gelatin silver prints, 11" x 14" each (279 x 356 mm)
Collection: The Minneapolis Institute of Arts, The John R.
    Van Derlip Fund

218. Jean Dubuffet
French, 1901-1985
Exhibition poster, 1960
Published by Berggruen, Paris
Color lithograph, 26" x 15-3/8" (661 x 391 mm)
Collection: Private

The subject, a wall- or ground-like surface, is from the
series *Phénomènes*.

219. Aaron Siskind
American, born 1903
Chicago, 1960
Gelatin silver print, 13-3/4" x 10-1/4" (349 x 261 mm)
Collection: Hallmark Collections

220. Jean Dubuffet
French, 1901-1985
Insouciance (Carelessness), 1961
Plate IV of ten lithographs, *Spectacles*, 1959-61
Lithograph, 17-5/8" x 14-5/8" (448 x 371 mm) on sheet 25"
    x 17-7/8" (635 x 454 mm)
Collection: Solomon R. Guggenheim Museum, New York,
    Gift, Mr. and Mrs. Ralph F. Colin, 1971

Both *Fragilité* (No. 215) and *Insouciance* are part of the
Phenomena series, 1958-1963, twenty-four albums of
lithographs encyclopedically depicting the appearances of
natural surfaces. These prints are closely related to the
artist's series of paintings *Célébrations du sol* (Celebrations
of the soil), 1957-1959, including *Texturologies* and
Topographies, that focus on sections of the earth, illimitable
fields of material "at once abstract and representational,
and can be read as tiny patches of ground, dense clouds of
gas or vast galaxies of stars—micro- and macrocosms of
concrete matter" (Sue Taylor, *Jean Dubuffet: Forty Years of
His Art*, p. 67). "What," said Dubuffet, "I had in mind was
to portray these surfaces without using lines or forms"
(Jean Dubuffet, *A Retrospective Glance at Eighty*, p. 17). In
the paintings, the artist sometimes used "a special
technique. It consisted in shaking a brush over the
painting spread out on the floor, covering it with a spray
of tiny droplets. This is the technique, known as
'Tyrolean,' that masons use in plastering walls to obtain
certain mellowing effects" (*Ibid.*, p. 18). In the graphic
Phenomena several key plates were combined. Dubuffet
described the process as involving "inscribing on stones
(or sheets of zinc) a generous series of pictures of diverse
aspects which would constitute my basic source, my basic
keyboard. ... These basic plates were not to depict
anything in particular but ... take on the appearance of
indeterminate textures historiated with tiny spots or
accidents so they would be interchangeable and any one
of them could be used on top of any other. ..." (quoted in
Prints from the Guggenheim Museum Collection, No. 4,
p. 14).

221. Minor White
American, 1908-1976
Moencopi Strata, Capital Reef, Utah, 1962
Silver print, 10-1/4" x 7-7/8" (261 x 200 mm)
Collection: Spencer Museum of Art, The University of
    Kansas

222. Jim Dine
American, born 1935
Seven Days of Creation, 1966 (Mikro 33, as *The Creation
    (Rainbow)*, 1965)
a. Untitled [void?]
b. *Earth*
c. *Light*
d. *Snow*
e. *Grass*
f. *Six Clouds*
g. *Water - Sea*
Seven lithographs, each 24" x 13-1/2" (610 x 343 mm)
Collection: North Carolina Museum of Art, Raleigh,
    purchased with funds from the National Endowment
    for the Arts and the North Carolina Art Society (Robert
    F. Phifer Bequest)

223. Edward Ruscha
American, born 1937
Every Building on the Sunset Strip
Los Angeles: Edward Ruscha, 1966
52 folds, 7" x 5-1/2" (180 x 150 mm), accordion format
    extending to 23' 10-1/2" long
Collection: Private

Appropriately presented in a mylar-mirrored slipcase, this
record of both sides of the Hollywood street is more

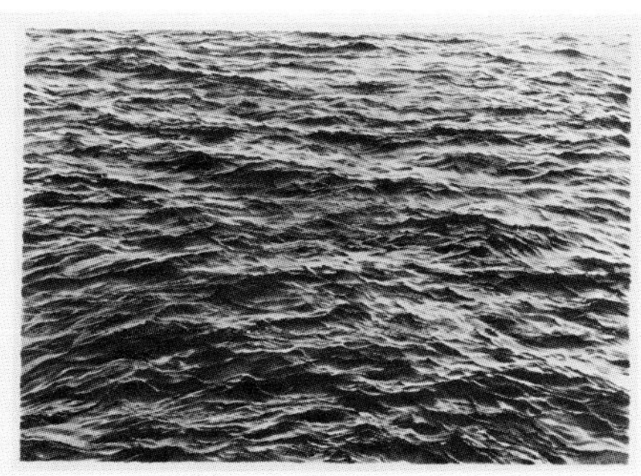

231. Vija Celmins, 1970

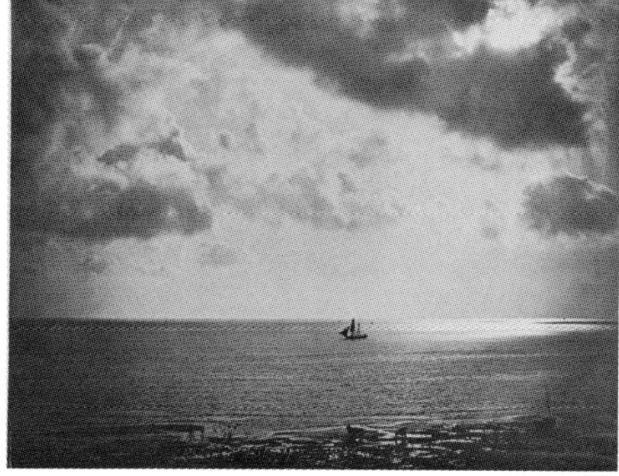

182. Gustave Le Gray, 1856

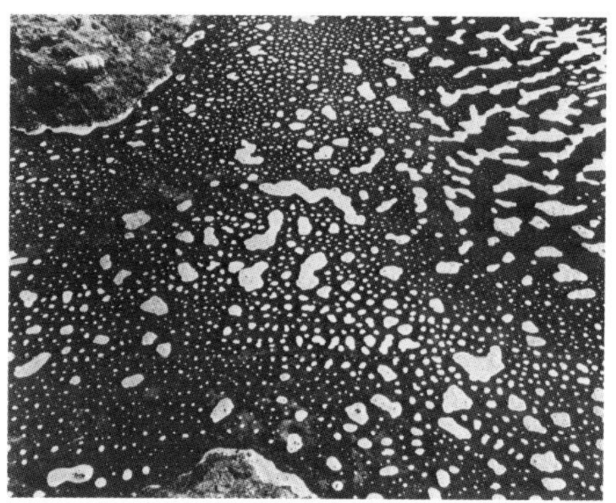

200. Edward Weston, 1938

complete and deadpan documentary than Henderikse's later perspectival Broadway (No. 267).

224. Aaron Siskind
American, born 1903
Arizpe 14, 1966
Gelatin silver print, 7-15/16" x 9-15/16" (202 x 252 mm)
Collection: The Art Museum, Princeton University, Gift of
    Robert Menschel

225. Daniel Spoerri
French, contemporary
An Anecdoted Topography of Chance
New York: Something Else Press, 1966
234 pp., 8" x 5-3/8" (203 x 136 mm)
Collection: Private

Eighty objects accumulated at random on the artist's table are described and furnished with exhaustive detailed anecdotal annotations—a veritable festival of footnotes.

226. Elliott Erwitt
American, born France, 1928
Beach Group, Sylt, West Germany, 1968, from portfolio
    published 1977 by Acorn Editions, Ltd., Geneva,
    Switzerland
Gelatin silver print
6-5/16" x 9-7/16" (161 x 240 mm) on sheet 7-31/32" x 9-
    15/16" (202.5 x 252 mm)
Collection: The Nelson-Atkins Museum of Art, Gift of Dr.
    Carl Melcher

227. Andreas Feininger
American, born 1906
Coney Island Beach in July
Gelatin silver print, 11-1/8" x 14" (282 x 356 mm)
Collection: The Nelson-Atkins Museum of Art, Gift of
    Mrs. George H. Bunting, Jr.

228. Edward Ruscha
American, born 1937
Four sheets from *Stains*, 1969, portfolio of 75 loose sheets,
    published in Hollywood by Heavy Industry
    Publications, ed. 70 (Foster B10)
Each sheet, 11-1/2" x 10-1/2" (292 x 266 mm)
Collection: The Minneapolis Institute of Arts, The William
    Hood Dunwoody Fund, by exchange

Each sheet bears the evidence of an organic material, the artist's first use of such substances, some of which he had previously portrayed in simulacra. The unpredictable original impression is subject to later alteration depending upon physical and chemical changes in the contents.

229. Robert Stanley
American, born 1932
Paul's Mud, 1969
Silkscreen, 30" x 37" (762 x 940 mm)
Collection: The artist

According to Stanley, the print is based on photographs he made in the winter of 1968 in Stonington, Connecticut, showing the glitterings of light on the mud flats oozing into Long Island Sound (in letter to the curator, December 2, 1987).

230. Garry Winogrand
American, 1928-1984
Cape Kennedy, Florida, 1969: Apollo Moon Shot, from
    portfolio published by Hyperion Press, Ltd., 1978, AP
    III/XIII
Gelatin silver print
9" x 13-3/8" (228 x 340 mm) on sheet 10-15/16" x 13-7/8"
    (279 x 352 mm)
Collection: The Nelson-Atkins Museum of Art, Gift of Dr.
    Carl Melcher

231. Vija Celmins
American, born Latvia, 1939
Untitled (Waves), 1970
Lithograph, 20-7/16" x 29-7/16" (520 x 748 mm)
Collection: The Art Museum, Princeton University, Laura
    P. Hall Memorial Fund

"With vision immersed in the sea or the night, one can think one's way to chaos, that entropic state from which difference, the distinction between one entity and the next, has disappeared. ... How can the eye drive mind, hand, all of the artist's being to renderings as meticulously accurate as Celmins'—and renderings of the empty surface of the sea, at that? The answer has to do with the fact that her images of waves are not really accurate. Nor are they inaccurate. In a manner of speaking, they're not meticulous either, but sweepingly visionary" (Ratcliff, "Vija Celmins: An Art of Reclamation," pp. 194-5).

232. Joseph D. Jachna
American, born 1935

Blurred Waterscape, Door County, Wisconsin, 1970
Gelatin silver print, 9" square (229 mm) on sheet 15" x 18"
   (381 x 457 mm)
Collection: Hallmark Collections

The striated random sweeping effect is caused by moving the camera rapidly from one side to another during exposure.

233. James Rosenquist
American, born 1933
Silver Skies, 1970, 38/65 (Varyan 15, Tucker 29)
Published by Castelli Graphics and Hollander Workshop
Color lithograph on Arches paper
34" x 29-3/4" (865 x 755 mm)
Collection: The Nelson-Atkins Museum of Art, Gift of
   Mrs. Jean S. Lighton

Against a randomly dotted mottled sky, three colored plumes of smoke rise from the stacks of an Edison plant.

234. Juan Genovés
Spanish, born 1930
Many Men, 1971
Monoprint, 12-1/16" x 17-5/8" (320 x 447 mm)
Collection: The Nelson-Atkins Museum of Art, Gift of
   Paula N. Dorman, The Print Society of the Friends of
   Art, and Miscellaneous Nelson Gallery Foundation
   Funds

The seemingly non-objective shapes are actually human bodies seen from above, silhouetted against a boundless gold ground—figures meeting in motion, perhaps in conflict, perhaps in coalescence—a visual ambiguity as puzzling as much of the behavior of people in the mass.

235. Joe Goode (Jose Bueno)
American, born 1937
Untitled (Large Folded Clouds), 1971, 96/100 from
   Fourteen Big Prints Portfolio
Published by Bernard Jacobson, Ltd., London
Printed by the Curwen Press, London
Color lithograph, 39" x 55" (991 x 1398 mm)
Collection: Des Moines Art Center, Gift of Margo Leavin
   Gallery, Los Angeles

236. Cristos Gianakos
Greek, contemporary
The White Pit of Mykonos
New York: Cristos Gianakos, 1971
12 pp.; 5 3/8" square (137 mm)
Collection: Private

Photographic details of a six-foot square pit of white casein used for whitewashing present a variety of textural and tonal aspects altering with time and daily use.

237. Agnes Denes
American, contemporary
Introspection III: "Les Demoiselles d'Avignon," 1972
"Aesthetograph," transfer monoprint on photographic
   paper, printed in brown
68-1/2" x 42-1/2" (1740 x 1080 mm)
Collection: The Nelson-Atkins Museum of Art, Gift of Mr.
   and Mrs. Stephen Tabb

The "Introspection" series is devoted to revealing the "inner life of paintings," based on positive and negative aspects of X-rays of canvases, showing layers of paint, enlarged details, pentimenti, etc., not visible from inspection of the surface and seldom made accessible to museum visitors. In this instance, the subject is the heads in Picasso's painting of 1906-7 in which he first applied the principles of cubism, derived from his study of African masks. The revisions the artist made to the originally more conventional realistic likenesses are apparent.

238. Alen MacWeeney
Irish, born 1939
Flies in the Window, Castletown House, Ireland, 1972, from
   portfolio published by Hyperion Press, Ltd., 1979
Gelatin silver print, 10-11/32" x 15-5/8" (271 x 398 mm)
Collection: The Nelson-Atkins Museum of Art, Gift of Dr.
   Carl W. Melcher

239. Aaron Siskind
American, born 1903
Jalapa 43, from *Homage to Franz Kline*, 1974
Gelatin silver print, 14-7/8" x 14-3/4" (378 x 375 mm) on
   sheet 19-1/16" x 15-7/8" (484 x 430 mm)
Collection: Milwaukee Art Museum, Gift of friends of
   Robert W. Moon in his memory

240. Vija Celmins
American, born Latvia, 1939
Untitled (Water), 1975, 59/75
Lithograph, 12-3/8" x 16-3/8" (315 x 416 mm) on sheet 16-
   3/8" x 20" (416 x 508 mm)
Collection: The Nelson-Atkins Museum of Art, Gift of The
   Print Society

241. William Clift
American, born 1944
Sheep and Petroglyphs, Canyon del Muerto, Arizona, 1975
Gelatin silver print, 7-1/2" x 10-1/2" (191 x 261 mm)
Collection: Hallmark Collections

242. Scott Hyde
American, born 1926
Morning/Evening Cloud, 1975, 22/75
Silkscreen, 9" x 14-1/2" (229 x 360 mm)
Collection: Spencer Museum of Art, The University of
   Kansas

243. Roger Shimomura
American, born 1939
Oriental Masterprint #16, 1975
Silkscreen, 24" square (610 mm)
Collection: Hallmark Collections

This print, derived from Hokusai's *Waterfall of Kirifuri* (No. 156), is from a series of such graphic adaptations which revise and update their famous prototypes, sometimes adding Occidental elements to them. *#16* is one of the least Westernized of the group. It is shown here as an instance of the pictorial embodiment of the unpredictable flow of a watery cascade, made even more fortuitous as a modification of an artistic precedent.

244. Al Souza
American, born 1944

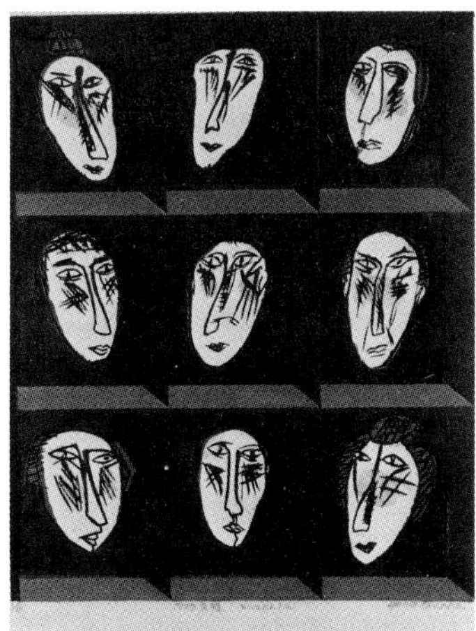

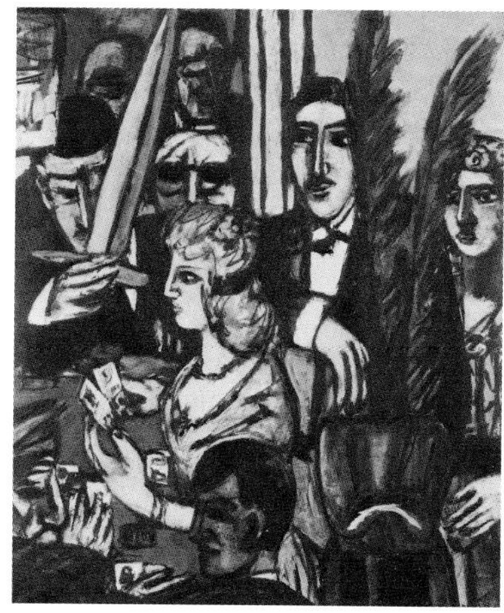

311.   Max Beckmann, 1947

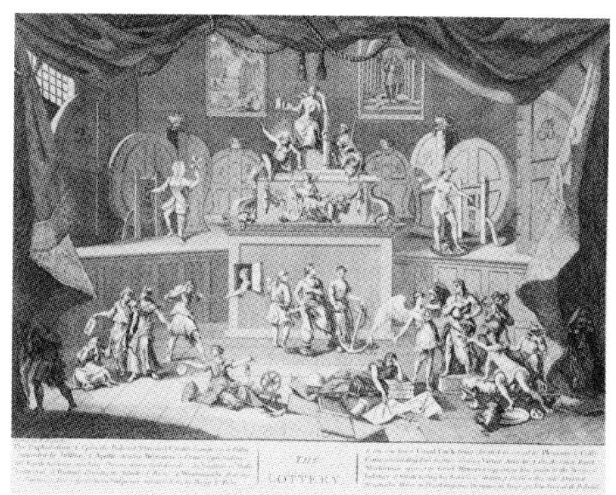

303.   William Hogarth, 1721

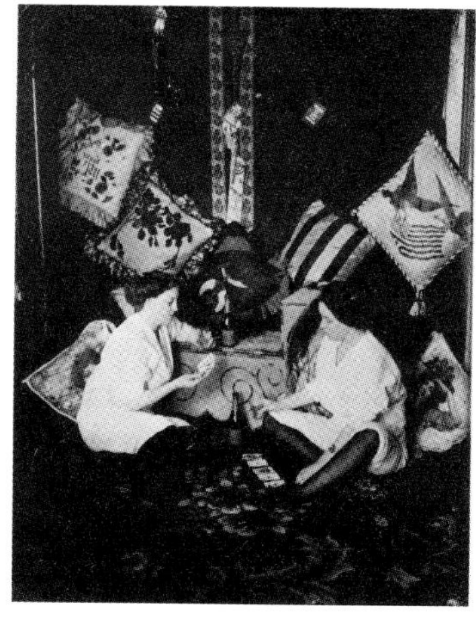

310.   Eugene J. Bellocq, about 1911-13

probably an ironic contraction of *'hourra'* and *'loupe'* (argot: *fainéantise, flânerie*)—Hurrah for do-nothingness. If the world is personified and linked with the slang *'enterlouper,'* to play a trick on someone, the artist is both joker and victim, for surely he is L'Hourloupe" (Ossorio, "The Hour of the Hourloupe," p. 48).

First created in 1964, the cards, in Dubuffet's now familiar palette of red, blue, black, and white, have images of commonplace objects in home and neighborhood, representing a sort of universe of anti-matter, with which one may play a game of chance.

314. Amy N. Worthen
American, born 1946
A Deck of Playing Cards, 1974, 5/25
Engraving and water color
Title card and 52 playing cards, each 5" x 3" (127 x 76.5 mm)
Collection: Des Moines Art Center, Gift of William S. Doan, Fort Dodge, in memory of Vernon Hill, Des Moines

The four suits, two of them hand-colored in red, depict birds, fish, insects, and reptiles (*The Print Collector's Newsletter,* Vol. V, No. 6, Jan.-Feb., 1975, p. 153).

315. Bea Nettles
American, born 1946
Mountain Dream Tarot, 1975
Seventy-eight photographic half-tone cards
Each card, 4-1/2" x 3-11/16" (114 x 93 mm)
Collection: The Nelson-Atkins Museum of Art, Gift of Mr. and Mrs. George L. McKenna

Picturing models and locations in North Carolina, this is the first known photographic version of the symbolist deck that perhaps originated in the ancient Orient (Dugan, *Photography Between Covers,* pp. 116, 118-119).

316. Richard Diebenkorn
American, born 1922
Black Club, 1981, 6/35
Etching, aquatint, and drypoint
13-1/2" x 9-1/2" (343 x 241 mm) on sheet 30-1/4" x 22-5/8" (769 x 574 mm)
Collection: The Whitney Museum of American Art, New York; Purchase, with funds from the Print Committee, 83.10

The austere, almost diagrammatic compositions of the paintings and drawings of the artist's Ocean Park period (echoed in the *Six Softground Etchings,* of 1978) were supplanted from 1980 to 1982 by a series of nearly fifty drawings of variations on the playing-card motifs of club and spade. These themes had been used by Diebenkorn as early as the 1950s: in prints, first, in an unpublished etching of 1963. Like his canvases, "often modulated with the muddied, unplanned tailings and by-products of the painting process" (Newlin, *Richard Diebenkorn Works on Paper,* p. 12), the prints bear evidences of voluntary and involuntary revision: scratching, scraping, smudging, and foul-biting. The drawings alternate between versions of the subjects entirely in curved outline, more or less compressed, and those filled partly or wholly with a single tone, as in this *Black Club.*

317. Peter Downsbrough
Contemporary
Notice
Munich: Rupert Walser, 1985
78 pp.; 11-9/16" x 8-3/16" (293 x 207 mm)
Collection: Private

"The arbitrary assignment of exchange value, and the still more random opportunities for realizing that value, are aspects of the global art game (it might be called a crap shoot) that this book addresses. The rules of this particular version, given in eleven languages, constitute the text … A ghostly photograph of a pair of dice appears next to each translation" (Nancy Princenthal, *Printed Matter Catalogue 86/87,* p. 58).

318. Steven Cortright
American, contemporary
East-West: A Book of Fortune
New York: Chicago Books, 1986
110 pp.; 13-3/4" x 11-3/4" (349 x 298 mm)
Collection: Private

Alternating a horizontal with a vertical page, affording a glimpse of the recto of the following page, the book contrasts Oriental with Occidental images and concepts. Aphorisms on simulated printed strips are mingled with representations of the fortune cookies from which they might have emerged.

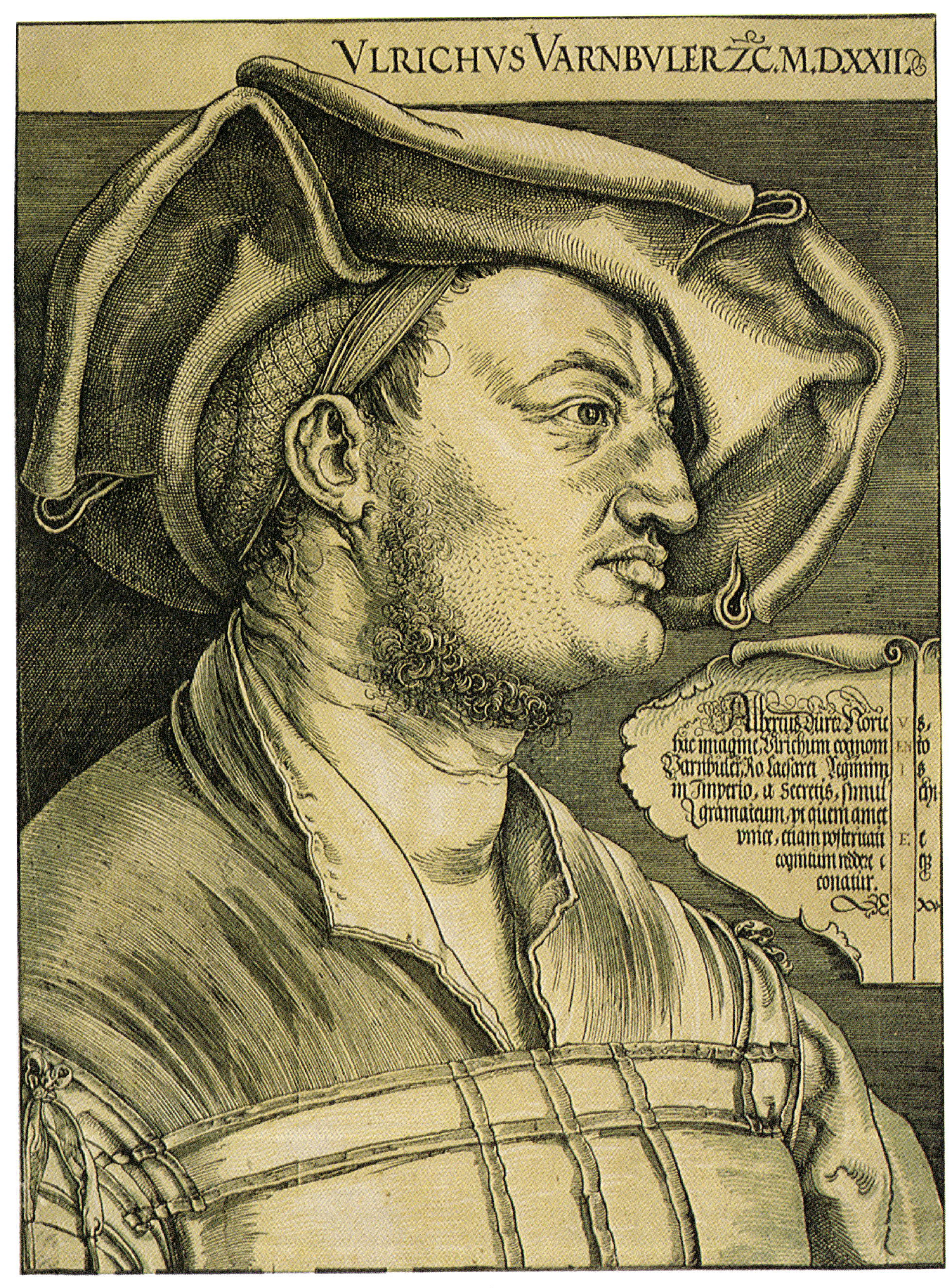

320.   Albrecht Dürer
        German, 1471-1528
        Portrait of Ulrich Varnbüler, 1522
        Chiaroscuro woodcut
        Collection: The Minneapolis Institute of Arts, Bequest of Herschel V. Jones, 1968

VI. Forces of Circumstance: Involuntarily Altered States and Unforeseen Versions

States of original prints are, as succinctly defined by Arthur M. Hind, records of "the separate stages through which a print passes when new work is added to the plate itself."[70] The successive impressions drawn from the inked matrix (plate, block, or stone) show, if examined in order, the progress of the artist's revisions—additions or deletions of strokes, for instance—toward the formation of the image intended. Degas's intaglio print *Mary Cassatt at the Louvre: The Paintings Gallery* involved no fewer than twenty states, while some of Zorn's sweepingly etched portraits, like the procedure of an artist painting *a la prima*, were completed in a single state. The presence or absence of inscriptions on the matrix, any change in its size, and editions on different types of paper all define states. In the case of many artists, catalogues raisonnés have been compiled, listing all known stages, which serve to guide those attempting to determine the state of a print in hand. Not indications of state are tonal variations in impressions of a single plate, occasioned by more or less ink film left on its surface: as Rembrandt selectively wiped to enhance chiaroscuro effects, or as Whistler, Appian, and Lepic similarly aimed in the 19th century perhaps to emulate the dusky atmosphere of the then newly popular photographs. Further, impressions of color prints sometimes vary in the nature and extent of their polychromy, and each edition of the same print may be issued in a different hue.

Often the revision in a matrix leaves little trace on the impression taken from it, just as the *pentimenti* of a painting are not usually visible to the unaided eye.

Agnes Denes's grid of transferred X-rays of Picasso's *Demoiselles d'Avignon* (Section III, No. 237) is an uncommon revelation of a painter's early touches later overlaid. Since the latter 19th century, after the complete editions of a multiple graphic have been pulled, the matrix is often cancelled by drawing an "X" or diagonals across the surface, or by perforating a plate. Impressions from the defaced plates or photographs of such impressions are sometimes taken to attest to the cancellation. One impression, from the canceled plate of Tissot's *October, 1878* (No. 328), is shown here for its surprising associative time-warp appearance: as the art historian Heinrich Wolfflin said, "not everything is possible in every period."[71]

Following the printing of planned editions but before cancellation, impressions made after an artist's death or after the conveyance of a matrix to a printer or publisher for publication without the artist's supervision or signature, are restrikes or reprints. As Old Master print matrices were not cancelled and were not often intentionally destroyed, impressions of some have continued to be pulled on into modern times, pale images from worn-out, or darkened shades from reworked, originals. Not really in this opprobrious category are the later, revised versions of Dürer's *Varnbüler* (No. 320), Vicentino's *Healing of the Lepers* (No. 321) and Oursel's *Peinture Lyonnaise* become Picasso's *L'Italienne* (No. 329), which, in a sense, are creative recastings.

In some instances, our perception of the visual character of certain prints encompasses without particular alarmed remark (except for possible memory of comments once read on states in the catalogues raisonnés) the evident damages sustained by matrices before printing, or later, during vicissitudes before subsequent reissues. As they were, so shall they ever be. Thus Dürer's *Rhinoceros* (No. 319), Van Dyck's *Erasmus* (No. 322), Dusart's *Village Fair* (No. 323), Géricault's *Horses Going to a Fair* (No. 326), and Duncan's *Cua Viet* (No. 332) remain, in their ultimate states, blemished by chance. An analogy is possibly the quite recognizable "extra arm" of Michelangelo's unfinished Rondanini *Pietà* (Castello Sforzesco, Milan), which often is, as Arthur Danto notes, unseen by some observers "because there is no room in their preformed concept of a statue for detached and disembodied arms, and hence no room in their constitution of the work for what, if noticed at all, is read out as perceptual excrescence under inductive habit."[72] Such are the powers of human schemata, or inattentiveness. What we seek we find.

A contemporary Dada-derived attitude regards all incidents, including the accidental, to be germane to the creation of a work of art and essential to its completeness. This divine receptivity of the unpredictable is surely the raison d'être for "action painting." Related is the apparent calamity of the unexpectable breaking of the two successive lithograph stones of Rauschenberg's *Accident* (No. 331), 1963. This was accepted by the artist with as much nonchalance as Marcel Duchamp had manifested in 1931 when his *Bride Stripped Bare by the Bachelors, Even (The Large Glass)* was accidentally cracked in transport and the fractures were welcomed by him as another worthy addition to the many evidences of chance imagery in the work. The actual incorporation of the evidence of accident aligns the art work with the chaotic unruliness of nature, and, indeed, is nature itself. In Rauschenberg's lithograph, the impression of the fortuitous fissure (and the drawn image of the fallen fragments) became as integral as the surrounding collage-like content, an example of harmonized disorderliness: "Critics picked up the term random order to describe the heterogeneous quality of Rauschenberg's work, to what on the surface appears to be an 'irrational juxtaposition of things'"[73] Does not Rauschenberg's complex organization of disparate elements echo Arnhem's conclusion?: "The arts, as a reflection of human existence at its highest, have always and spontaneously lived up to [the] demand of plenitude."[74]

---

319. Albrecht Dürer
German, 1471-1528
The Rhinoceros, 1515 (H273f of h)
Woodcut, 8-1/2" x 11-3/4" (216 x 300 mm)
Collection: The Nelson-Atkins Museum of Art, Purchase, Nelson Fund

Drawn from a written description of the beast, which Dürer himself had not seen before its drowning while being shipped by the King of Portugal to Pope Leo X, this frequently reprinted image served for some two hundred years as the standard likeness of the species. Among the damages the oft-used block progressively suffered that can be descried in this impression from it are the crack extending through all four legs and the cracks in the right border, here filled in with ink.

320. Albrecht Dürer
German, 1471-1528
Portrait of Ulrich Varnbüler, 1522 (Hollstein 256), III/III
Chiaroscuro woodcut, 17" x 12-13/16" (432 x 325 mm)
Collection: The Minneapolis Institute of Arts, Bequest of Herschel V. Jones, 1968

It was over-printed in light green and dark green by Willem Janssen Blaeu, Amsterdam, about 1620.

321. Giuseppe Nicolò Rossigliani, called Vicentino
Italian, active 1510-1540

Christ Healing the Lepers (B. 39.15), II/II
Chiaroscuro woodcut, 11-1/2" x 16-1/4" (293 x 412 mm)
Collection: The Nelson-Atkins Museum of Art, Purchase, Nelson Fund

Andrea Andreani (about 1540-1623) acquired the Vicentino block, added his monogram to it (over the traces in white of Vicentino's original signature), and republished the print in 1608. Inspired by a Raphael tapestry cartoon, the original drawing of the subject by Parmigianino (now in the Chatsworth collection: Popham, *Catalogue of the Drawings of Parmigianino*, I, No. 690, p. 204; II, Pl. 133) was among the plates, blocks, and drawings, which, according to Vasari (II, pp. 1143-4), Antonio da Trento, Parmigianino's chiaroscuro woodblock cutter, stole one night from his master. Apparently (*Ibid.*, I, p. 27), Vicentino later had access to the drawing to make his print.

322. Anthony Van Dyck
Flemish, 1599-1641
Desiderius Erasmus, after 1626 - about 1636 (Wibiral 5, Dutuit 4), IV/IV
Etching, 9-9/16" x 6-1/8" (242 x 158 mm)
Collection: The Nelson-Atkins Museum of Art, Gift of Mr. and Mrs. Robert L. Bloch

The prominent pitting of the plate was caused by foul-biting at the outset (the effect of acid eating under a poorly laid or damaged ground).

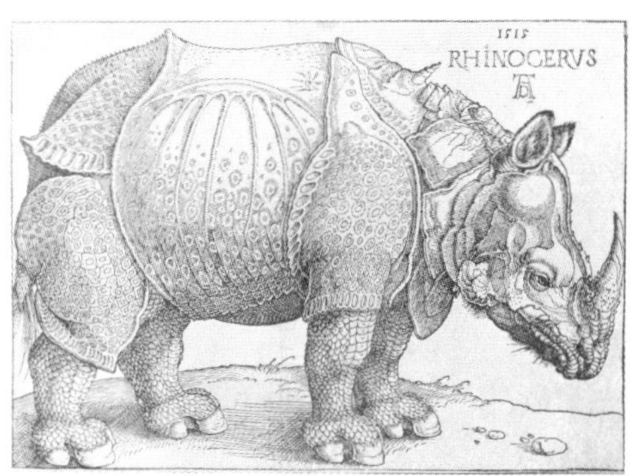
319. Albrecht Dürer, 1515

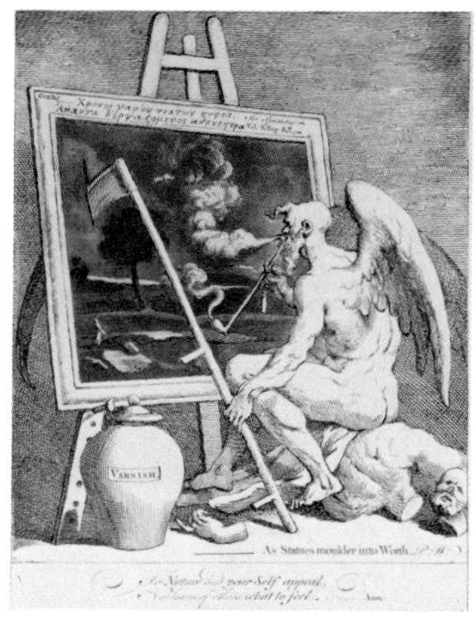
324. William Hogarth, 1761

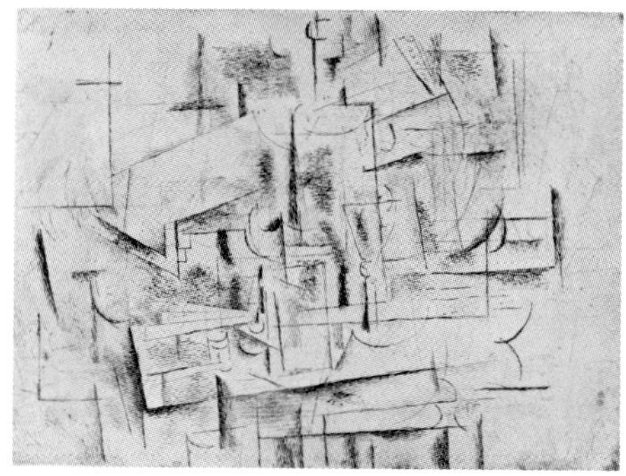
330. Georges Braque, 1912

323. Cornelius Dusart
Dutch, 1660-1704
Village Fair, 1685 (B., H. 16), II/III
Etching, 9-3/4" x 12-7/8" (248 x 327 mm) on sheet 10-1/2"
x 13-1/2" (268 x 342 mm)
Collection: The Nelson-Atkins Museum of Art, Purchase,
Nelson Fund

There is an acid spot in the sky, upper left.

324. William Hogarth
English, 1697-1764
Time Smoking a Picture (Paulson 207)
March, 1761
Etching and mezzotint: pl., 9-5/8" x 7-3/16" (244 x 183 mm)
From *The Works of William Hogarth,* 1837-8
Collection: The Nelson-Atkins Museum of Art, Gift of
Mrs. James C. Lysle, Mr. John F. Fennelly, and Mr.
Joseph C. Fennelly in memory of Mrs. John F. Fennelly

Hogarth here ridicules the prevailing preferences by
connoisseurs for old paintings rendered dark by the
effects of aging and for classical statuary altered by
damage. He quotes the Greek playwright Crates, about
450 B.C., in the legend at the top of the frame: "For time is
not a great artist, but weakens all he touches." (Paulson,
Hogarth's Graphic Works, I, p. 242) The patina of time was
often artificially induced by just such practices as smoking
pictures. "The fragmented hand of the statue points at the
'Varnish' jar, equating it with Time's scythe as a
destroyer." (*Loc. cit.*) The etching *Time Smoking* was
designed as a subscription ticket for an (ultimately
unrealized) engraving of Hogarth's painting *Sigismunda,* a
poorly received picture the artist conceived as surpassing
a then popular painting of the same subject by the 17th
century Florentine baroque master Furini. "In fact
Hogarth said in his *Epistle* that when his *Sigismunda* had
become black through age, people would find it a good
picture." (Antal, *Hogarth,* n. 66, p. 246)

A century later, bewailing the continuing public liking for
pictures seen through discolored, darkened varnish,
Constable wrote, "Dodsworth shall have his picture when I
can find an opportunity of sending it. Had I not better
grime it down with slime and soot, as he is a connoisseur,
and perhaps prefers filth and dirt to freshness and beauty?"
(C. R. Leslie, *Memoirs of the Life of John Constable,* p. 96)

325. Joseph Haynes
English, 1760-1829
Debates on Palmistry, III/III
February 1, 1782, after 1729 oil sketch by William Hogarth
(1697-1764)
Etching and engraving: pl., 12-1/16" x 14-15/16"
From *The Works of William Hogarth,* 1837-8
Collection: The Nelson-Atkins Museum of Art, Gift of
Mrs. James C. Lysle, Mr. John F. Fennelly, and Mr.
Joseph C. Fennelly in memory of Mrs. John F. Fennelly

Applied after Hogarth's death, the titles of this picture have
varied. The first state of the print, without the letters, was
untitled. The second state and the painting are designated
as *A Consultation of Physicians,* showing, according to
Nichols's commentary, "Physicians and Surgeons in an
Hospital, who are debating the most commodious method
of receiving a fee …" (Dobson, *William Hogarth,* p. 293).
Quennel (*Hogarth,* p. 145) describes the print as "a rogues'
gallery of celebrated London doctors, all nuzzling the
knobs of their canes with true professional *sangfroid,*
headed by Mrs. Sarah Mapp, a muscular giant of a
woman, who at that period was doing a brisk trade as a
bone-setter." The title of the third state, *Debates on
Palmistry,* interprets the openhanded, palm-up gesture of
the figure seated at the left of the table as a demonstration
of diagnosis guided by the lines of the hand. Whatever the
appropriate appellation chanced upon, Gowing (*Hogarth,*
p. 27), sees the scene of the early prototype painting as at
the beginning of the artist's "comedy of manners."

326. Jean Louis André Théodore Géricault
French, 1791-1824
Horses Going to a Fair, from the series *Various Subjects
Drawn from Life and on Stone,* 1821 (D. 32), II/II
Crayon lithograph, 9-7/8" x 14" (253 x 355 mm) on sheet
14-7/16" x 21-1/16" (373 x 535 mm)
Collection: The Nelson-Atkins Museum of Art, Purchase,
Anonymous Fund

A crack in the stone extends from the upper right corner
diagonally downward to the white back of the horse in
the center foreground.

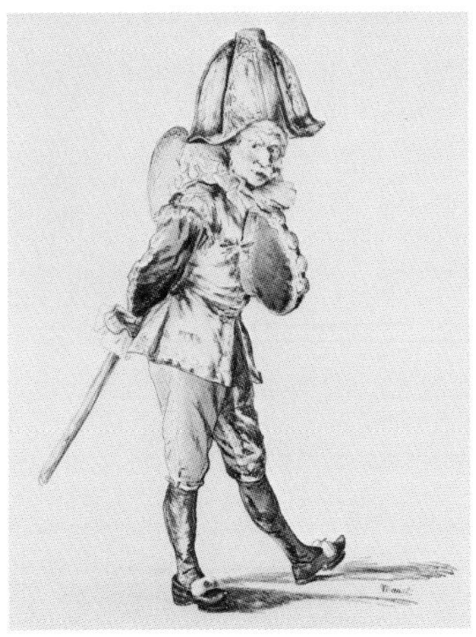

327. Edouard Manet, 1874

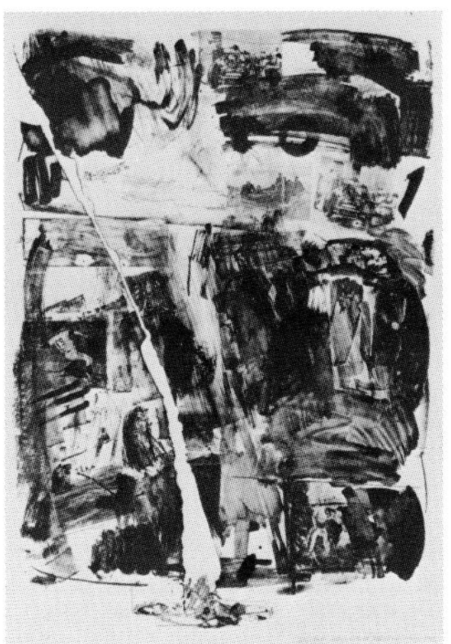

331. Robert Rauschenberg, 1963

327. Edouard Manet
French, 1832-1883
Le Polichinelle, 1874, printed 1876 (Guerin 79, Harris 80, Moreau-Nelaton 87), III/III
Seven-color lithograph, 16-3/4" x 12-3/16" (425 x 310 mm) on sheet 21-7/8" x 14-3/16" (556 x 360 mm)
Collection: The Nelson-Atkins Museum of Art, Nelson Gallery Foundation Purchase

This picture was preceded by a first printing, intended for the subscribers of the periodical *Le Temps,* but forbidden by the police and the stones destroyed because it was falsely believed that the image was a caricature of General MacMahon, respected marshal and president of the Republic. Actually the model was Edmond André, a friend of Manet, and his posture is typical of that of the male component of the Punch and Judy entertainments the French enjoyed for centuries. A new set of stones was prepared, from which this impression of the published edition of 1876 was made.

328. James Joseph Jacques Tissot
French, 1836-1902
October, 1878 (Wentworth 33)
Etching and drypoint, 21-9/16" x 10-15/16" (548 x 278 mm)
Collection: The Nelson-Atkins Museum of Art, Gift of Mr. John S. Bender

This impression was made from a canceled plate so precisely scored, in the adventitious guise of a chain-link fence, that it has a striking new, anachronistic appearance. It depicts Mrs. Kathleen Newton, in a favorite black and silver coat, silhouetted against a background of chestnut leaves, and stooping in the fashionable "Grecian bend" of the 1870s (Wentworth, *James Tissot,* p. 150).

329. Pablo Picasso
Spanish, 1881-1973
L'Italienne, January 21, 1953 (Bloch 740), 19/50
Lithograph and engraving on photolithographic plate 17-1/2" x 13-7/8" (445 x 352 mm)
Collection: Museum of Fine Arts, Boston, George Peabody Gardner Fund, 1986.561

To the image Victor Oursel had drawn on a zinc plate,

announcing the 1948 exhibition of *Peinture Lyonnaise,* Picasso added scratched-in figures, brushwork on the outline of the woman, and his own signature (Gilmour, *The Mechanised Image,* No. 226, pp. 106-107).

330. Georges Braque
French, 1882-1963
Cubist Still Life II, 1912 (Engelberts 10), 8/50
Printed by Visat, published by Maeght, 1953
Etching with drypoint, 12-15/16" x 17-15/16" (329 x 455 mm) on sheet 19-1/2" x 25-7/8" (495 x 656 mm)
Collection: The Nelson-Atkins Museum of Art, Nelson Gallery Foundation Purchase

"Of the ten Cubist drypoints Braque drew on copper between 1907 and 1912, only *Fox* and *Job* were published by Kahnweiler. ... But, in 1948, when The Museum of Modern Art in New York was researching its important Braque retrospective to be held the following year, William S. Lieberman discovered the rejected plates in the artist's studio. Although they were battered and Braque was reluctant to retouch them, Lieberman persuaded him to do so, suggesting which imperfections might be burnished." (Conversation with Lieberman, reported by Donna Stein, "Cubist Prints from the Weiss Collection" in *Cubist Prints/Cubist Books,* p. 13.) "The plates were subsequently printed as etchings by Visat between 1950 and 1954, in editions of twenty-five, thirty, and fifty and published by Braque's French dealer Aimé Maeght. All of the late printings have dates allocated by Braque in 1950" (*Loc. cit.*).

331. Robert Rauschenberg
American, born 1925
Accident, 1963 (Foster 12), ed. 29
Lithograph, 41" x 29" (1042 x 737 mm)
Collection: The Minneapolis Institute of Arts, The Mr. and Mrs. Hall James Peterson Fund

Printed from a broken stone, the second state shows the simulacra of the fragments, in the lower part of the picture. The mistaken, but charming notion that impressions were printed from the very bits of the debris occasioned an amusing exchange between Clinton Adams and Pat Gilmour in *The Print Collector's Newsletter* (Vol. XVII, No. 3, July-August, 1986, p. 108; No. 4, September-

October, 1986, pp. 138-139) that involved quoting from the master's thesis of Mrs. Kase of this city *(loc. cit.)*.

332. David Douglas Duncan
American, born 1916
Cua Viet, Viet Nam, September 17, 1967,
   from *War Without Heroes* (Marine Capt. Reginald G. Ponsford, III, telephoning for naval shelling)
Gelatin silver print, 26-3/4" x 40" (680 x 1016 mm)
Collection: The Nelson-Atkins Museum of Art, gift of the artist

The photographer states: "Later it was discovered that the monsoon storm had left its marks upon the negatives taken that day. Fearsome streaks ripped through every picture made when the amtracs were being showered by air bursts: apparently the column was at the epicenter of the tempest. Static electricity crackled everywhere, especially inside the camera" (Duncan, *War Without Heroes,* p. 39).

333. Sam Francis
American, born 1923
Spleen (Red), 1971, 24/27
Printed and published by Gemini G.E.L., Los Angeles
Lithograph from two aluminum plates and two stones
35" x 78-3/4" (889 x 2001 mm)
Collection: The High Museum of Art, Museum purchase with funds from the Members Guild for the Ralph K. Uhry Collection, 1974

One of the two stones was cracked during printing.

Sources of Quotations

Introduction. Gerard Manley Hopkins, in Richard Aldington, ed., *The Viking Book of Poetry of the English-Speaking World*, New York: The Viking Press, 1958, rev. ed., Vol. II, p. 1062.

I. Samuel Palmer, letter to Mrs. Robinson (formerly his pupil Miss Julia Richmond), December 9, 1872, in Alfred Herbert Palmer, *The Life and Letters of Samuel Palmer*, London: Seeley and Co., Ltd., 1892, p. 343.

Joan Miró, in "VII Orange Notebook, 1940-1941," in Joan Miró and Gaeton Picon, *Joan Miró, Catalan Notebooks*, New York: Rizzoli International Publications, Inc., 1977, p. 136.

Frederick Sommer, "The Mistress of this World Has No Name," in *Where Images Come From*, Denver Art Museum, 1987, exhibition catalogue, p. 13.

II. John Ford, from "Can You Paint a Thought?," in Richard Aldington, ed., *The Viking Book of Poetry of the English-Speaking World*, Vol. I, p. 308.

III. Robert Herrick, from "Delight in Disorder," in Richard Aldington, ed., *The Viking Book of Poetry of the English-Speaking World*, Vol. I, p. 326.

Wassily Kandinsky, from "Little Articles on Big Questions, II. On Line," published in *Iskusstvo*, Moscow, 1919, quoted in Kenneth C. Lindsay and Peter Vergo, *Kandinsky Complete Writings on Art*, Vol. I (1901-1921), Boston: G. K. Hall and Co., 1982, p. 426.

IV. Epictetus, from *Discourses*, Chapter 27; translation, 1865, by Thomas Wentworth Higginson (1823-1911), based on that, 1758, of Elizabeth Carter (1717-1806), quoted in John Bartlett, *Familiar Quotations*, 11th ed. revised and enlarged; Christopher Morley, ed., Boston: Little, Brown and Company, 1940, p. 1007.

V. Publilius Syrus, Maxim 280, quoted in Bartlett, *Familiar Quotations*, p. 987.

Edward Bulwer Lytton, in *Eugene Aram*, Chapter 10, quoted in Bartlett, *Familiar Quotations*, p. 426.

Paul Klee, in Jürg Spiller, ed., *Paul Klee Notebooks*, Vol. I. The thinking eye, New York: George Wittenborn, 1961, p. 9.

John Cage, quoted in Calvin Tomkins, *Ahead of the Game; Four Versions of Avant-garde*, Harmondsworth: Penguin Books, 1968, p. 11.

VI. Marcel Duchamp, quoted in Calvin Tomkins, *Ahead of the Game; Four Versions of Avant-garde*, p. 66.

Catalogue Notes

I. Unpremeditated and Invented Tracks: Random Loci

[1]Breuil and Berger-Kirchner in Bandi *et al., The Art of the Old Stone Age*, p. 23.

[2]In mathematical terms, marbled ware is as visually demonstrative as "Smale's horseshoe" of the chaotic properties of dynamic systems in the universe: "A pair of points that end up close together may have begun far apart," Gleick, *Chaos: Making a New Science*, pp. 51-52.

[3]"The results are predictable only within general categories, but the potters would have acquired empirical knowledge of the positions in the kilns favourable for certain effects," Gray, *Sung Porcelain and Stoneware*, p. 130.

[4]"There is nothing that gives such tastefulness as the melted running glazes of *raku chawan* [tea bowls]," Masatoshi Okochi, quoted in Jenyns, *Japanese Pottery*, p. 255.

[5]Gray, *Early Chinese Pottery and Porcelain*, p. 39.

[6]Hobson, *A Guide to the Pottery and Porcelain of the Far East*, p. 77.

[7]Shimizu and Rosenfield, *Masters of Japanese Calligraphy 8th - 19th Century*, p. 72.

[8]Weimann, "Techniques of Marbling in Early Indian Paintings," p. 134.

[9]De Voogd, "Laurence Sterne, the marbled page, and 'the use of accident,'" pp. 279-287.

[10]Hay, *Kernels of Energy, Bones of Earth*, p. 53.

[11]*Ibid.*, p. 48.

[12]*Ibid.*, p. 49.

[13]Ortega y Gasset, in *The Dehumanization of Art*, p. 41, asserts that "an ever growing mass of traditional styles hampers the direct and original communication between the nascent artist and the world around him ... tradition stifles all creative power—as in Egypt, Byzantium, and the Orient in general." Laurence Sickman's penciled notation in the margin of his copy of the book states "not so—19th cent. idea."

[14]Oppé, *Alexander & John Robert Cozens*, pp. 155-156.

[15]*Ibid.*, p. 34.

[16]*Ibid.*, pp. 169-170.

[17]*Ibid.*, p. 170.

[18]Quotation from the notes of Henry Trimmer, Jr., in Beckett, *John Constable's Correspondence*, V, p. 69.

[19]*Ibid.*, VI, p. 77.

[20]Greenberg, Art and Culture, p. 218.

[21]Danto, *The Transfiguration of the Commonplace*, p. 108.

[22]Duchamp, *Notes and Projects for The Large Glass*, [99].

[23]Eisler, *Charles Maurin; The Vaporizer Watercolors: A hitherto unknown development of the 1890's*, n.p.

II. Dreams, Miracles, Disasters, and Coincidences

[24]Quoted in Sakanishi, *The Spirit of the Brush*, p. 19. Chang Yen-yüan recorded similar observations by the painters Ku K'ai-chih (about 344-406) and Lu T'an-wei (5th century) in his compilation, 845 - 847, of the words of earlier artists, *Li Tai Ming Hua Chi* (Famous Pictures of Antiquity), *ibid.*, p. 79.

[25]Mayor, *Prints and People*, 231-236; Gombrich, *Art and Illusion*, pp. 157-168.

[26]Wang Qingzheng, "The Arts of Ming Woodblock-printed Images and Decorated Paper Albums," in *The Chinese Scholar's Studio*, pp. 56-60.

[27]Gombrich, *Art and Illusion*, pp. 208-9, quoting Sze, *The Tao of Painting*.

[28]F. de Coulon, *Signal Theory and Processing*, quoted in Peitgen and Saupe, *The Science of Fractal Images*, p. 220.

[29]Nierendorf, preface to *Urformen der Kunst* quoted in Elliott, *Karl Blossfeldt Photographs,* p. 8. This translation differs slightly from that of Nierendorf's introduction in the 1985 Dover publication, *Art Forms in the Plant World,* n.p.

[30]Bernstein, "The Joy of Ornament: The Prints of Robert Kushner," p. 194.

[31]Quoted in Leslie's *Memoirs of the Life of John Constable,* p. 9.

[32]Gombrich, *op. cit.,* p. 317.

[33]Quoted by Sheldrake, *The Presence of the Past,* p. 268.

[34]*Ibid.,* p. 321.

[35]Gablik, *Progress in Art,* 1977, quoted by Sheldrake, *op. cit.,* p. 268.

[36]J. Monod, *Chance and Necessity,* 1972, quoted by Sheldrake, *op. cit.,* p. 312.

III. Captured Transiences and Appearances of Spontaneity

[37]"With them [the landscape sketches painted in oil] he created a new type of picture which has become typical of nineteenth century painting, sketches made out of doors." Badt, *John Constable's Clouds,* p. 44.

[38]Hawes, "Constable's Sky Sketches," p. 345.

[39]Ruskin, *Modern Painters,* quoted by Badt, *op. cit.,* p. 6.

[40]Peckham, "Triumph of Romanticism," p. 297.

[41]Quoted in Norman, *Alfred Stieglitz,* p. 14.

[42]Greenough, *Alfred Stieglitz's Photographs of Clouds,* p. 165.

[43]The physicist Mitchell Feigenbaum quoted in Gleick, *Chaos,* p. 186.

[44]Mason, "On the Shapes of Snow Crystals," in Kepler, *The Six-Cornered Snowflake,* p. 45.

[45]McNulty, Miller, *The Lithographs of Jean Dubuffet,* n.p.

[46]Quoted in *ibid., The Lithographs of Jean Dubuffet,* n.p.

[47]Gombrich, *Art and Illusion,* p. 60.

[48]Benjamin, "The Work of Art in the Age of Mechanical Reproduction," in *Illuminations,* p. 251, n. 21.

[49]Quoted in Sheldrake, *The Presence of the Past,* p. 233.

[50]Goldschmidt and Naef, *The Truthful Lens,* No. 58, p. 199.

IV. Expectations Confounded and Realizations Deferred

[51]Duchamp, "The creative act," p. 29.

[52]Gombrich, *Art and Illusion,* p. 262.

[53]Sheldrake, *The Presence of the Past,* pp. 264-5.

[54]Gombrich, *op. cit.,* p. 243.

[55]Arnhem, *Entropy and Art,* p. 54.

[56]Gombrich, *op. cit.,* p. 87.

[57]Bowness, *Robert Rauschenberg,* n.p.

[58]Quoted in *ibid.,* n.p.

[59]Stereograms are obtained by photographing the subject through a lenticular screen, consisting of thin, parallel, transparent half-round strips. When another such screen is fixed over the printed picture, dividing it into countless minute areas acting as lenses in some parts and barriers in others, the eye sees different images simultaneously in three-dimensional simulation, Mahoney, "The Third Dimension," p. 42.

[60]Tzara, "5. manifesto on feeble love and bitter love," VIII, in Motherwell, ed., *The Dada Painters and Poets: An Anthology,* p. 92.

V. Harbingers and Manipulators of Fate

[61]Carter, *The Invention of Printing in China,* pp. 140-1.

[62]*Ibid.,* p. 141.

[63]*Ibid.,* p. 140 and n. 4, pp. 243-4.

[64]Mayor, *Prints and People,* 109.

[65]Loewe and Blacker, *Oracles and Divination,* p. 41.

[66]Mayor, *op. cit.,* 115-116.

[67]Benjamin, "On Some Motifs in Baudelaire," in *Illuminations,* n. 11, p. 198.

[68]*Ibid.,* p. 175.

[69]*Ibid.,* p. 177.

VI. Forces of Circumstance: Involuntarily Altered States and Unforeseen Versions

[70]Hind, *A History of Engraving and Etching,* pp. 15-16.

[71]Quoted by Gombrich, *Art and Illusion,* p. 4.

[72]Danto, *The Transfiguration of the Commonplace,* p. 115.

[73]Bolmeier, *Response and Documentation: Aesthetic Inquiry Relevant to Selected Works of Robert Rauschenberg,* p. 95.

[74]Arnhem, *Entropy and Art: An Essay on Disorder and Order,* p. 49.

Bibliography

Adams, Brooks, "Report from Yale; German Drawings of the '60s," *The Print Collector's Newsletter,* Vol. XIII, No. 2 (May-June, 1982), pp. 49-52.

Adams, Clinton, *American Lithographers 1900-1960.* Albuquerque: Univ. of New Mexico Press, 1983.

Akademie der Künste, *Dubuffet Retrospektive.* Berlin: Akademie der Künste, 1980. Exhibition catalogue.

Adler, Eric, "The Beauty of Chaos," *Kansas City Star,* August 16, 1988, pp. 1-2 Tech.

Adrian, Dennis and Born, Richard A., *The Chicago Imagist Print: Ten Artists' Works, 1958-1987; A Catalogue Raisonné.* Chicago: David and Alfred Smart Gallery, University of Chicago, 1987. Exhibition catalogue.

Alexandrian, Sarane, *Max Ernst* (Eleanor Levieux, transl.). Chicago: J. Philip O'Hara, Inc., 1972.

Allen, Virginia (intro.), *Drawings: Jean Dubuffet, Gift of Mr. and Mrs. Lester Francis Avnet.* New York: Museum of Modern Art, 1968.

Alloway, Lawrence, "The Graphic Art of Robert Rauschenberg," in *Rauschenberg Graphic Art,* Institute of Contemporary Art, University of Pennsylvania, Philadelphia, 1970. Exhibition catalogue.

Alloway, Lawrence, *Robert Rauschenberg Drawings 1958-1968.* New York: Acquavella Contemporary Art, Inc., 1986. Exhibition catalogue.

Andrews, Natalie T. and Bridwell, Margaret M., *The Inimitable George Cruikshank: An Exhibition of Books, Prints, Drawings, and Manuscripts from the Collection of David Borowitz.* Louisville: J. B. Speed Art Museum, 1968. Exhibition catalogue.

Antal, Frederick, *Hogarth and His Place in European Art.* London: Routledge and Kegan Paul, 1962.

Arnheim, Rudolf. *Entropy and Art; An Essay on Disorder and Order.* Berkeley: University of California Press, 1971.

Arping, Michael, *Marcel Duchamp: Works from the John and Mable Ringling Museum of Art Collection.* Sarasota: John and Mable Ringling Museum of Art Foundation, 1983. Exhibition catalogue.

Attwood, Martin, *Artists' Books.* London: Arts Council of Great Britain, 1976. Exhibition catalogue.

Austin, Gabriel, "The Modern Illustrated Book: A Neglected Field for Collectors," *The Print Collector's Newsletter,* Vol. IV, No. 6 (Jan.-Feb., 1974), pp. 130-131.

Badt, Kurt, *John Constable's Clouds.* London: Routledge and Kegan Paul, 1950.

Bandi, Hans-Georg; Breuil, Henri; Berger-Kirchner, Lilo; Lhote, Henri; Holm, Erik; Lommel, Andreas, *The Art of the Old Stone Age; Forty Thousand Years of Rock Art.* New York: Crown Publishers, Inc., 1961.

Barret, Richard Carter, *Bennington Pottery and Porcelain.* New York: Crown Publishers, Inc., 1958.

Barthes, Roland (Henry Martin, transl.), "Non Multa Sed Multum," in Yvon Lambert, *Catalogue raisonné des oeuvres sur papier de Cy Twombly,* Vol. VI, 1973-1976. Milan: Multhipla Edizioni, 1979.

Bastian, Heiner, *Cy Twombly; A Catalogue Raisonné of the Printed Graphic Work.* New York: New York University Press, 1975.

Beazley, J. D., *The Development of Attic Black-Figure.* Berkeley: University of California Press, 1951.

Benjamin, Walter (Harry Zohn, transl., Hannah Arendt, ed.), *Illuminations.* New York: Schocken Books, 1969.

Bernstein, Barbara, "The Joy of Ornament: The Prints of Robert Kushner," *The Print Collector's Newletter,* Vol. XI, No. 6 (Jan.-Feb., 1981), pp. 193-197.

Binyon, Laurence, *British Water-Colours,* 1933. New York: Shocken Books, 1969. 1st paperback ed.

Binyon, Laurence, *The Engraved Designs of William Blake.* New York: Charles Scribner's Sons, 1926.

Binyon, Laurence and Keynes, Geoffrey, *Illustrations of the Book of Job by William Blake.* New York: The Pierpont Morgan Library, 1936. 6 Fascicles.

Birnholz, Alan C., "On the Meaning of Kazimir Malevich's 'White on White,'" *Art International,* Vol. XXI/I (1977), pp. 9-16.

Blofeld, John (transl., ed.), *I Ching (The Book of Change).* New York: E. P. Dutton and Co., Inc., 1968.

Blossfeldt, Karl, *Art Forms in the Plant World* (Karl Nierendorf, intro.). New York: Dover Publications, Inc., 1985.

Blossfeldt, Karl, *Urformen in Kunst: Photograpische Pflanzenbilder.* Berlin: Verlag Ernst Wasmuth A.G., 1929.

Boardman, John, *Athenian Black Figure Vases.* New York: Oxford University Press, 1974.

Bogle, Andrew, *Chance and Change; a century of the avant-garde.* Auckland, New Zealand: Auckland City Art Gallery, Oct. 25-Dec. 8, 1985. Exhibition catalogue.

Bogle, Andrew, *Graphic Works by Edward Ruscha.* Auckland, New Zealand: Auckland City Art Gallery, 1978. Exhibition catalogue.

Bolmeier, Jane, *Response and Documentation: Aesthetic Inquiry Relevant to Selected Works of Robert Rauschenberg* (NYU dissertation). Ann Arbor: University Microfilms International, © 1984; 1986.

Boorsch, Suzanne, and Lewis, Michal and R. E., *The Engravings of Giorgio Ghisi.* New York: The Metropolitan Museum of Art, 1985. Exhibition catalogue.

Boultenhouse, Charles, "Poems in the Shapes of Things," *Art News Annual,* XXVIII (1959), pp. 64-83, 178.

Bowlt, John E., *Journey into Non-Objectivity: The Graphic World of Kazimir Malevich and Other Members of the Russian Avant-Garde.* Dallas: Dallas Museum of Fine Art, 1980. Exhibition catalogue.

Bowness, Alan, *Robert Rauschenberg.* London: The Tate Gallery, 1981. Exhibition catalogue.

Boyd, Malcolm, "Three Attic Black Figure Kylikes," *Indiana University Art Museum Bulletin,* Vol. I, No. 1 (Fall, 1977), pp. 20-29.

Boyle-Turner, Caroline, *The Prints of the Pont-Aven School: Gauguin and His Circle in Brittany.* New York: Abbeville Press, 1986. Exhibition catalogue.

Brecht, George, *Chance-Imagery.* New York: Something Else Press, Inc. (A Great Bear Pamphlet), 1966.

Broun, Elizabeth, *Form Illusion Myth: Prints and Drawings of Pat Steir.* Lawrence, Kansas: Spencer Museum of Art, 1983.

Brown, Kathan (intro., ed.), *John Cage Etchings 1978-1982.* Oakland: Crown Point Press, 1982.

Brown, Kathan (ed.), Plous, Phyllis, and Stevens, Mark, *Richard Diebenkorn Etchings and Drypoints 1949-1980.* Houston: Houston Fine Art Press, 1981. Exhibition catalogue.

Cahill, James, *Fantastics and Eccentrics in Chinese Painting.* New York: Asia Society, Inc., 1967. Exhibition catalogue.

Calvocoressi, Richard, *A. R. Penck: Brown's Hotel and Other Works.* London: Gallery of New Art, The Tate Gallery, 1984. Exhibition folder.

Carter, Thomas Francis, *The Invention of Printing in China and Its Spread Westward.* New York: Columbia University Press, 1925.

Cassan, Arnold (intro.), *Petroglyphs of the Heart: photographs by Connie Sullivan.* Dobbs Ferry, New York: Morgan and Morgan, 1983.

Castleman, Riva, *American Impressions; Prints since Pollock.* New York: Alfred A. Knopf, 1985.

Castleman, Riva (intro.), Upright, Diane, and Wye, Deborah, *Surrealist Prints from the Collection of the Museum of Modern Art.* Fort Worth: Fort Worth Art Museum, 1985. Exhibition catalogue.

Chang, Kuang-yüan (Kamen, David M., transl.), "Late Shang Divination: An Experimental Reconstruction of Methods of Preparation, Use and Inscription of Oracle Bone Materials," Abridged Versions, Part I and II, *National Palace Museum Bulletin,* Vol. XVIII, No. 1-2, 3/4 (March-April/May-June, 1983; July-August/September-October, 1983).

Charlesworth, Sarah, "Movie - Television - News - History, June 21, 1979," *Aperture,* No. 100 (Fall, 1985), pp. 54-59.

Chiarenza, Carl, *Photographs by Aaron Siskind in Homage to Franz Kline.* Chicago: The David and Albert Smart Gallery, the University of Chicago, 1975. Exhibition catalogue.

Cohen, Ronny, "New Abstraction V," *The Print Collector's Newsletter,* Vol. XVIII, No. 1 (March-April, 1987), pp. 9-14.

Cohn, Albert M., *George Cruikshank; A Catalogue Raisonné of the Works Executed during the Years 1806-1877.* London: from the office of "The Bookman's Journal," 1924.

Compton, Michael (intro.), *Malcolm Morley Paintings 1965-82.* London: The Whitechapel Art Gallery, 1983. Exhibition catalogue.

(Constable) Beckett, R. B. (ed.), *John Constable's Correspondence.* 6 vol.; vol. 7, *John Constable's Discourses.* Ipswich: Suffolk Records Society, 1962-1970.

(Constable), *Memoirs of the Life of John Constable, Composed Chiefly of His Letters; by C. R. Leslie, R.A.* Ed. by Jonathan Mayne. London: Phaidon Press, 1951.

Cornack, Malcolm, *Constable.* Oxford: Phaidon Press, Ltd., 1986.

Courtney, David W., "The Autoportraits of Arnulf Rainer," *Arts Magazine,* Vol. 61, No. 2 (October, 1986), pp. 80-83.

Cowling, Elizabeth, "The Eskimo, the American Indian, and the Surrealists," *Art History,* Vol. I, No. 4 (Dec., 1978), pp. 484-499.

Crone, Rainer, *Andy Warhol.* New York: Praeger Publishers, Inc., 1970.

Curtis, Verna Posever and Holo, Selma Reuben, *La Tauromaquia: Goya, Picasso, and the Bullfight.* Milwaukee: Milwaukee Art Museum, 1986. Exhibition catalogue.

Dabrowski, Magdalena, "Malevich-Mondrian: Geometric Form as the Expression of the Absolute," *The Nelson-Atkins Museum of Art Bulletin,* Vol. V, No. 7 (Oct., 1982), pp. 19-34.

Damon, S. Foster, *Blake's Job.* New York: E. P. Dutton and Co., Inc., 1969.

Danto, Arthur C., *The Transfiguration of the Commonplace.* Cambridge: Harvard University Press, 1981.

Davies, Hugh M. and Castelman, Riva, *The Prints of Barnett Newman.* New York: The Barnett Newman Foundation, 1983. Exhibition catalogue.

Davis, Bruce, *Mannerist Prints: International Style in the Sixteenth Century.* Los Angeles: Los Angeles County Museum of Art, 1988. Exhibition catalogue.

De Voogd, Peter J., "Laurence Sterne, the marbled page, and 'the use of accidents,'" *Word and Image,* Vol. 1, No. 3 (July-Sept., 1985), pp. 279-287.

d'Harnoncourt, Anne, *John Cage: Scores and Prints.* Philadelphia: Philadelphia Museum of Art, 1982. Exhibition catalogue.

Dietrich, Dorothea, "A Talk with A. R. Penck," *The Print Collector's Newsletter,* Vol. XIV, No. 3 (July-Aug., 1983), pp. 91-94.

Dietrich-Boorsch, Dorothea, *German Drawings of the 60s.* New Haven: Yale University Art Gallery, 1982. Exhibition catalogue.

Dobson, Austin, *William Hogarth.* London: Sampson Low, Marston and Co., 1981.

Dodds, E. R., *The Greeks and the Irrational.* Berkeley: University of California Press, 1968.

D'Oench, Ellen G., and Feinberg, Jean E., *Jim Dine Prints 1977-1985.* New York: Harper and Row in assoc. with the Davison Art Center, 1986. Exhibition catalogue.

Douglas, Charlotte, *Swans of Other Worlds: Kazimir Malevich and the Origins of Abstraction in Russia.* Ann Arbor: UMI Research Press, 1980.

Duchamp, Marcel, *Notes and Projects for The Large Glass* (Arturo Schwartz, ed.). New York: Harry N. Abrams, Inc., 1969.

Dugan, Thomas, *Photography Between Covers: Interviews with Photo-Bookmakers.* Rochester, New York: Light Impressions Corp., 1979.

Duncan, David Douglas, *War Without Heroes.* New York: Harper and Row, 1971.

Dupin, Jacques, *miró engraver, I. 1928-1960.* Paris: Daniel Lelong, 1984.

Edel, Leon, *Stuff of Sleep and Dreams.* London: Chatto and Windus, 1982.

Edwards, Edward, *Anecdotes of Painters, 1808.* London: Cornmarket Press Ltd., 1970. Reprint ed.

Eisler, Colin (intro.), *Charles Maurin: The Vaporizer Watercolors.* New York: Lucien Goldschmidt, Inc., 1986. Exhibition brochure.

Elliott, David, *Karl Blossfeldt Photographs.* Oxford: Museum of Modern Art, 1978.

Essick, Robert N. (ed.), *The Visionary Hand; Essays for the Study of Blake's Art and Aesthetics.* Los Angeles: Hennessey and Ingalls, Inc., 1973.

Faust, Wolfgang Max (Gabriel, J.W., transl.), "'Du Hast Keine Chance. Nutze Siei' With It and Against It: Tendencies in Recent German Art," *Artforum,* XX, 1 (Sept., 1981), pp. 33-39.

Faxon, Alicia, "German Expressionist Prints, A Persistent Tradition," *The Print Collector's Newsletter,* Vol. XIV, No. 1 (March-April, 1983), pp. 3-4.

Feinblatt, Ebria and Davis, Bruce, *Los Angeles Prints, 1883-1980.* Los Angeles: Los Angeles County Museum of Art, 1980. Exhibition catalogue.

Feldman, Freyda and Schellmann, Jörg, *Andy Warhol Prints.* New York: Ronald Feldman Fine Arts, Inc., Editions Schellmann, and Abbeville Press, 1985.

Fichner-Rathus, Lois, "Pollock at Atelier 17," *The Print Collector's Newsletter,* Vol. XIII, No. 5 (Nov.-Dec. 1982), pp. 162-165.

Field, Richard, *Prints and Drawings by Lee Bontecou.* Middletown, Conn.: Davison Art Center, 1975. Exhibition catalogue.

Field, Richard S. and Fine, Ruth E., *A Graphic Muse: Prints by Contemporary American Women.* New York: Hudson Hills Press in association with the Mount Holyoke Art Museum, 1987. Exhibition catalogue.

Fleming-Williams, Ian, *Constable Landscape Watercolours and Drawings.* London: The Tate Gallery, 1976.

Foster, Edward A., *Robert Rauschenberg: Prints 1948/1970.* Minneapolis: The Minneapolis Institute of Arts, 1970. Exhibition catalogue.

Foster, Stephen C. (ed.), *Dada/Dimensions.* Ann Arbor: UMI Research Press, 1985.

Francis, Richard; Atwood, Martin; Phillpot, Clive; and Taylor, Brandon, *Artists' Books.* London: Arts Council of Great Britain, 1976.

Friedman, B. H., *Jackson Pollock: Energy Made Visible.* New York: McGraw-Hill Book Co., 1974.

Friedman, Martin, *Michelangelo Pistoletto: A Reflected World.* Minneapolis: Walker Art Center, April 4-May 8, 1966.

Friedman, Martin (intro.) and Armstrong, Elizabeth, *Prints from Tyler Graphics.* Minneapolis: Walker Art Center, 1984. Exhibition catalogue.

Frumkin, Allan Gallery, "Westermann Woodcuts," *Allan Frumkin Gallery Newsletter,* No. 3 (Spring, 1977), p. 3.

Ganse, Elizabeth, Shirley H., *Chinese Ceramics: Art and Technology.* Atlanta: High Museum of Art, 1985. Exhibition catalogue.

Garver, Thomas H., *Robert Rauschenberg in Black and White.* Newport Harbor: Newport Harbor Art Museum, 1970. Exhibition catalogue.

Garvey, Eleanor M., *Artist Books of the Kaldewey Press.* New York: Thomas J. Watson Library, The Metropolitan Museum of Art, 1988. Exhibition catalogue.

Gernsheim, Helmut and Alison, *The History of Photography, from the camera obscura to the beginning of the modern era.* New York: McGraw-Hill Book Company, 1969.

Geske, Norman A., *Photographs; Sheldon Memorial Art Gallery Collections, University of Nebraska - Lincoln.* Lincoln: Nebraska Art Assoc. with the assistance of the University of Nebraska Foundation and the National Endowment for the Arts, 1977.

Gettings, Fred, *Ghosts in Photographs.* New York: Harmony Books, 1978.

Ghyka, Matila, *The Geometry of Art and Life.* New York: Dover Publications, Inc., 1977.

Gilmour, Pat, *The Mechanised Image; An Historical Perspective on 20th Century Prints.* London: Arts Council of Great Britain, 1978. Exhibition catalogue.

Giuliano, Charles, "Bruce Conner," *Artist's Proof,* Vol. VII, 1967, p. 56.

Glassman, Elizabeth and Symmes, Marilyn F., *Cliché-verre: Hand-Drawn, Light Printed, A Survey of the Medium from 1839 to the Present.* Detroit: Detroit Institute of Arts, 1980. Exhibition catalogue.

Gleick, James, *Chaos: Making a New Science.* New York: Viking Penguin, Inc., 1987.

Goldman, Judith, *American Prints: Process and Proofs.* New York: Whitney Museum of American Art, 1982. Exhibition catalogue.

Goldman, Judith, *Jasper Johns Prints 1977-1981.* Boston: Thomas Segal Gallery, 1981.

Goldman, Judith, *Print Acquisitions 1974-1984.* New York: Whitney Museum of American Art, 1984.

Goldman, Judith, *James Rosenquist.* New York: Viking Penguin, 1975.

Goldschmidt, Lucien and Naef, Weston J., *The Truthful Lens; A survey of the photographically illustrated book 1844-1914.* New York: The Grolier Club, 1980.

Goldwater, Marge, Smith, Roberta, and Tomkins, Calvin, *Jennifer Bartlett.* New York: Abbeville Press, Inc., 1985. Exhibition catalogue.

Gombrich, Ernst H., *Art and Illusion.* Princeton: Princeton University Press, 1984.

Gombrich, Ernst H., "Image and word in twentieth-century art," *Word and Image,* Vol. I, No. 3 (July-Sept., 1985), pp. 213-241.

Gowing, Lawrence, *Hogarth.* London: The Tate Gallery, 1972. Exhibition catalogue.

Gray, Basil, *Early Chinese Pottery and Porcelain.* London: Faber and Faber, 1953.

Gray, Basil, *Sung Porcelain and Stoneware.* London: Faber and Faber, 1984.

Greenberg, Clement, *Art and Culture; Critical Essays.* Boston: Beacon Press, 1961.

Greenough, Sarah Eden, *Alfred Stieglitz's Photographs of Clouds.* Doctoral dissertation. UMI facsimile. Albuquerque: University of New Mexico, 1984.

Gullick, Michael, *Prospectus for Poems of Majnun Laila.* Hitchin: The Red Gull Press, 1985.

Haftmann, Werner, *The Mind and Work of Paul Klee.* New York: Frederick A. Praeger, 1967.

Halasz, P., "Stanley William Hayter: Pollock's Other Master," *Arts,* Vol. 59, No. 3 (Nov., 1984), pp. 73-75.

Hamilton, Richard and Hamilton, George Heard (transl.), *The Bride Stripped Bare by her Bachelors, Even; A Typographic Version of Marcel Duchamp's Green Box.* New York: Jaap Rietman Inc., Art Books, 1976.

Hamilton, Richard, "Duchamp," *Art International,* Vol. VII, No. 10 (Jan. 16, 1964), pp. 22-28.

Hardie, Martin, *Water-colour Painting in Britain. I, The Eighteenth Century.* London: B. T. Batsford Ltd., 1966.

Harris, Tomás, *Goya Engravings and Lithographs.* Oxford: Bruno Cassirer, 1964. 2 vol.

Harrison, Martin and Waters, Bill, *Burne-Jones.* London: Barrie and Jenkins Ltd., 1973.

Haus, Andras, *Moholy-Nagy: Photographs and Photograms.* New York: Holt, Rinehart and Winston, 1982.

Hawes, Louis, "Constable's Sky Sketches," *Journal of the Warburg and Courtauld Institutes,* Vol. XXXII (1969), pp. 344-365.

Hawes, Louis, *Presences of Nature: British Landscape 1780-1830.* New Haven: Yale Center for British Art, 1982. Exhibition catalogue.

Hay, John, *Kernels of Energy, Bones of Earth: The Rock in Chinese Art.* New York: China House Gallery, China Institute in America, 1986. Exhibition catalogue.

Hayes, John, *The Drawings of Thomas Gainsborough.* New Haven: Yale University Press, 1971. 2 vol.

Hayes, John, *Gainsborough as Printmaker.* New Haven: Yale University Press, 1972.

Hayes, John, *The Landscape Paintings of Thomas Gainsborough.* London: Sotheby Publications, 1952. 2 vol.

Heartney, Eleanor, "Sarah Charlesworth Tartan Sets" in "New Editions," *Art News,* Vol. 86, No. 8 (Oct., 1987), pp. 135-6.

Heffernan, James A. W., *The Re-creation of Landscape; A Study of Wordsworth, Coleridge, Constable, and Turner.* Hanover: University Press of New England for Dartmouth College, 1984.

Heinemann, Susan, "Nancy Graves: The Painting Seen," *Arts,* 51 (March, 1977), pp. 139-41.

Hight, Eleanor M., *Moholy-Nagy: Photography and Film in Weimar Germany.* Wellesley, Mass.: Wellesley College Museum, 1985. Exhibition catalogue.

Hind, Arthur M., *A History of Engraving and Etching.* New York: Houghton Mifflin Co., 1927.

Hobson, R. L., *A Guide to the Pottery and Porcelain of the Far East.* London: British Museum, 1924.

Hoffmann, Donald, "Computer-generated 'Chaos' dazzles with its detail," *The Kansas City Star,* September 11, 1988, p. 6E.

Hofmann, Julius, *Francisco de Goya: Katalog Seines Graphischen Werkes.* Vienna: Gesellschaft für Vervielfältigende Kunst, 1907.

Hogben, Carol and Watson, Rowan (ed.), *From Manet to Hockney: Modern Artists' Illustrated Books.* London: Victoria and Albert Museum, 1985.

(Howell) "Douglass Howell: Poet in Pulp and Rag," *Artist's Proof,* No. 6 (Fall - Winter, 1963-4), Vol. III, No. 2, pp. 30-31 (intro. by Fritz Eichenberg?).

Hugunin, James R. and Ollman, Arthur (intro.), *Victor Landweber Photographs, 1967-1984.* San Diego: Museum of Photographic Arts, 1985. Exhibition catalogue.

Hunter, Sam (intro.), *Joan Miró. His Graphic Work.* New York: Harry N. Abrams, Inc., 1958.

Janis, Eugenia Parry, *The Photography of Gustave Le Gray.* Chicago: The Art Institute of Chicago and the University of Chicago Press, 1987. Exhibition catalogue.

Jenyns, Soame, *Japanese Pottery.* London: Faber and Faber, 1971.

Johnson, Elaine, "The 'Phenomena' of Jean Dubuffet," *Artist's Proof,* Vol. II, No. 1, Issue No. 3 (Spring, 1962), pp. 27-29.

Jones, Trevor, "The Featured Bookbinding: James Joyce's *Tales of Shem and Shaun, Three Fragments from Work in Progress,*" *Fine Print,* Vol. 11, No. 2 (April, 1985), pp. 119, 128.

Kandinsky Complete Writings on Art, Vol. I (1901-1921), Vol. II (1922-1943). Ed. by Kenneth Lindsay and Peter Vergo. Boston: G. K. Hall and Co., 1982.

King, Susan E., "Recent Press Books: The New Pyramid Press," *Fine Print,* Vol. 11, No. 3 (July, 1985), pp. 166-167.

Karshan, Donald, *Malevich: The Graphic Work: 1913-1930; A Print Catalogue Raisonné.* Jerusalem: The Israel Museum, 1975.

Kepler, Johannes, *The Six-Cornered Snowflake* (ed. and transl. from the Latin by Colin Hardie, with essays by L. L. White and B. F. J. Mason). Oxford: Clarendon Press, 1966.

Paul Klee Notebooks, Vol. I. The thinking eye. Ed. by Jürg Spiller. New York: George Wittenborn, 1961.

Kok, J. P. Filedt, *Rembrandt etchings and drawings in the Rembrandt House.* Maarssen: Gary Schwartz, 1972.

Konheim, Linda, *Prints from the Guggenheim Museum Collection.* New York: The Solomon R. Guggenheim Foundation, 1978. Exhibition catalogue.

Koslow, Francine Amy and Harding, Walter, *Henry David Thoreau As a Source for Artistic Inspiration.* Lincoln, Mass.: DeCordova and Dana Museum and Park, 1984. Exhibition catalogue.

Kostelanetz, Richard (ed.), *John Cage.* New York: Praeger Publishers, 1970.

Kostelanetz, Richard (ed.), *John Cage.* London: Allen Lane The Penguin Press, 1971.

Kovel, Ralph and Terry, "Potters once favored 'coleslaw' decoration," *The Kansas City Star,* June 28, 1987, p. 2K.

Kozloff, Max, "Pygmalion Reversed," *Artforum,* Vol. 14, No. 3 (Nov., 1975), pp. 30-37.

Kren, Alfred, "Aspects of German Prints after 1945," *The Print Collector's Newsletter,* Vol. XIV, No. 1 (March-April, 1983), pp. 5-8.

Krens, Thomas, *Jim Dine Prints: 1970-1977.* New York: Harper and Row in assoc. with Williams College, 1976. Exhibition catalogue.

Lassam, Bert, *Fox Talbot Photographer*. Wiltshire: Compton Press, 1979.

Late Japanese Lacquers. San Francisco: Asia Art Museum, 1987. Exhibition catalogue.

Lavezzari, Paolo (intro., transl.), *Alexander Cozens, A New Method of Assisting the Invention in Drawing Original Compositions of Landscape* (1785). Treviso: Libreria Editrice Canova, 1981.

Legge, James (transl.), *I Ching; Book of Changes*. Ed. and intro. by Ch'u Chai with Winberg Chai. New York: Bantam Books, 1969.

The Notebooks of Leonardo da Vinci. Transl. by Edward MacCurdy. New York: Reynal and Hitchcock, 1938. 2 vol.

Lerner, Abe, *Poems by Majnun Laila*, "Recent Press Books," *Fine Print*, Vol. XII, No. 3, July, 1986, pp. 144-146.

Leroil-Gourhan, André, *Treasures of Prehistoric Art*. New York: Harry N. Abrams, Inc., 1967?.

Lightbrown, Ronald, *Mantegna*. Oxford: Phaidon. Christie's, 1986.

Lippard, Lucy, "James Rosenquist: Aspects of a Multiple Art," *Artforum*, Vol. IV, No. 4 (Dec., 1965), pp. 41-44.

Lippard, Lucy (ed.), *Surrealists on Art*. Englewood, New Jersey: Prentice-Hall, Inc., 1970.

Livesay, Thomas A., Rudisill, Richard, and Turner, David, *Approaches to Photography; A Historical Survey*. Amarillo, Texas: Amarillo Art Center, 1979. Exhibition catalogue.

Livet, Anne, *The Works of Edward Ruscha*. San Francisco: San Francisco Museum of Modern Art, 1982.

Loehr, Max, *Chinese Landscape Woodcuts*. Cambridge: Belknap Press of Harvard Univ. Press, 1968.

Loewe, Michael and Blacker, Carmen (ed.), *Oracles and Divination*. Boulder: Shambhala, 1981.

López-Rey, José, *Goya's Caprichos: Beauty, Reason, and Caricature*. Princeton: Princeton University Press, 1953. 2 vol.

Lucquet, Georges-Henri, *The Art and Religion of Fossil Man*. Transl. by J. Townsend Russell, Jr. New Haven: Yale University Press, 1930.

MacAgy, Jermayne, *Out of This World; An Exhibition of Fantastic Landscapes from the Renaissance to the Present*. Houston: University of St. Thomas, 1964. Exhibition catalogue.

Mahoney, Thomas P., "The Third Dimension," *Graphic Arts Monthly*, July, 1967, pp. 40-43.

Marrow, James H. and Shestack, Alan, *Hans Baldung Grien Prints and Drawings*. New Haven: Yale University Press, 1981. Exhibition catalogue.

Martin, Kenneth, *Chance and Order* (The Sixth Annual William Townsend Lecture). London: Waddington Galleries, 1979.

Maurer, Paul and Diane Philippoff, *An Introduction to Carrageenan and Watercolor Marbling*. Centre Hall, Pa.: The Maurers' Hand-Marbled Papers, 1984.

Mayor, A. Hyatt, *Giovanni Battista Piranesi*. New York: H. Bittner and Co., 1952.

Mayor, A. Hyatt, *Prints and People: A Social History of Printed Pictures*. New York: The Metropolitan Museum of Art, 1971.

McNulty, Kneeland, Miller, N. Richard, and Dubuffet, Jean, *The Lithographs of Jean Dubuffet*. Philadelphia: Philadelphia Museum of Art, 1964. Exhibition catalogue.

Medley, Margaret, *The Chinese Potter: A Practical History of Chinese Ceramics*. New York: Charles Scribner's Sons, 1976.

Mikami, Tsugio, *The Art of Japanese Ceramics*. Transl. by Ann Herring. New York: Weatherhill/Heibonsha, 1972.

Miller, George and Dorothy, *Picture Postcards in the United States 1893-1918*. New York: Clarkson N. Potter, Inc., 1976.

Miró, Joan and Picon, Gaëtan, *Joan Miró, Catalan Notebooks*. New York: Rizzoli International Publications, Inc., 1977.

Moes, Robert, *Japanese Ceramics*. Brooklyn: The Brooklyn Museum, 1979. Exhibition catalogue.

Moon, Warren G., *Greek Vase Paintings in Midwestern Collections*. Chicago: Art Institute of Chicago, 1980. Exhibition catalogue.

Motherwell, Robert (ed.), *The Dada Painters and Poets: An Anthology* (Documents of Modern Art). New York: Wittenborn, Schultz, Inc., 2nd ed., 1981.

Mueller, Robert E., *The Science of Art; The Cybernetics of Creative Communication*. New York: The John Day Company, 1967.

Münz, Ludwig, *A Critical Catalogue of Rembrandt's Etchings*. London: Phaidon Press, 1952. 2 vol.

Murdoch, Iris, *Acastos: Two Platonic Dialogues*. New York: Viking, 1986.

Murray, Julia K., "An Album of Paintings by Yun Shou-p'ing, the Recluse of Nan-t'ien," *Record of the Art Museum, Princeton University*, Vol. 37, No. 1 (1978), pp. 3-25.

Musée des Arts Décoratifs, *Retrospective Jean Dubuffet 1942-1960*. Paris: Musée des Arts Décoratifs, 1960. Exhibition catalogue.

Naef, Weston J., *Counterparts; Form and Emotion in Photographs*. New York: Metropolitan Museum of Art and E. P. Dutton, 1982. Exhibition catalogue.

Nakaya, Ukichiro, *Snow Crystals, Natural and Artificial*. Cambridge: Harvard University Press, 1954.

Nakov, Andréi B. (Railing, Patricia A., transl.), "Malevich as Printmaker," *The Print Collector's Newsletter*, Vol. VII, No. 1 (March-April, 1976), pp. 4-10.

Newlin, Richard (ed.), *Richard Diebenkorn Works on Paper*. Houston: Houston Fine Arts Press, 1987.

New York Times News Service, "Don't fool around with Mother Nature," *The Kansas City Star*, March 27, 1988, p. 2-I.

Norman, Dorothy, *Alfred Stieglitz*. Millerton, N.Y.: Aperture, 1976.

O'Connor, Francis V. and Thaw, E. V., *Jackson Pollock: A Catalogue Raisonné of Paintings, Drawings, and Other Works*. New Haven: Yale University Press, 1978. 4 vol.

O'Connor, Patrick, *Nancy Graves*. New York: Associated American Artists, 1988. Exhibition brochure.

O'Hara, Frederick, "*Comanches* and *Antelope Priest*," *Artist's Proof*, Issue No. 4, Vol. II, No. 2 (Fall, Winter, 1962), pp. 30-31.

Ollman, Arthur and Hugunin, James R., *Victor Landweber Photographs: 1967-1984*. San Diego: Museum of Photographic Arts, 1985. Exhibition catalogue.

Oppé, A. P., *Alexander and John Robert Cozens*. Cambridge: Harvard University Press, 1954.

Oppé, A. P., "New Light on Alexander Cozens," *Print Collector's Quarterly*, Vol. 8 (1921), pp. 62-90.

Orange, James, *The Chater Collection: Pictures Relating to China, Hongkong, Macao, 1655-1860*. London: Thornton Butterworth, Ltd., 1924.

Ortega y Gasset, José, *The Dehumanization of Art*. Garden City: Doubleday and Co., Inc., 1956.

Ossorio, Alfonso, "The Hour of the Hourloupe," *Art News*, Vol. 67, No. 3 (May, 1968), pp. 48-66.

Panofsky, Erwin, *Albrecht Dürer*. Princeton: Princeton Univ. Press, 1945. 2 vol.

Paoletti, John T., "Arnulf Rainer: Prints as Encounter and Event," *The Print Collector's Newsletter*, Vol. XVIII, No. 1 (March-April, 1987), pp. 1-6.

Parris, Leslie, Fleming-Williams, Ian, and Shields, Conal, *Constable Paintings, Watercolours and Drawings*. London: The Tate Gallery, 1976. Exhibition catalogue.

Parris, Leslie, *Landscape in Britain c. 1750-1850*. London: The Tate Gallery, 1973. Exhibition catalogue.

Passeron, René, *The Concise Encyclopedia of Surrealism*. Secaucus, New Jersey: Chartwell Books, Inc., 1975.

Paulson, Ronald, *Hogarth's Graphic Works*. New Haven: Yale University Press, 1965. 2 vol.

Paulson, Ronald, *Hogarth: His Life, Art, and Times*. New Haven: Yale University Press, 1971. 2 vol.

Paulson, Ronald, *Literary Landscape: Turner and Constable*. New Haven: Yale University Press, 1982.

Peckham, Morse, "Constable and Wordsworth," *College Art Journal*, Vol. 12 (1952), pp. 196-209.

Peckham, Morse, *Man's Rage for Chaos; Biology, Behavior, and the Arts*. New York: Schocken Books, 1967.

Peckham, Morse, "Triumph of Romanticism," *The Magazine of Art*, Vol. XLV, No. 7 (Nov., 1952), pp. 291-299.

Peitgen, Heinz-Otto and Saupe, Dietmar (ed.), *The Science of Fractal Images*. New York: Springer-Verlag, 1988.

Pekarik, Andrew J., *Japanese Lacquer, 1600-1900*. New York: The Metropolitan Museum of Art, 1980. Exhibition catalogue.

Pennell, E. R. and J., *The Life of James McNeill Whistler*. Philadelphia: J. W. Lippincott Co., 1909. 2 vol.

Pilat, Bianca Maria, *Man Ray Opera Grafica*. Milan: Studio Marconi, 1984.

2 vol.

Pillsbury, Edmund P. and Richards, Louise S., *The Graphic Art of Federico Barocci*. New Haven: Yale University Art Gallery, 1978. Exhibition catalogue.

Pindell, Howardena, "Words with Ruscha," *The Print Collector's Newsletter*, Vol. III, No. 6 (Jan.-Feb., 1973), pp. 125-128.

Popham, Arthur E., *Catalogue of the Drawings of Parmigianino*. New Haven: Yale University Press, for the Pierpont Morgan Library, 1971. 3 vol.

Porter, Fairfield, "Reviews and Previews," *Art News*, Vol. 50, No. 8 (Dec., 1951), p. 48.

Printed Matter, Inc., *Books by Artists*, catalogues. New York, 1981-1986.

Prokopoff, Stephen S., *Against Order: Chance and Art*. Philadelphia: Institute of Contemporary Art, Univ. of Pennsylvania, 1970. Exhibition catalogue.

Quennell, Peter Courtney, *Hogarth's Progress*. New York: The Viking Press, 1955.

Quinn, Edward, *Max Ernst*. Barcelona: Ediciones Poligrafa, S.A., 1984.

Ratcliff, Carter, *Pat Steir Paintings*. New York: Harry N. Abrams, Inc., 1986.

Ratcliff, Carter, "Vija Celmins: An Art of Reclamation," *The Print Collector's Newsletter*, Vol. XIV, No. 6 (Jan.-Feb., 1984), pp. 193-196.

Reynolds, Graham, *The Later Paintings and Drawings of John Constable*. New Haven: Yale University Press, 1984. 2 vol.

Robison, Andrew, *Piranesi Early Architectural Fantasies; A Catalogue Raisonné of the Etchings*. Washington: National Gallery of Art, 1986.

Rosenberg, Harold, *The Tradition of the New*. 2nd ed. New York: McGraw-Hill, 1965.

Rosenberg, Jakob, *Rembrandt*. Cambridge: Harvard University Press, 1948. 2 vol.

Rowell, Margit, *Jean Dubuffet; A Retrospective*. New York: Solomon R. Guggenheim Foundation, 1973. Exhibition catalogue.

Rueppel, Merrill, *Jean Dubuffet Retrospective*. Dallas: Museum of Fine Arts, 1966. Exhibition catalogue.

Sakanishi, Shio (transl.), *The Spirit of the Brush*. London: John Murray, 1939.

Samachon, Dorothy and Joseph, *The First Artists*. Garden City: Doubleday and Co., Inc., 1970.

Samuel, Arthur, *Piranesi*. London: B. T. Batsford, 1912. 2nd ed.

Sayre, Eleanor, *The Changing Image: Prints by Francisco Goya*. Boston: Museum of Fine Arts, 1974. Exhibition catalogue.

Schaefer, Vincent J., "Winter Photography—Snowflakes," *The Complete Photographer: The Encyclopedia of Photography*. New York: National Educational Alliance, Inc., 1949. Vol. 9, pp. 3509-3514.

Scharf, Aaron, *Art and Photography*. Baltimore: Penguin Books, Inc., 1974.

Schwartz, Arturo, *The Complete Works of Marcel Duchamp*. London: Thames and Hudson, 1969.

Schwartz, Arturo, *Marcel Duchamp, The Lovers; nine original etchings for The Large Glass and Related Works, Vol. II*. Milan: Galleria Schwartz, 1969. Exhibition catalogue.

Seattle Art Museum, *Ceramic Art of Japan*, 1972. Exhibition catalogue.

Seckler, Dorothy Gees, "The Artist Speaks: Robert Rauschenberg," *Art in America*, 54 (May/June, 1966), pp. 73-84.

Selz, Peter, *Sam Francis* (with essays on his prints by Susan Einstein and Jan Butterfield). Rev. ed. New York: Harry N. Abrams, Inc., 1982.

Selz, Peter, *The Work of Jean Dubuffet*. New York: Museum of Modern Art, 1962. Exhibition catalogue.

Senefelder, Alois, *A Complete Course of Lithography*. London: R. Ackermann, 1819.

Sheldrake, Rupert, *The Presence of the Past; Morphic Resonance and the Habits of Nature*. New York: Times Books, 1988.

Shestack, Alan, "Lift-Ground Prints by Alexander Cozens," *Artist's Proof*, Vol. VIII, 1968, pp. 82-86.

Shimizu, Yoshiaki, and Rosenfield, John M., *Masters of Japanese Calligraphy 8th-19th Century*. New York: The Asia Society Galleries and Japan House Gallery, 1984. Exhibition catalogue.

Simon, Sidney, "Michelangelo Pistoletto," *Art International*, Vol. X, No. 6 (Summer, 1966), pp. 69-71, illus. p. 76.

Sloan, Kim, *Alexander and John Robert Cozens: The Poetry of Landscape*. New Haven: Yale University Press in association with the Art Gallery of Ontario, 1986.

Smith, Keith A., *The Structure of the Visual Book*. Rochester: Visual Studies Workshop Press, 1984.

Sobieszek, Robert A., *Masterpieces of Photography from the George Eastman House Collections*. New York: Abbeville Press, 1985.

Solomon, Alan R., *Robert Rauschenberg*. New York: The Jewish Museum, 1963. Exhibition catalogue.

Spargo, John, *The Potters and Potteries of Bennington*. Boston: Houghton Mifflin Co. and Antiques Inc., 1926.

Spies, Werner, *Max Ernst. Loplop; The Artist in the Third Person*. New York: George Braziller, 1983.

Spurlock, William (ed.), Klausner, Betty, and Dole, William, *Santa Barbara Museum of Art Contemporary Graphics Center, William Dole Fund Collection*. Exhibition catalogue. Santa Barbara: Santa Barbara Museum of Art, 1980.

Stainton, Lindsay, *J.M.W. Turner Watercolors from the British Museum*. Athens: Georgia Museum of Art, 1982. Exhibition catalogue.

Steadman, David, *The Graphic Art of Francisco Goya*. Claremont, Calif.: The Galleries of the Claremont Colleges, 1975. Exhibition catalogue.

Stein, Donna, *Cubist Prints/Cubist Books*. New York: Franklin Furnace, 1983.

Stein, Aurel. *Serindia*. 5 vol. Oxford: Clarendon Press, 1921.

Steinberg, Norma S., *Monstrosities and Inconveniences: Works by George Cruikshank*. Worcester: Worcester Art Museum, 1986. Exhibition catalogue.

Stevens, Mark, "The Haunted Studio," *Vanity Fair*, Vol. 51, No. 7, (July, 1988), pp. 70-75. (Photographs by Evelyn Hofer)

Strauss, Walter L., *Chiaroscuro*. Greenwich: New York Graphic Society, Ltd., 1973.

Strauss, Walter L., *Albrecht Dürer Intaglio Prints, Engravings, Etchings, and Drypoints*. New York: Kennedy Galleries, Inc., 1975.

Strauss, Walter L., *The Wood Cuts and Wood Blocks of Albrecht Dürer*. New York: Abaris Books, Inc., 1980.

Sundell, Nina, *Rauschenberg/Performance 1954-1984*. Cleveland: Cleveland Center for Contemporary Art, 1984. Exhibition catalogue.

Surrealism in Perspective, The Cleveland Museum of Art, 1979. Exhibition catalogue.

Taggart, Ross E., *The Burnap Collection of English Pottery*. Kansas City: Nelson Gallery-Atkins Museum, 1967. 2nd, revised edition.

Talbot, Charles W. (ed.), *Dürer in America*. Washington: National Gallery of Art, 1971. Exhibition catalogue.

Tammeus, Bill, "Scientists' new *chaosmology* has long been know[n] to lay types," *The Kansas City Times*, July 28, 1988, p. A-13.

Taylor, Basil, *Constable Paintings, Drawings, and Watercolors*. London: Phaidon, 1973.

Taylor, Sue, *Jean Dubuffet: Forty Years of His Art*. Chicago: The David and Alfred Smart Gallery, The University of Chicago, 1984. Exhibition catalogue.

Teuber, Marianne L., "New Aspects of Paul Klee's Bauhaus Style," intro. in *Paul Klee; Paintings and Watercolors from the Bauhaus Years 1921-1931*, Des Moines Art Center, Sept. 18-October 28, 1973.

Tirenzio, Stephanie and Belknap, Dorothy C., *The Painter and the Printer: Robert Motherwell's Graphics 1943-1980*. New York: The American Federation of Arts, 1980.

Tomkins, Calvin, *Ahead of the Game*. Harmondsworth: Penguin Books, 1968.

Tomkins, Calvin, *The Bride and The Bachelors*. New York: The Viking Press, 1965.

Tomkins, Calvin, *Off the Wall: Robert Rauschenberg and the Art World of Our Time*. New York: Penguin Books, 1982.

Tousley, Nancy, "Artists' Books," *The Print Collector's Newsletter*, Vol. IV, No. 6 (Jan.-Feb., 1974), pp. 131-134.

Towle, Tony, "Two Conversations with Lee Bontecou," *The Print Collector's Newsletter*, Vol. II, No. 2 (May-June, 1971), pp. 25-28.

Trini, Tommaso (Rodney Stringer, transl.), "Michelangelo Pistoletto," *Data* (Fall, 1974), pp. 42-45.

Tucker, Marcia, *James Rosenquist*. New York: Whitney Museum of American Art, 1972. Exhibition catalogue.

Turner, Anne Wilkes (ed.), *Target III: In Sequence*. Houston: Museum of Fine Arts, 1982.

Tyler, Parker, "Hopper/Pollock, The Loneliness of the Crowd and the Loneliness of the Universe: An Antiphonal," *Art News Annual* 26 (Nov., 1956), pp. 86-107.

Ucko, Peter J. and Rosenfeld, Andrée, *Paleolithic Cave Art.* New York: McGraw-Hill Book Co., 1967.

Vaizey, Marina, *The Artist as Photographer.* New York: Holt, Rinehart, and Winston, 1982.

Various authors, *Minor White: A Living Remembrance.* Millerton, N.Y.: Aperture, 1984.

Varyan, Elayne H., *James Rosenquist Graphics Retrospective.* John and Mable Ringling Museum of Art and Fort Lauderdale Museum of the Arts, 1979. Exhibition catalogue.

Vasari, Giorgio, *Lives of the Most Eminent Painters, Sculptors, and Architects.* Transl. by Gaston Du C. de Vere. New York: Harry N. Abrams, Inc., 1979. 3 vol.

Verdi, Richard, *Klee and Nature.* New York: Rizzoli, 1985.

Volger, Richard, *Reading Hogarth.* Los Angeles: Grunwald Center for the Graphic Arts, Wight Art Gallery, UCLA, 1988. Exhibition catalogue.

Walch, Peter and Barrow, Thomas (ed.), *Perspectives on Photography: Essays in Honor of Beaumont Newhall.* Albuquerque: Univ. of New Mexico Press, 1986.

Wallace, Richard W., *The Etchings of Salvator Rosa.* Princeton: Princeton University Press, 1979.

Wattenmaker, Richard J., *Puvis de Chavannes and the Modern Tradition.* Toronto: Art Gallery of Ontario, 1975. Exhibition catalogue.

Watts, Harriett, *Chance: A Perception on Dada.* Ann Arbor: UMI Research Press, 1975.

Welsh-Ovcharov, Bogomila, *Vincent van Gogh and the Birth of Cloisonism.* Toronto: Art Gallery of Ontario, 1981. Exhibition catalogue.

Wentworth, Michael Justin, *James Tissot: Catalogue Raisonné of His Prints.* Minneapolis: The Minneapolis Institute of Arts, 1978. Exhibition catalogue.

White, Minor, *Mirrors/Messages/Manifestations.* Millerton, N.Y.: Aperture, Inc., 1982. 2nd ed.

Willetts, William, *Chinese Calligraphy; Its History and Aesthetic Motivation.* Hong Kong: Oxford University Press, 1977. Exhibition catalogue.

Williams, Reba and Dave, "The Prints of Jackson Pollock," *Print Quarterly*, Vol. V, No. 4 (Dec., 1988), pp. 347-373.

Wilton, Andrew, *The Art of Alexander and John Robert Cozens.* New Haven: Yale Center for British Art, 1980.

Wünsche, Hermann, *Andy Warhol; Das Graphische Werk 1962-1980.* Bonn: Herman Wünsche, 1981.

Yalkut, Jud, "Towards an Intermedia Magazine" (Review of *S.M.S.* and *Aspen* Magazine), *Arts*, Vol. 42, No. 8 (June/Summer, 1968), pp. 12-14.

Yashiro, Yukio, *Sandro Botticelli and the Florentine Renaissance.* Boston: Hale, Cushman, and Flint, 1929.

Yonemura, Ann, *Japanese Lacquer.* Washington: Freer Gallery of Art, 1979. Exhibition catalogue.

Young, Blamire, *The Proverbs of Goya.* Boston: Houghton Mifflin Co., n.d.

Zukav, Gary, *The Dancing Wu Li Masters; An Overview of the New Physics.* New York: Bantam Books, 1980.